THE SHAKESPEAREAN
INTERNATIONAL YEARBOOK

GENERAL EDITORS

Tom Bishop, University of Auckland, Auckland, New Zealand
Alexa Huang, George Washington University, Washington, D.C., USA

EDITOR EMERITUS

Graham Bradshaw, Chuo University, Japan

GUEST EDITOR

Susan Bennett, University of Calgary, Canada

ADVISORY BOARD

Supriya Chaudhuri, Jadavpur University, Kolkata, India
Natasha Distiller, University of Cape Town, Cape Town, South Africa
Jacek Fabiszak, Adam Mickiewicz University, Poznan, Poland
Atsuhiko Hirota, University of Kyoto, Kyoto, Japan
Ton Hoenselaars, University of Utrecht, Utrecht, Netherlands
Peter Holbrook, University of Queensland, Brisbane, Australia
Jean Howard, Columbia University, New York, USA
Ania Loomba, University of Pennsylvania, Philadelphia, USA
Kate McLuskie, University of Birmingham, Birmingham, UK
Alfredo Modenessi, Universidad Nacional Autónoma de México, Mexico City, México
Ruth Morse, Université Paris VII, Paris, France
W. B. Worthen, Barnard College, New York, USA

The Shakespearean International Yearbook

16: Special Section, Shakespeare on Site

General Editors
Tom Bishop and Alexa Huang

Guest Editor
Susan Bennett

LONDON AND NEW YORK

First published 2016
by Routledge
2 Park Square, Milton Park, Abingdon, Oxon OX14 4RN

and by Routledge
711 Third Avenue, New York, NY 10017

Routledge is an imprint of the Taylor & Francis Group, an informa business

© 2016 selection and editorial matter, Tom Bishop, Alexa Huang, and Susan Bennett; individual chapters, the contributors

The right of Tom Bishop, Alexa Huang, and Susan Bennett to be identified as the authors of the editorial material, and of the authors for their individual chapters, has been asserted in accordance with sections 77 and 78 of the Copyright, Designs and Patents Act 1988.

All rights reserved. No part of this book may be reprinted or reproduced or utilised in any form or by any electronic, mechanical, or other means, now known or hereafter invented, including photocopying and recording, or in any information storage or retrieval system, without permission in writing from the publishers.

Trademark notice: Product or corporate names may be trademarks or registered trademarks, and are used only for identification and explanation without intent to infringe.

British Library Cataloguing in Publication Data
A catalogue record for this book is available from the British Library

Library of Congress Cataloging-in-Publication Data
A catalog record for this book has been requested

ISBN: 978-1-4724-8891-6 (hbk)
ISBN: 978-1-3154-0598-8 (ebk)

Typeset in Times New Roman
by Apex CoVantage, LLC

Printed and bound by CPI Group (UK) Ltd, Croydon, CR0 4YY

Contents

List of illustrations vii
Preface xi

PART ONE

1 Shakespeare on site: here, there and everywhere 1
  Susan Bennett

2 Proximal dreams: Peter Sellars at the Stratford Festival
  of Canada 11
  Margaret Jane Kidnie

3 The site of burial in two Korean *Hamlet*s 29
  Yu Jin Ko

4 The merchant of Ashland: the confusing case of an organized
  minority response at the Oregon Shakespeare Festival 49
  Jason Demeter and Ayanna Thompson

5 Exhibiting the past: Globe replicas in Shakespearean
  exhibitions 65
  Clara Calvo

6 Spatial negotiations in the Brazilian street production
  Sua Incelença, Ricardo III by Clowns de Shakespeare 87
  Anna Stegh Camati and Liana de Camargo Leão

7 Shakespeare going out here and now: travels in China
  on the 450th anniversary 109
  Li Jun and Julie Sanders

PART TWO

8 "What ceremony else?" Images of Ophelia in Brazil:
   the politics of subversion of the female artist 129
   Cristiane Busato Smith

9 Mapping Shakespeare in street art 147
   Mariacristina Cavecchi

10 Collaborations and conversations: the year in Shakespeare
   studies, 2012–2013 177
   Elizabeth Pentland

Notes on contributors *191*
Index *195*

Illustrations

2.1 Festival Theatre (panorama). Stratford Festival of Canada. Photo by Richard Bain. 11
2.2 *A Midsummer Night's Dream: A Chamber Play*. Set and installation artist, Abigail DeVille. Photo by Abigail DeVille. The space (auditorium and stage) is suffused indigo in the original colour photograph. 15
2.3 *A Midsummer Night's Dream: A Chamber Play*. Set and installation artist, Abigail DeVille. Photo by Abigail DeVille. The ceiling lighting is a yellowish-green in the original colour photograph. 16
2.4 Mike Nadajewski (left), Dion Johnstone and Trish Lindström in *A Midsummer Night's Dream: A Chamber Play*. Photo by Michael Cooper. 21
2.5 From left: Sarah Afful, Dion Johnstone, Mike Nadajewski and Trish Lindström in *A Midsummer Night's Dream: A Chamber Play*. Photo by Michael Cooper. 23
5.1 Proposed permanent Shakespeare Village for Boston. "Boston to Have Permanent Shakespeare Village," *The New York Times*, 25 June 1916. Public domain. 67
5.2 Frank Chouteau Brown. Plans for the Shakespeare Memorial Village in Back Bay Fens, Boston, Massachusetts. Proposed by the Shakespeare Festival Guild of Boston. Reverse brown print. Courtesy of Historic New England. 70
5.3 Frank Chouteau Brown. Elevation of Shakespeare's Old "Globe" Theatre. Reverse brown print. Courtesy of Historic New England. 71
5.4 The Globe Theatre, Shakespeare's England, Earl's Court, 1912. Author's collection. 72
5.5 Bird's-Eye View of "Shakespeare's England," *The New York Times*, 23 June 1912. Public domain. 73
5.6 Postcard showing timber-framed and gabled houses by Edward Lutyens in the Earl's Court exhibition "Shakespeare's England." Author's collection. 74

5.7	Postcard showing timber-framed and gabled houses by Edward Luytens in the Earl's Court exhibition "Shakespeare England." Author's collection.	76
5.8	Advertisement for the Shakespeare Exhibition. *The Sunday Times*, 26 April 1964, p. 33. By permission of News Syndication.	77
5.9	The replica of the Globe interior under construction, showing the sloping uprights. The Shakespeare Exhibition. *The Birmingham Post*, 9 April 1964. Author's collection.	78
6.1	The circus ring used as performance space. *Sua Incelença, Ricardo III* (2011), by Shakespeare's Clowns.	95
6.2	Seduction scene. Ricardo's vulgar gesture when he asks Lady Anna to wear his ring. Pablo Pinheiro, photographer.	98
6.3	Tyrrel Jararaca dressed as a *cangaceiro*. Pablo Pinheiro, photographer.	99
6.4	Stylization of violence: the heads of the young princes are represented by two coconuts. Pablo Pinheiro, photographer.	100
6.5	The chorus chants "Acauã" (bird of ill omen). The curved bamboo stalks suggest birds' wings. Pablo Pinheiro, photographer.	103
7.1	*Romeo and Juliet*, 2014: the transformative power of love. The protagonists develop from suppressed and twisted animal figures who can stand only with support to awakened and free-moving bodies. The iconic balcony scene is staged with a trampoline in a moment potentially influenced by the work of UK physical theatre company Kneehigh. Images courtesy of Zhao Miao and photographer Guo Xiaotian and integrated by Li Jun with their kind permission.	119
7.2	*Romeo and Juliet*, 2011, 2014: Chinese shadow puppetry reimagined in Zhao Miao and Theatre SanTuoQi's production melding ancient and modern approaches to theatre. Image courtesy of Theatre SanTuoQi.	120
7.3	*Macbeth*, 2014: 'A *Macbeth* adapted for the Chinese here and now': note the presence of the English text on stage. Image courtesy of Huang Ying.	121
7.4	*Macbeth*: Note the basin Lady Macbeth uses to wash her bloody hands: it is a red enamel basin painted with floral designs, typically used by Chinese people as an auspicious	

	and festive household utensil before the period of opening-up and reform. Image courtesy of Huang Ying.	123
8.1	*Face do Amor* (2012)	135
8.2	*Ofélia Piscina 1* (2009)	137
8.3	*Ofélia Piscina 2* (2012)	138
8.4	*Ofélia Explica*, 2008. Screen capture from *Ofélia Explica* (Sander 2009).	141
9.1	The photograph of "Shakespeare toilet" (Matt from London) (Ian Press Photography) is published on the website The World's Best Photos of Shoreditch (www.flickr.com/photos/londonmatt/9580501367; last access 30 August 2016). CC creative commons.	147

Preface

Literature has always been enjoyed "on site" – quotidian, local, national, colonial, fictional, international and so on – and plays *a fortiori* when they are performed. Shakespeare's works, like others, are enacted in specific places, not in a vacuum, or nowhere, or everywhere. Still, there can be complexities. A broadcast performance is both produced and witnessed at specific places, but different ones in this case. Even a performance in a virtual world is witnessed somewhere, though just where it is produced is an interesting question.

Sites, like books, have their fates. Shakespearean performances have been located at both historic sites and sites of putative and peculiar authority, locations overdetermined and with complex resonance, such as Shakespeare's Globe Theatre in London and the royal castle of *Hamlet* – Elsinore – in Denmark. When staged in Denmark, the fictional setting interacts with the real Kronborg Castle to create a unique hybrid locality. The Globe in London, though it is not the only venue associated with the playwright, has generated from its particular authority many portable ideas and tropes about Shakespearean performance that have in turn affected other sites. The flurry of commemorative events passed around the world in the landmark year of 2016 suggests that Shakespeare is an adaptably mobile floating signifier moving across geographic spaces and touching down variously. How do these sites differ and how are they implicated in one another?

Among the many ambitious projects of this anniversary year is the Shakespeare Theatre Association's "400 Dreams: Shakespeare Around the Globe," a year-long celebration of user-generated digital videos from every time zone in the world. This is an instance where arts activity makes sites legible. On the other hand, as Britain's vote to leave the European Union reminds us, performances can radically change the meanings of place in short order. Some instances of "global" Shakespeare seem to belong more to particular geohistorical sites, others are designed to signify across several international sites and festivals – the London Globe's *Hamlet*, directed by Dominic Dromgoole, has toured to more than 200 countries and regions – and still others adapt themselves to site-specific performances, such as the long list of experimental and mainstream productions staged at Kronborg Castle's annual *Hamletsommer* festivals. The sites of performance can change, challenge, or sustain collective memory.

The meanings of various sites of performance also go beyond mere brute location. Our knowledge of sites is skewed by available histories offered by various archives and by collective memory. Scholars' and educators' own site-specific ideologies and knowledge influence how they historicize and how they teach about global Shakespeares and their sites of origin and reception. Audiences' historical baggage from their own "sites of origin" influences their perception of performances in different sites. As much as we recognize and celebrate the mobility of global Shakespeare, the complexities of site remind us that Shakespeare can be as grounded and site-specific in articulation as it can also be ungrounded and fluid in discursive formation. There's always a place elsewhere, as Coriolanus almost says (though experience may change his mind), but we can't appreciate the journey unless we understand the situation of specific sites and the dynamics that unfold between them.

In the Special Section of this year's volume of *The Shakespearean International Yearbook*, guest-edited by Susan Bennett, the contributors explore Shakespearean performances, exhibitions, and festivals in relation to the idea of site – of space and place produced and modified through cultural enactment and of performance inflected by its location. Additional essays consider the history of a single character, Ophelia, in the shaping location of Brazil, and the intriguing character of Shakespeare on the specific site of the urban wall – as graffiti. The volume concludes with the annual review of recent work in the field of Shakespeare studies.

The Shakespearean International Yearbook surveys annually the present state of Shakespeare studies, addressing issues fundamental to our interpretive encounter with Shakespeare's work and his time, across the whole spectrum of his literary output and across historical periods and media. We invite potential contributors of individual essays or edited groups to contact the general editors with proposals.

Tom Bishop
Alexa Huang

General Editors

1 Shakespeare on site: here, there and everywhere

Susan Bennett

In 2016 it will have been difficult, likely impossible, in England to avoid Shakespeare. The 400th anniversary of the playwright's death has prompted a wealth of programming to ensure that his cultural legacy, entertainment value and economic impact are recognized nationwide. The Shakespeare 400 "consortium of leading creative, cultural and educational organisations"[1] advertise "a year of celebrations"; Shakespeare's Globe will return to its London stage a touring production of *Hamlet* that will, by then, have visited "all nations on earth"[2]; and the British Council has announced its own roster of arts events, teaching materials and education projects. In the words of the council's chief executive, Sir Martin Davidson: "Shakespeare provides an important connection to the UK for millions of people around the world, and the world will be looking to celebrate this anniversary with the UK. We hope that the UK's cultural organisations will come together to meet these expectations and ensure that 2016 is our next Olympic moment."[3] As both Davidson's aspiration and the Globe's tour recognize, 2016 will be, not just England's year of commemoration and revels, but also a recognition of this anniversary that will extend across the world. The essays I have assembled for this 2016 volume of the *Shakespeare International Yearbook* form, certainly, another testament to the scope of attention Shakespeare and his plays now garner in both national and international contexts. Across the sites that these essays explore, I hope to illustrate the complexity and diversity of this globally relevant and recognized Shakespeare – to understand the reproduction of his plays in the twenty-first century in those places well-known and often recognized for their contributions to contemporary knowledge of the works, but also in geographic and historical contexts less often acknowledged or explored. The idea of "site" invoked by this collection of essays is informed by Mike Pearson's expansive sense of the term to include "the role of human agency in place-making in a transitory moment of absorption of actors and things and an intensification of affect," instructive, he suggests, "for both the critical apprehension of and creative initiatives in performance."[4]

Shakespeare on Site examines, then, how cultural performances of many kinds contribute to the experiences and meanings of place – whether local, regional or national – and how these different practices elaborate our notions of what has come to be called, both in popular and scholarly discourses, "global Shakespeare." How do we understand productions of Shakespeare's plays that "belong" to a particular geographical setting and a specific historical moment? How do they inform, challenge or contradict the everyday sense(s) of place? How should we think about productions of Shakespeare's plays that are designed with an eye to travel? What do audiences understand by "site" of performance for productions that circulate internationally? How do the various sites of Shakespearean performance create and sustain cultural memory? What relationship(s) do we have to the varied sites of performance for Shakespeare's plays? These are some of the key questions that the 2016 celebrations provoked and that the authors here explore.

British Council executive Davidson's anticipation of 2016 as "our next Olympic moment" is, of course, deliberate. It served to remind British citizens of the pervasive excitement and national pride that the 2012 summer games produced as well as the gaze of the world's media and general public attention directed that year towards London. As well as the abundance of sports competitions that made up the Olympic and Paralympic Games, the attendant Cultural Olympiad (required by rule 39 of the International Olympic Committee's Charter) involved 12,000 events, 25,000 artists and 5.9 million participants.[5] Its centerpiece was the World Shakespeare Festival (WSF), itself comprising seventy-three productions and a major exhibition at the British Museum, under the direction of Deborah Shaw at the Royal Shakespeare Company.[6] Within the WSF, the complete works performances at Shakespeare's Globe over a six-week period (known as the Globe to Globe Festival), all staged in languages other than English, drew large and generally enthusiastic audiences – 80 per cent of whom were first-time visitors to the theatre, a statistic that lent credibility to the idea that this was Shakespeare for "all." Moreover, as Christie Carson and I noted in our introduction to *Shakespeare Beyond English* (a critical record of the Globe to Globe Festival), "the experience of watching a Shakespeare play with audiences drawn predominantly from non-English-language communities in London changed the conditions of reception in ways that few of us well-rehearsed in Shakespeare spectatorship could ever have imagined."[7] In other words, those first-time audiences changed the Globe by revealing other dramatic traditions and cultural priorities as equally viable and deserving in this place of performance. Nonetheless, whether it was Globe to Globe or the larger World Shakespeare Festival in 2012, these were Shakespeare celebrations that insisted that the world come to Britain as the appropriate – indeed, authentic – site for his work.

But festivals far from Shakespeare's homeland have long been places where audiences enjoy productions of his plays, even if otherwise those spectators might be neither Shakespeare enthusiasts nor regular theatregoers. These are sites that rely, like Stratford-upon-Avon itself, on visitor populations who may be local, regional, national or international but who have committed, in a premeditated or spontaneous decision, to include Shakespeare on their entertainment "to do" list. The Stratford Festival in Ontario, Canada, is one of the best-known and longest-running in North America. Incorporated in 1952, this festival has grown to become "home of the largest classical repertory theatre in North America,"[8] although it has regularly included guest actors and directors in delivery of its annual season. Margaret Jane Kidnie's essay "Proximal Dreams: Peter Sellars at the Stratford Festival of Canada" charts the affirmation *and* the re-scripting of Stratford as place of production by way of two versions of *A Midsummer Night's Dream* in the 2014 season. Festival artistic director Antonio Cimolino's invitation to international superstar opera and theatre director Peter Sellars led to the remaking of Shakespeare's drama as *A Midsummer Night's Dream: A Chamber Play*, performed not in one of the festival's four theatre spaces but in the town's Masonic Hall. With a more conventional production of *Dream* on the Festival Theatre stage in the same year, Sellars's "chamber play" unraveled typical expectations and challenged ideas of site through his version's script adaptation, narrative structure, rehearsal process, lighting and sound design, and acting style – producing cumulatively, Kidnie suggests, an "affective battering" that the audience underwent. Familiarity with the Stratford Festival – where it takes place and the kind of work it typically produces – was no preparation for Sellars's *Dream*. Instead the director took the play "off site," both geographically and in his performance methodology, challenging how we know and understand Stratford, Ontario, as a festival place and, equally, how we know and understand the play itself (how we might think of *A Midsummer Night's Dream*'s charming, holiday world of noble lovers, rude mechanicals and generous fairies).

If Sellars's *Dream* opens up new sites for play and place alike, the Korean *Hamlet*s discussed by Yu Jin Ko navigate a complex and freighted relationship between ideas of the play's "universal" address and specifically Korean affects and meanings. It is at such junctures, as Alexa Huang has written in a discussion of two other Asian *Hamlet*s, that " 'Shakespeare' is manufactured and consumed."[9] Ko takes up the assumed site of the intercultural encounter (Korean theatre practitioners with Shakespeare's play) but, in his nuanced analysis of the two subject productions by companies Yonhuidan Gureepe and Yohangza, finds "distinctly local or Korean spaces." In other words, these two Korean *Hamlet*s do not necessarily – or, at least, not only – speak to the burgeoning repertoire of global Shakespearean production; rather, they are addressed particularly to Korean subjectivities and sensibilities (including the author's own). As Ko demonstrates, these performances exploit an affective register of Korean experience and resonate with the specificity of the country's history, both recent and more distant.

Hamlet becomes very much a site-specific drama as it is rendered within nationally meaningful frameworks in which both the play and the titular character speak Korean. The careful elaboration of how productions of this play can be both conceived as a universally significant text and a profoundly local one asks us to think about the limitations of discourses about "global Shakespeare," where the endpoint is, too often, a recuperation of performance for entertainment and/or scholarly enterprise in the West. We might agree that Shakespeare's plays hold a universal – global – appeal, but their sites of production, expressed as translated texts and the places of performance, sometimes refuse to be understood through conventional interpretive paradigms.

There is a tension in expressions of geography that is characteristic to the contemporary condition of production for Shakespeare's plays. In her landmark collection *World-wide Shakespeares*, Sonia Massai reminded us to pay attention "to differential strategies of appropriation, ranging from the use of uncompromisingly local, to a blend of local and more widely recognizable, frames of reference."[10] Yet site is not only a crucial variable in contemporary performance practice. Indeed, casting site in historical contexts shows, too, that many of the questions demanded of contemporary work – be they creative or critical – have prior articulations that not only inform scholarly knowledge, theatre history and archival record but also shape the possibilities of production in our own moment.

Jason Demeter and Ayanna Thompson examine a fraught history for performances of *The Merchant of Venice* at the other North American site of a major Shakespeare festival: Ashland, Oregon. Although *The Merchant of Venice* had been staged regularly at the Oregon Shakespeare Festival (OSF) since its founding in 1935, a production in 1991 incited protests by local and regional Jewish communities. The charge of anti-Semitism, as Demeter and Thompson explain, was in significant part provoked by the modernization of the play and the deployment of "recognizable signifiers from contemporary Orthodox Judaism." The waves of objection from audience members and the local population made palpable the place that the OSF occupied not just in Ashland itself, but in the broader north-west region. As well, it showed quite precisely that commitment to produce the works of Shakespeare – OSF's mission statement today still includes the early modern playwright as an inspiration for their work to "reveal our common humanity"[11] – did not necessarily imply a compliant and like-thinking audience. More recently, however, commonplaces of contemporary theatrical production such as educational programming and materials, talk-back sessions and "expert" lectures, whether at the OSF or elsewhere and whether of Shakespeare or another playwright, have extended and reformed the spectatorial experience. And at Ashland, recent productions of *The Merchant of Venice* have been carefully mediated by these kinds of strategic "offstage" engagements so as to divest the site from its troubling past with this play.

At the same time, the modulating history of *The Merchant* at the OSF belongs with a more detailed historical and geographic mapping so as to understand the significance of place of production for this particular play and for the "universal" status of Shakespeare's oeuvre. The performance of this play by Tel Aviv's Habima National Theatre at the Globe to Globe Festival in London engendered protests both outside and inside the theatre and, as Suzanne Gossett noted, the production "inevitably raised the question of how, and how much, artistic works and artistic organizations should be forced to participate in, or be judged by, cultural conflict."[12] Whether at the Globe on London's Southbank or in the more bucolic setting of Ashland, *The Merchant of Venice* tests the relationships produced in, for and among the inhabitants of the play, the spectatorship and the general population. The instability that this particular play brings to places that otherwise share few, if any, points of resemblance, suggests that local histories can productively elucidate not only the changing environment for Shakespearean production and reception at a specific site, but can also provide telling points of reference for other moments of contest and (potential) censorship.

Theatres are, of course, not the only places where Shakespeare frequently appears. Perhaps the best-attended and most distinctive event of the World Shakespeare Festival in 2012 was the British Museum's "Shakespeare: Staging the World" exhibition. As Neil MacGregor (director of the museum) described it, "As the world comes to London in 2012, it is timely to explore how the world came to London, and was viewed from London, four hundred years ago, in the era when so many aspects of global modernity had their origins."[13] The exhibition's curator, Dora Thornton, in collaboration with "Shakespearean consultant"[14] Jonathan Bate, assembled a compelling collection of period artifacts that could, through their links to Shakespeare's life and works, "create an innovative cultural anthropology of Shakespeare's key characters, suggesting the range of associations . . . upon which they drew and to which they contributed in his culture."[15] Whether "key characters" from the plays or, more often (as Clara Calvo demonstrates in her essay here), putatively "authentic" replicas of the Globe Theatre and/or sham Elizabethan villages, components of Shakespeare's life and works have been instrumentalized to create and sustain social memory. This has been a common, if not always effective, practice, and Calvo draws our attention to a variety of exhibitions staged over the past hundred years where Baudrillardian simulacra of

Shakespeare "environments" were deployed so as to foster a shared sense of the past in their intended audiences.

While exhibitions of this kind have been almost a regular feature in London (from the "Shakespeare's England" exhibition at Earl's Court in 1912 to the British Museum in 2012, the Victoria and Albert Museum in 2014 and the British Library in 2016),[16] other cities have sought to produce as site a Shakespearean past, but one useful to a particular and local project of memory creation and circulation. Calvo describes the ambitions behind a proposal for an Elizabethan village in Boston (1916) and for the construction of a replica Globe theatre at the 1934 Chicago World's Fair, among other non-English examples. She suggests how the replica is a particularly privileged locus of meaning that allows for the production of invented traditions that undergird politically motivated acts of identity- and nation-building. And if replicas of the Globe have, by now, become iconic features in many of the world's cities, it is equally important to think through how particular productions of a Shakespeare play become iconic as representative of the theatre of a particular place – whether that is a city, a festival locale or a nation.

At a time when audiences in the West have developed hearty appetites for Shakespearean productions that visit from elsewhere in the world, Grupo Galpão's *Romeu y Julieta* (*Romeo and Juliet*) has been one of the most far traveled, extensively analyzed and best admired of non-English-language productions. As Jacqueline Bessell notes, the Brazilian company started work on its adaptation in 1991 and the play has since become a definitive production in the group's thirty-year history, with more than 300 performances across Latin America, Europe and the United States, including appearances in 2002 and 2012 at Shakespeare's Globe in London.[17] In short, this company and its street-theatre-styled adaptation of *Romeo and Juliet* have been assumed, in the global cultural marketplace and on the scholarly map, to be "Brazilian Shakespeare." Anna Stegh Camati and Liana de Camargo Leão, however, focus on another Brazilian street theatre, Clowns de Shakespeare, and their adaptation of *Richard III* as a play about (and set in) northeast Brazil at the turn of the twentieth century. To grasp the importance of this text in both local and national geographies, the authors provide a contextual history of Shakespeare's place in Brazil's theatre history that reveals companies like Clowns de Shakespeare and Grupo Galpão as simply more recent instantiations in Brazil's long history of engagement with Shakespeare and his writing. They outline a colonially inflected tradition of adapting the English playwright for the social and political conditions of a specifically Brazilian experience and illustrate, too, how many English-language productions of Shakespeare's plays have traveled there – a reminder that the "trade routes" of today's global Shakespeare often occupy a map created by the European colonial enterprise that burgeoned in Shakespeare's own time.

The Clowns de Shakespeare take their methodological lead from a distinctively Brazilian publication, the 1928 "Cannibalist Manifesto," that informs their radical rewriting of the source text, a strategy that combines with their own development of an outdoor circus ring as signature performance space. The contradictions and conflicts of local history become part of Richard III's story and vice versa. The staging, buoyed by song and music, transforms urban space to recognize native performance traditions as much as Shakespearean ones, recent Brazilian political scandals as much as the intrigues of a distant time in the English monarchy. This critical account cautions against tendencies to pigeonhole too easily one production as representative of a country's past and present relationships to Shakespeare.

In a similar vein, the National Theatre of China's production of *Richard III*, premiered at the Globe to Globe Festival in 2012 (and since seen at the Skirball Center for the Performing Arts in New York in 2014 and back at the Globe in 2015), has become a flagship production for China's interest in Shakespeare's plays as well as its pursuit of (cultural and business) trading partners. Li Jun and Julie Sanders contextualize the National Theatre of China's export with an overview of the country's Shakespeare performance history from 1986, the year of "the first Shakespeare Festival in post–Cultural Revolution China" to a present characterized by a density and diversity of Shakespearean adaptations and productions. They address how interactions between locally created and touring productions from elsewhere create the complex horizon that comprises a twenty-first-century "Shakespeare in China." Productions of *Romeo and Juliet* (directed by Zhao Miao) and *Macbeth* (directed by Huang Ying), the two Chinese-originated shows in Beijing's 2014 "Salute to Shakespeare" festival, are understood as exemplary of a new and less defensive approach to staging Shakespeare on mainland China. At the same time, the authors point to the Royal Shakespeare Company's plans as part of the 2016 celebrations to travel to the country, supported financially by the UK government.[18] Moreover, the British Council established a research and development programme, "Shakespeare Reworked," that saw a number of British artists travel abroad in 2015 to develop Shakespeare-oriented projects with local cultural producers: among them were Peter McMaster, a performance practitioner collaborating "with communities, artists and land-based practitioners in China" to explore how human connection to landscape has changed since Shakespeare's time, and physical theatre company Gecko which worked with the Shanghai Dramatic Arts Centre on a creative ensemble Shakespearean production. A council review of November 2015 declared that "the most promising will receive further investment to bring their projects to full production in 2016 overseas, and potentially in the UK."[19]

The anniversary year of 2016 and the acceleration of Shakespearean event production that this has precipitated cannot fail to bring new material and challenging questions to what Huang has already described as an endeavour "to transform global Shakespeares from centerpieces in exotic displays into critical methodologies."[20] As the essays for *Shakespeare on Site* emphatically demonstrate, the relationships between local specificities and global routes are multilayered and sometimes unpredictable. How we report on and understand a particular Shakespearean production staged in a particular place, and how this work contributes to a worldwide knowledge about Shakespeare (in his time and ours), continues as a demanding, but vital, project. Yet it remains difficult to detach global Shakespeare from the long shadows of histories of colonialism and, as Yu Jin Ko warns, the "center could simply grow stronger as an increasingly wide periphery circulates around it."

Perhaps it is the snowball of Shakespeare celebrations – the World Shakespeare Festival in 2012, the 450th anniversary of his birth in 2014, and the 400th anniversary of his death in 2016 – that must take the blame for the emergent fantasy that imagines theatregoers as passport holders in Shakespeare nation, at the very least an oddly timed initiative when the "migrant crisis" dominates daily news and the right of possession of particular countries' passports has never been more valuable. In this regard, Demeter and Thompson point out that the Oregon Shakespeare Festival embarked in its eightieth anniversary season (2015) on a commitment to produce the complete works over the course of a decade – a project where audience members are encouraged to acquire a "Shakespeare Passport" and have it stamped at each play they attend. The 2012 Globe to Globe Festival similarly provided ticket buyers with a passport that might incentivize and inspire attendance.[21] The U.S.-based Shakespeare Theatre Association (STA), a coalition that fosters "artistic, managerial, educational leadership for theatres primarily involved with the production of the works of William Shakespeare,"[22] has created a Shakespeare Passport app that promises free entrance and discounts to their fifty-plus participant organisations.[23] This Shakespeare Passport is but one feature of an extensive programme planned for the STA's "Shakespeare's Legacy 400."[24] Among the other celebratory events they advertise are the American Library Association/Folger Shakespeare Library tour of "Shakespeare and His First Folio" (an exhibition that will spend a month in each of all fifty states, the District of Columbia, Puerto Rico and the U.S. Virgin Islands) and "400 Dreams – Shakespeare in Space," a real-time performance and readings event on 23 April 2016, staged in every time zone in the world. They had hoped that NASA would agree to a reading at the International Space Station, but that appears not to have happened: even for 2016, Shakespeare is not yet beyond the globe.

In 2012, however, the context of London's Olympic Games encouraged a national demonstration of ownership of Shakespeare to which non-English Shakespeare performances were invited. But 2016 is surely not what British

Council executive Davidson imagines as "our next Olympic moment";[25] rather, this anniversary year has the potential not only to provide an altogether different mapping that better recognizes the mobilities of contemporary Shakespearean production and one that does not inevitably recognize Stratford-upon-Avon and London as the centres of its landscape. The year 2016 could emerge as the year when, across geographies familiar and unfamiliar, Shakespeare happened with a much more expansive sense of site. I think here of Miwon Kwon's suggestion that *site* is no longer singularly defined as physical location, "grounded, fixed, actual" but becomes, too, a "discursive vector – ungrounded, fluid, virtual."[26] In this way, in 2016, global Shakespeare might be appropriately here, there and everywhere.

NOTES

1 shakespeare400.org
2 www.shakespearesglobe.com/theatre/whats-on/globe-theatre-on-tour/globe-to-globe-hamlet
3 "British Council announces global celebration of Shakespeare, 23 April 2014, www.britishcouncil.org/organisation/press/british-council-announces-global-celebration-shakespeare
4 Mike Pearson, *Site-Specific Performance* (New York: Palgrave Macmillan, 2010), 13.
5 See Tim Masters, "London 2012 Festival: An Olympian Feat?" 21 June 2012, www.bbc.co.uk/news/entertainment-arts-18505885, and Beatriz Garcia with Tamsin Cox, "London 2012 Cultural Olympiad Evaluation: Executive Summary," 25 April 2013, 6. Garcia's report can be downloaded at www.beatrizgarcia.net/?p=1182.
6 Paul Edmonson, Paul Prescott and Erin Sullivan's *A Year of Shakespeare: Re-living the World Shakespeare Festival* (London: Bloomsbury, 2013) provides a useful collection of reviews of all the festival events.
7 Susan Bennett and Christie Carson, "Introduction: Shakespeare Beyond English," *Shakespeare Beyond English* (Cambridge: Cambridge UP, 2013), 3.
8 See "The Stratford Story" on the festival's website: www.stratfordfestival.ca/about/history.aspx?id=8217
9 "Site-Specific *Hamlet*s and Reconfigured Localities: Jiang'an, Singapore, Elsinore," *Shakespeare International Yearbook*, 7 (December 2007), 42. Huang's discussion is of Jiao Juyin's staging at a Confucian temple in Jiang'an in China and Ong Ken Sen's direction of the play for the Singaporean company Theatre Works, staged at Kronborg Castle in Elsinore, Denmark.
10 Sonia Massai, *World-Wide Shakespeares* (Abingdon: Routledge, 2005), 10.
11 https://www.osfashland.org/about/what-is-osf.aspx. The mission statement in full reads: "Inspired by Shakespeare's work and the cultural richness of the United States, we reveal our collective humanity through illuminating interpretations of new and classic plays, deepened by the kaleidoscope of rotating repertory."
12 Suzanne Gossett, "Habima *Merchant of Venice*: Performances Inside and Outside the Globe," in Susan Bennett and Christie Carson, eds. *Shakespeare Beyond English* (Cambridge: Cambridge University Press, 2013), 271.
13 Neil MacGregor, "Director's Foreword," in Jonathan Bate and Dora Thornton, eds. *Shakespeare: Staging the World* (London: British Museum, 2012), 8.

14 MacGregor, "Director's Foreword," 9.
15 MacGregor, "Director's Foreword," 8.
16 "Shakespeare: Staging the World" was at the British Museum from 19 July to 25 November, 2012; the Victoria and Albert Museum celebrated the 450th anniversary of Shakespeare's birth (2014) with museum-wide events including "a special Shakespeare Festival" that ran from 21 April to 4 May (http://www.vam.ac.uk/page/s/shakespeare/); and the British Library was one of the lead partners of Shakespeare 400 (2016).
17 See Grupo Galpão's website for a fuller performance history: http://www.grupogalpao.com.br/?p=173. Bessell's *"Romeu e Julieta (Reprise):* Grupo Galpão at the Globe, Again," in S. Bennett and C. Carson, eds. *Shakespeare Beyond English* (Cambridge: Cambridge University Press, 2003), 212–20. W. B. Worthen considered the production exemplary of modern intercultural performance in his detailed case study in *Shakespeare and the Force of Modern Performance*, 153 and following. Grupo Galpão's *Romeu y Julieta* is pictured on the book's front cover.
18 The company's productions of *Henry IV (1 & 2)* and *Henry V* were staged at the National Centre for the Performing Arts in Beijing, the Shanghai Grand Theatre and as part of the Hong Kong Arts Festival (February and March 2016) before traveling to the Brooklyn Academic of Music in New York City for performances there (March 2016).
19 The British Council, "Shakespeare Reworked," http://theatreanddance.britishcouncil.org/projects/2015/shakespeare-reworked/. Other incubator collaborations included India, Nigeria, Russia, South Africa, South Korea, Tunisia and Hong Kong.
20 Alexa Huang, "Global Shakespeares as Methodology," *Shakespeare*, 9, no. 3 (2013): 274.
21 Anecdotal evidence suggests more than 100 people completed their Globe to Globe passports, including my co-editor Christie Carson, whose fully stamped document is pictured on the back cover of *Shakespeare Beyond English*.
22 See the Shakespeare Theatre Association (STA) website: http://www.stahome.org/mission/. Their mission also includes the sharing of resources and advocacy issues.
23 http://shakespearepassport.com/what-is-it. Versions are available for both iPhone and Android devices.
24 Details are posted at http://www.stahome.org/2016/.
25 See note 3.
26 Miwon Kwon, *One Place after Another* (Cambridge, MA: MIT Press, 2004), 29–30.

2 Proximal dreams: Peter Sellars at the Stratford Festival of Canada

Margaret Jane Kidnie

Figure 2.1　Festival Theatre (panorama). Stratford Festival of Canada. Photo by Richard Bain.

The Stratford Festival of Canada performed *A Midsummer Night's Dream* in 2014 on the prestigious festival stage in Stratford's largest theatre. To get to this performance, you might have driven along Stratford's picturesque river, admiring the swans and landscaping until you saw the iconic architecture of the Festival Theatre loom in view (Figure 2.1). This space comes freighted with Ontario history. In the first half of the twentieth century, Stratford's economy was endangered by the relocation of the railway industry. The idea for a classical repertory theatre was the brainchild of Tom Patterson, a local journalist, who saw the opportunity to reinvent Stratford as a destination site for culture and arts. Tyrone Guthrie was invited to serve as artistic director, and he in turn commissioned Tanya Moiseiwitsch to design the stage. Moiseiwitsch's conception of a flexible, multi-tiered thrust space was first realized in Ontario, and has since inspired such auditoriums as Lincoln Center's Beaumont Theater in New York, the Crucible Theatre in Sheffield, and the Guthrie Theater in Minneapolis. Guthrie's opening season in the summer of 1953, starring Alec Guinness as Richard III and Irene Worth as Helena in *All's Well That Ends Well*, was played in a tent, and spectators sat on metal-frame wooden chairs, the backs of which were stencilled with seat numbers. In 1957 the Stratford Festival gained a permanent home, and the award-winning theatre's tent-like roof, topped with its signature crown, provides a visual reminder of the festival's origins, its classical mandate, and its earliest seasons in the open air.[1]

Once you sighted the Festival Theatre on your way to the 2014 production of *A Midsummer Night's Dream*, you perhaps parked by the river on Lakeside Drive and walked the short distance up the hill to admire the gardens planted with flowers mentioned in Shakespeare's plays, eventually walking in to take your seat in the Festival Theatre. This is where the sense of pilgrimage, if that's what you were looking for, ended. There was nothing particularly reverent about Chris Abraham's production of *Dream*, which a disgruntled and exasperated audience member (in fact, Ben Carlson in character as Christopher Sly) disparaged at the beginning of Abraham's 2015 production of *The Taming of the Shrew* as "my big fat gay Shakespearean wedding."

Sly's in-joke was especially directed at festival patrons who had seen Abraham's popular and critically well-received *Dream* the previous year. In the specific context of a second main-house Abraham production of one of Shakespeare's comedies, the joke depends on spectators recognizing the caricature while also, to some extent, disallowing the view of this particular "spectator" – Carlson, tellingly, played the patron/Sly with a British accent, imposing an audible culture gap between this character and a festival audience base drawn largely from Canada and the United States. The joke marks Abraham's staging of *Dream* as unexpected or exceptional, arguably even "un-Shakespearean." Yet at the same time, by locating the complaint with a disruptive spectator who (in the character of Sly) falls asleep on stage and eventually, naively, takes performance for reality, it no less firmly marginalizes that opinion as ill-judged and precious. It is not the outlandish spectator, but the outlandish staging, that is marked as belonging to this mainstream festival space.

Abraham's innovation in 2014 was to introduce a framing device to *Dream* that situated the enactment of the play as the entertainment at a same-sex wedding in Stratford, Ontario, attended by festival actors. The grooms (Josue Laboucane and Thomas Olajide) sat front row centre throughout the staging, Lysander was cross-cast as a woman (played by Tara Rosling), and Jonathan Goad and Evan Buliung played Oberon and Titania, switching the roles on alternate nights. Although some of the sight gags and tongue-in-cheek metatheatricality may have startled some patrons – a rumour circulated during the summer of several school groups leaving in haste after the grooms' kiss in the opening scene – it was a show that remained fairly easily legible as Shakespeare's *Dream*, right down to the fairies' rendition of Bruno Mars' "Grenade" in Titania's bower.[2] There was an imaginative proximity between Abraham's production and expectations of this comedy in performance, a nearness that was reinforced by the staging's physical location in the Festival Theatre, squarely at the heart of the season's theatrical programming.

What was really surprising, however, was that Antoni Cimolino, artistic director of the Stratford Festival, programmed not one, but two, productions of *A Midsummer Night's Dream* in the summer of 2014 as part of a season designed to explore "Minds Pushed to the Edge." This second production was also called *A Midsummer Night's Dream*, but it was subtitled "a chamber play." Issues of proximity immediately press more insistently to the fore. The subtitle marks this staging as Shakespeare's play, but not quite Shakespeare's play – it is not even "the" chamber play, it is "a" chamber play, one potentially among many. And that sense of a slight distance from the thing itself was reinforced by the production's physical location. Stratford has four world-class theatres. *A Chamber Play* was not staged at any of them. Instead, it was performed at the Masonic Concert Hall, slightly renovated for the purpose. Rather than motoring along the familiar Lakeside Drive, patrons found themselves on mapquest.com, in search of Church Street.

A Chamber Play was directed by Peter Sellars. There are perhaps only three or four other directors currently working today whose international reputations would be sufficient to persuade the festival to invest in the expense of borrowing and modifying the Masonic site, especially given the disorientation and potential loss of brand recognition this temporary location might entail for spectators. The Stratford Festival press release communicating their choice of theatrical space for this production explains that "a non-traditional venue was central" to Sellars' vision, and further clarifies that "the venue's location in a combined commercial-residential neighbourhood makes [the Masonic Concert Hall] a perfect choice."[3] The hall's neighbourhood, however, is not unique; the Studio Theatre is likewise situated in an area of town where shops and homes co-exist. The advantage of the Concert Hall is perhaps rather that it could be constructed – literally and ideologically – as a Stratford (Festival) theatre, the parenthesis marking the production's geographical and artistic proximity to, yet distance from, the festival and its history. This complex sense of place is further enhanced by a production team which included, in addition to James F. Ingalls (lighting), the Harlem-based visual artist Abigail DeVille (set and installation) and the Mexican composer Tareke Ortiz (sound). Sellars' creative "home" in Stratford was grounded in

Canadian regional and national histories – theatrical and otherwise – while also deliberately reaching out to stories from other communities, other cultures. "Let 100,000 flowers bloom," as Sellars puts it in interview with J. Kelly Nestruck, talking about audience expectations and Cimolino's decision to program two productions of *Dream*. "Shakespeare by nature is not a narrow playwright."[4]

The Masonic Concert Hall, with its sprung dance floor and raised stage, was built in 1930 and is best known as a venue for live music. The rectangular hall floor measures forty-one feet by fifty-six feet, with the stage positioned on the narrow length of the rectangle, furthest from the entrance.[5] The stage itself is a somewhat shallow three-sided proscenium space with a twenty-one foot arch; there is a door on stage left and another, stage right. Although the venue offers a stage extension (twenty-four feet by eight feet), in effect transforming the space into a partial thrust stage, *A Chamber Play* was staged entirely behind the proscenium. "Backstage" at the Masonic Concert Hall is limited to tiny spaces at extreme right and left, behind the stage doors, and actors have backstage access to the stage only from stage right – Sellars' actors approached the stage from the back of the house at the beginning of the show, remained visible onstage throughout the performance, and exited back through the audience at the show's end. With room for 168 spectators, the capacity of the hall was significantly smaller than that offered even by the Studio Theatre, which is otherwise the festival's most intimate performance space, seating 260 spectators.

DeVille's installation transformed the hall. The stage took on an almost cavernous feel – the area behind the proscenium was empty of set, and the walls were painted a dark colour with variations of tone that could suggest landscape, or at least texture and depth, when Ingalls' lighting design played on them. The walls and ceiling of the auditorium, on the other hand, were filled, literally, with junk (Figure 2.2). DeVille describes her materials for this project as "accumulated debris from two junkyards in Stratford Ontario."[6] There were pieces of scrap wood, and large sheets of rusty corrugated metal and plywood, but the bulk of the suspended objects were household items: ironing boards, a couple of busted-out televisions, thin single mattresses, a wooden six-armed chandelier, a broom, a "Swiffer" mop, a newel post, a toilet seat, a white ceramic sink, a screen door, at least four or five bedsprings, a pogo stick.

And there were chairs – lots of chairs – some of them wood and metal frame chairs with white, stencilled seat numbers on their wooden backs. Not only did DeVille draw inspiration from the local public junkyards, but she also raided the Stratford Festival's metaphorical attic, blending together remnants and offcasts from the early days with Alec Guinness, Tyrone Guthrie, and Tanya Moiseiwitsch, when the plays were performed in a tent.[7] DeVille's installation encouraged spectators to reflect on any number of local dreams – those unwritten

Figure 2.2   *A Midsummer Night's Dream: A Chamber Play.* Set and installation artist, Abigail DeVille. Photo by Abigail DeVille. The space (auditorium and stage) is suffused indigo in the original colour photograph.

stories to which we no longer have access, some of them domestic, some of them theatrical – the traces of which linger in the "junk" they leave behind.

All of these items were displayed and arranged on silver foil crumpled against the ceiling and walls. Strands of light were woven through the foil on the ceiling, through which pulsed vibrant electric colours, the design rippling like waves, in no discernible pattern, from pink to orange to blue to indigo to green to purple. Figure 2.2 is a photograph taken during rehearsal from a spot near the back of the hall (the auditorium was raked to facilitate sightlines); in addition to partially documenting DeVille's installation, this view of the stage suggests how lighting could transform flat, dark stage walls into something suggestive of landscape. As spectators walked into the space, the light rippling through the installation was complemented by an echoing, ghostly, metallic soundscape that sounded something like the hum of a Tibetan singing bowl.

The photograph in Figure 2.3 was taken looking into the auditorium from a position just in front of the stage. The installation and house lights are both on. Stills

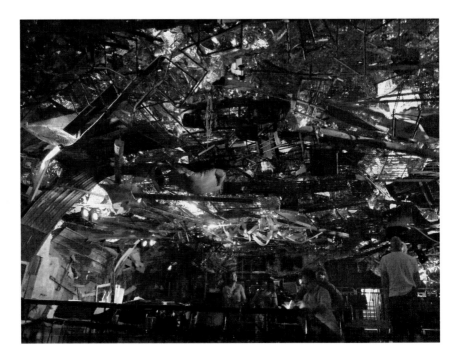

Figure 2.3   *A Midsummer Night's Dream: A Chamber Play*. Set and installation artist, Abigail DeVille. Photo by Abigail DeVille. The ceiling lighting is a yellowish-green in the original colour photograph.

capture inadequately the full impact of this aural and visual space: rippling lighting, a continuous soundscape, and an installation that covers the hall's interior shell created a kind of sensory bath into and around which spectators walked. It was an immersive – almost an oppressively immersive – space, and the festival encouraged spectators to arrive early to partake of it, blurring the lines between gallery and theatre, installation and performance. Once the show began, the installation lighting blacked out, and the stage was lit with saturated washes that steadily darkened throughout the lovers' night in the forest. The soundscape, however, continued to wash over the audience, underscoring the dialogue. There was no choice but to mic the actors, a necessity Jill L. Levenson describes as enriching *Dream*'s affective power: "Sellars uses soft microphones as film uses close-up. In this otherwise strenuous production the actors can whisper their most emotional lines."[8] Ortiz' sound design was reminiscent of the ocean, and closely tied to the characters' emotional journey. It could seem gentle and soothing – Richard Ouzounian heard in it "fragments of music, rushing winds, whispering voices" – moments later transforming into a thunderous, almost physically punishing roar, driving and underpinning the actors' dialogue.[9]

There was a sequence in this production – it maps onto Act 3.2, when Puck is misdirecting Lysander and Demetrius in the woods – which the stage manager's notes warn as the "gates of hell."[10] The bold lighting, rapidly scrolling through a series of monochromatic washes, in combination with the "violent rumbling of what sounds (and feels) like an earthquake," created the effect of a "world on the precipice of extinction, or perhaps rebirth."[11] Three of the actors cowered or crouched against the upstage wall, clawing at it, while Puck, seated on the floor upstage left and facing out to the audience, screamed above the visual and aural storm, "Up and down, up and down, / I will lead them up and down; / I am feared in field and town: / Goblin, lead them up and down."

One doesn't really "watch" a sequence like this – one is battered by it, one survives it. Reviewers repeatedly describe the sound at such moments in the show in terms of felt vibration.[12] When the crescendo of sound and light finally and suddenly ended after Puck's quatrain, the actors collapsed like marionette puppets whose strings had been cut. In the silence and stillness of the theatre, one sensed only the most intense feeling of relief that it was over. A theatre companion commented that it was only when the actors fell to the ground that he became aware that he had stopped breathing; Ouzounian's review describes "the [occasional, blessed] joy of sudden, magical silence."

I want to build on this analysis of ambient space to talk about the way rehearsal method and creative process shaped language and character, eventually concluding by thinking about the dynamic between space and storytelling in this production of *Dream*. Four actors played all of Shakespeare's parts. An interview with the actors taped for the Canadian Broadcasting Corporation (CBC) begins with each actor introducing himself or herself: "I'm Trish Lindström, and I play Titania, Hermia, Lion, and Wall as one individual." "I'm Mike Nadajewski, and I play one person, but with the words of Oberon, Lysander, Peter Quince, and a touch of Theseus." "I'm Sarah Afful. I play as one person Hippolyta, Puck, Helena, Starveling the Tailor, and Thisbe, and – am I missing one? – Flute. And Fairy." "I'm Dion Johnstone, and combined into one person I'm playing Bottom, Theseus, Demetrius."[13]

As their somewhat deliberate phrasing is careful to explain, this show's doubling strategies provided complicated interpretations of character. The script development was limited to cutting lines, rather than rewriting or rearranging Shakespeare's text, but the editing process was intensive and purposeful. The production's continuous action in combination with the actors' seamless shifts between characters made this familiar comedy seem like suddenly unfamiliar terrain, an effect which was often disorienting, and in places revelatory. Afful's character, to offer just one short example, speaks Helena's lines to Johnstone, accusing him of doing her "mischief," while he at the same time moves away from her to embrace Lindström: "Fie, Demetrius!," Afful says, "Your wrongs do set a scandal on my sex. / We cannot fight for love, as men may do; / We should be wooed, and were not made to woo. / I'll follow thee," she continues, "and make a heaven of hell, / To die upon the hand I love so well." Here, Nadajewski approaches Afful, and pulling her gently to one side, says to her, "Fare thee well, nymph; ere he do leave this grove / Thou shalt fly him, and he shall seek thy love. / Hast thou the flower there? Welcome, wanderer." And Afful replies, "Ay, there it is." In this passage familiar to us from Act 2.1, Afful shifts from the human world to the fairy world, from Helena to Puck, from rejection to revenge somewhere during the three lines Nadajewski addresses to her character.

At the beginning of the second week of rehearsals, in order to allow the actors more easily to follow their individual character arcs, the script was revised with the actors' names – Sarah, Dion, Trish, Mike – positioned in place of the character speech prefixes. This pragmatic rehearsal strategy, invisible to the audience since speech prefixes are not typically vocalized in performance, quietly asserts a particular kind of distance between Shakespeare's *Dream* and Sellars' *Chamber Dream*. Instead of doubling parts, each actor played a unified and coherent character. As Johnstone explains in interview, "I'm not switching from Bottom to Demetrius – I *am* Bottom/Demetrius/Theseus. I'm all of these; these are all facets of who I am."[14] To return to that brief example from Act 2.1, Afful was not asked to make sense of her reply about the flower "as" Puck instead of "as" Helena, but to conceptualize this narrative trajectory in terms of one self-consistent character called "Sarah."

This reinvention of character went hand in hand with Sellars' treatment of narrative. The actors, guided by Sellars in rehearsal, were led on intensive, and intensely personal, journeys of discovery, as they sought out the emotional through-line that for each of them could hold together the particular grouping of characters to which they had been assigned. Afful describes it as "a huge process of unlearning everything that I've learned in terms of how I thought Shakespeare was supposed to be done."[15] Rehearsals were enabled in the first instance by Sellars' determination to remove all of Shakespeare's "plot points." Their first week together was spent collaboratively cutting the play – Egeus was one of the first pieces of the original story to go – and the group continued to trim lines up to opening night. There was also no blocking. Sellars instead gave the actors positions from which to start at the beginning of the second week, and asked them to run their working script. This rehearsal method was entirely new to the actors, and challenging:

> We had our scripts and we were supposed to get up and do it. Do *what*? . . . It must have taken four hours to do our first pass-through of it. . . . It was only through time, by doing it, that the connections started to happen. "This might be what I'm

talking about." "This might be directed to so-and-so." And then Peter, looking at it from the outside, would say, "These things are starting to arise, you go in this direction." And then our own personal stories started to get mixed into it.[16]

The actors, as Johnstone puts it, "sniffed [their] way" through the play, following and developing particular threads that surfaced through rehearsal.[17]

The show's deep rootedness in the actors' personal stories along with its intimate, almost claustrophobic, performance space were inherent to Sellars' conception of the piece as "a chamber play." "We are playing *A Midsummer Night's Dream* not with an orchestra but with a string quartet," he explains in his director's notes, further clarifying in interview with *The Globe and Mail* that his subtitle alludes to the "really intense portraits of marriage" found in the chamber plays of August Strindberg.[18] For Strindberg, as for Sellars, the goal was to devise a method – and devised space is necessarily caught up in this project – able to capture the defining qualities of chamber music: "intimate approach, significant theme, careful treatment."[19] The show's unblocked, improvisational character was sustained throughout the run. An actor who found himself or herself "in a different place, emotionally or physically" in a certain performance could set in motion "the chamber effect": "one string plays a note different, and the whole balance shifts, it changes everything."[20] These personal stories, however, remained subterraneous – suggestive, rather than explicit – shaping the emotional texture of each performance without becoming themselves the narrative or message of the production. As Nadajewski explains, "Peter wasn't interested in the kind of Shakespeare where you stand up and you say, 'I know exactly what this means and I'm going to tell you exactly what this means.' He wants to allow for the opposite to be true, for one line to have many different meanings, different resonances."[21]

Without the "plot points" that tie Theseus and Hippolyta, Helena and Hermia, Puck, Oberon, and Bottom to Shakespeare's comedy, character names spoken in dialogue survived only as "archetypes," to use Nadajewski's term, within a drama about betrayed love and the opportunities for, and barriers to, reconciliation.[22] Johnstone, trying to describe language's inability to capture everything going on in this staging, sounds remarkably like Bottom trying to find words to describe his dream:

> There's so many layers of meaning to communicate . . . the way it plays for us is we reach a point where there aren't enough words, language fails to adequately describe the depth of the meaning so there are moments and times where we have to really stretch language to fully communicate the experience that we're having . . . the story that's emerging is amazing because it's so true to the words that are there on the page . . . but it's still only like a top 3% of the experience that's happening underneath it. Words can only just barely describe. . . . You

know – it feels like when we do this . . . it's very much submerged underneath an ocean of subconscious thoughts and dreams and nightmares and love and the pain of love and all of that.[23]

The "truth" of this staging is a recurrent theme in the interviews these actors gave, and as W. B. Worthen has analyzed, a discourse of authenticity is not uncommon in discussions of live Shakespearean performance.[24] Here, however, "truth" lies not with the essence of Shakespeare or his language, but with the actors' own personal truths as filtered through Shakespeare's language. By removing all "plot points" and assigning to his actors roles which are a blend of multiple characters, Sellars created a working environment in which his actors were led to draw creatively on their own life experiences in order to build stories and through-lines that they could play in performance. These narrative threads – as though in a dream – were both like, and unlike, Shakespeare's drama. Humour, it would seem, survives with difficulty the loss of plot. The tone of *A Chamber Play* was dominated by hurt, confusions, and anger, and the result was a production that seemed to mine relentlessly the dark subconscious of Shakespeare's romantic comedy.

As a spectator, the effect was disorienting because it was hard not to measure proximal distances. One could measure where the actors were in Shakespeare's story (had any plot points remained), but one could simultaneously measure where they were in a related, but different, narrative that involves four characters trying, and often failing, but then trying *again* to work through very precise, albeit unarticulated, stories of love and betrayal. One would imagine that as a spectator one would eventually let go of the traces of Shakespeare's plot that for the duration of this production exist only in memory, but my experience of it was that these plot points remained, ghosting the action playing out onstage. I saw these four actor/characters, but Shakespeare's characters, Shakespeare's plot points also kept flitting in and out of the stage action, enriching and complicating the narrative.

Lindström and Nadajewski – Hermia and Lysander, Titania and Oberon – enacted some of the production's rawest emotion (Figure 2.4). This couple seemed to start from a position of intense emotional loss. Nadajewski delivered his opening line, "How now, my love? Why is your cheek so pale?," as though he were utterly spent, completely emotionally drained. Lindström in turn replied to him with anger and resentment, "Belike for want of rain, which I could well / Beteem them from the tempest of my eyes," and she eventually turned sexually to Johnstone, groping his body while still verbally interacting with Nadajewski. One intuits from the tone and body language with which they interact with each other that this couple has not only been together a long time by the start of the play – more Titania and Oberon than Hermia and Lysander – but that they have suffered together. Not long after, they move into the argument between Titania

Figure 2.4   Mike Nadajewski (left), Dion Johnstone and Trish Lindström in *A Midsummer Night's Dream: A Chamber Play*. Photo by Michael Cooper.

and Oberon about possession of the changeling boy. This exchange is played as a tender moment of tentative reconciliation, and Lindström puts Nadajewski's hand on her belly, her womb, when she mentions the "childing autumn." That gesture – a Brechtian "gestus" might be the better term for it – is repeated over the course of the production, and the effect is to connect this couple's grief and anger, and sexual rejection of each other, to an unspoken story about the loss of a child. They are Hermia and Lysander, and they are also Titania and Oberon, *and* there is a changeling boy, but these characters get rolled together and played in a present moment when there may – or may not – have been a miscarriage or infant death.

One of the most moving exchanges in this production occurred when Lindström woke from the dream in which the serpent "ate [her] heart away." Nadajewski had just finished his "Hermia, sleep thou there" speech in which he rejects Lindström and turns to Afful, but instead of exiting (none of the actors left the stage at any point during this show), he remained seated on the stage, facing stage right towards Lindström. When Lindström wakes, she narrates her dream to Nadajewski, who impassively stares at her. The last lines of her speech were delivered kneeling over Nadajewski's extended legs, as she looked into his eyes:

> Lysander! What, removed? Lysander! Lord!
> What, out of hearing? Gone? No sound, no word?
> Alack, where are you? Speak, and if you hear;
> Speak, of all loves! I swoon almost with fear.
> No? Then I well perceive you are not nigh.
> Either death or you I'll find immediately.

At this, Johnstone led Lindström gently away, comforting her, and staring down Nadajewski. This moment's reinterpretation of literal sight as metaphorical sight brilliantly captured in Nadajewski's character that moment in a relationship when anguish and pain cuts out, as too much to bear, transforming into emotional emptiness.

Sellars' openness to modern identities and politics was an aspect of the process that the actors found especially enabling. To continue for the moment with the changeling child scene and Titania's "weather report," this was the speech that Afful brought into audition. Sellars asked Afful, who is from a village in Ghana, to try it again, but this time to picture herself in her village, and to imagine that all of the work her family has put into the land has been lost due to global warming. According to Afful, this brief exchange with the director opened her to the play, and the play to her, in a way that she had never before experienced:

> It's true, it's all happening at this moment right now, it's happening around the world and . . . people who aren't in power, who don't have what we have in

Canada, are suffering. It's . . . . to make [Shakespeare] real for yourself, which I never really thought I could do, I didn't think that was allowed. . . . [Peter] made me think I could take this text that isn't specifically written for my culture and use it. . . . There's a great sense of hope that yeah, this beautiful writer called Shakespeare can be used for telling stories of all sorts.[25]

In this same interview, Lindström passionately connects environmental politics and political agency to their staging of *Dream*, arguing that this production is not about being "clever," but getting the audience to connect as "humans": "they're actually hearing what the story is and they're actually seeing that global warming is affecting us right today, like *today*, *right* now, and so the very first line of our play is, "*Now* fair Hippolyta . . .". It's happening now. It's not happening in Elizabethan times, it's not in the sixteenth [century], it's *now*."

The "now" for Johnstone's character was further caught up in the politics of being young, black, and male. Nestruck praised his performance as a "tour de force," writing that Johnstone "dominates the production, physically but also in the compelling psychological journey he maps" (Figure 2.5).[26] Beginning the play against the back wall, looming over Afful, Johnstone infuses Theseus' opening

Figure 2.5   From left: Sarah Afful, Dion Johnstone, Mike Nadajewski and Trish Lindström in *A Midsummer Night's Dream: A Chamber Play*. Photo by Michael Cooper.

two and a half lines with an intense physical sexuality; when he is brushed off by Afful, he rotates to find Lindström, who responds to his caress. Tone and gesture once again modulate the signifying force of Shakespeare's lines. Johnstone's early reference to the "old moon" that "lingers my desires / Like to a step-dame or dowager / Long withering out a young man's revenue," figured his lust for Lindström, and since Afful was still clearly listening to his words, it doubled as an aggressive promise that he would cheat on her with this (white) woman. Djanet Sears' *Harlem Duet* – a Canadian "prequel" to *Othello* that tells the story of Billie, Othello's black wife, who is abandoned for Desdemona – suddenly became available as an unexpected intertext for Sellars' production of *Dream*.[27]

This love triangle darkened in the first mechanicals' scene, in which Johnstone directed squarely at Afful the violence of Bottom's audition piece for a role in "Ercles' vein, a tyrant's vein." After gently promising Lindström that he "will condole in some measure," he turned to Afful, shouting the "raging rocks" poem at her, and forcing her roughly into the upstage left corner. The exchange was deeply disturbing, bordering on assault, and Afful's character (Hippolyta? Helena? Thisbe?) remained visibly shaken when Nadajewski, jealous of Lindström, insisted that Afful must play the part of "the lady that Pyramus must love."

Johnstone's relationship with Lindström brought its own dangers, however, in terms of his perception of his character's social and mental vulnerability:

> I'm getting the sense that this is a guy who's done prison time, which has created a real fuck-up in our relationship [his with Afful]. Maybe it was abuse that happened in the past, maybe you called the cops, maybe I'm just one more strike from, like, twenty-five to life. And all my dallying with Trish's character is putting me in a position where all that can go to hell, because all she's got to do is phone the police and say this guy touched me, this guy fucking raped me, this guy, you know, killed my lover – anything.[28]

Johnstone's delivery of the sustained reference in Bottom's audition piece to the "raging rocks" and "shivering shocks" that "Shall break the locks / Of prison-gates" hints at this character's back story. He later collapses twice in this production, both times when threatened by the female characters with incarceration. In the first instance, the lighting shifts to blood red and the soundscape crescendoes to a howl, above which Afful yells Puck's promise to hunt him in the form of horse, hound, hog, bear, and fire. Johnstone desperately rattles the locked stage doors in a failed effort to escape the prison the stage space has suddenly become for him. Minutes later, as the lighting again bleeds red, Lindström accuses him of murdering Lysander, and this time it is Johnstone who, weeping and crouching against the assault of his lover's anger, braces himself in a corner.

There were moments in the action when it seemed as though these characters might be able to resolve their conflicts. Each time, however, one of them would reject the effort. The mechanicals' first rehearsal, in particular, offered an extended metatheatrical comment on their tangled relationships, and an opportunity for healing. Johnstone countered Afful's and Lindström's hesitant skepticism with variously conciliatory and reassuring speeches, carefully testing against the women's facial expressions and body language the words that he hoped might bring all of them together, "saying, 'Ladies,' or '*Fair* ladies, I would wish you' – or 'I would *request* you,' or 'I would *entreat* you, not to fear, not to tremble.' " Here Nadajewski, who was standing aloof from the others after the sequence in which he emotionally absents himself from Lindström, and channeling Peter Quince, suddenly and angrily intervenes to point out "two hard things." The opportunity for reconciliation founders with Lindström's acknowledgement, "You can never bring in a wall." The lighting darkened to red, the soundscape escalated to loud howling, and Afful, speaking Puck's words, verbally attacked a trapped Johnstone.

The play's eventual successful transition into what Sellars describes literally and metaphorically as "a new dawn," began in Titania's bower.[29] Stage lighting that had grown so dark that the stage manager in a windowed sound booth at the back of the hall felt it necessary to dim her table lamp, brightened to pale daylight, and the soundscape shifted for the first time to what the sound cue sheet calls "Fresh Ocean."[30] Behind the calm ocean effects, one discerned the faint sound of vocal music, or as described in the sound cues, "Esperanza." With Nadajewski's entrance into the bower to awaken a sleeping Lindström from Johnstone's embrace, and as the lighting continued to brighten, the bewildered characters gathered in their original pairings (Afful with Johnstone, and Lindström with Nadajewski). The dialogue of the fifth act "Pyramus and Thisbe" scored a complicated emotional choreography in which the characters helped each other shed, or at least set aside, the pain of their previous encounters. This process of healing remained provisional and conditional. Sellars instructed his actors in rehearsal not to "take care of" the audience: spectators were invited to witness the performance event in an immersive installation space, but they were conceived as being detached from the "chamber effect" playing out behind the proscenium. "It's almost like we're in an aquarium," Johnstone explains, and spectators "get to come in and watch the exhibit and make what they make of it."[31] This dynamic was nowhere more evident than in Afful's epilogue, which was delivered with her back to the audience as she spoke intently to the other three actors. The production's closing image was of the four of them briefly joining hands, "if we be friends," and releasing, as the lights blacked out.

The Stratford Festival at its inception in 1953 looked beyond national borders to import the kind of prestige and cultural cachet that a group of élite artists could bring to a small Ontario town with ambitions. Sellars' collaboration with Cimolino in 2014 as part of a season in which the festival mounted two productions of one of Shakespeare's best-known comedies was something different. "Place," in a new millennium, is a more unstable prospect than it was sixty years ago, and even a local destination site such as Stratford is now shot through with a spectrum of identities, cultures, and histories, homegrown and otherwise, all of which contribute to a particular perception of "space," and, for some, "home." And this space exists *now*, as Lindström puts it, in a world connected, not least, by global economics and climate change. *A Chamber Dream* was an intensive exploration of the ways in which the course of true love never does run smooth, and of how four damaged characters find their way through to healing and (provisional) reconciliation. "Now, fair Hippolyta," their play begins. Sellars took Shakespeare's theatrical language, and by releasing it from plot and opening it to rehearsal, immersed audiences in the under-belly of this almost too-well-known comedy. Surrounded by an installation that tunnelled down to four actor/characters on a stage from which it seemed they were unable to escape, it was as though we were floating beneath the flotsam of the twenty-first century – we were under the great Pacific junk patch, we were in the middle of hurricane Katrina, we were part of the history of Stratford and its festival – a world of love, and failed love, in which Shakespeare is caught up, and to which his plays continue to speak. Proximity, indeed.

Notes

1 Details about the genesis of the Stratford Festival are available in Tom Patterson and Allan Gould, *First Stage: The Making of the Stratford Festival*, rev. ed. (Willowdale, ON: Firefly Books, 1999), and in "The Stratford Story," now available on the Stratford Festival website: http://www.stratfordfestival.ca/about/history.aspx?id=8217 (accessed 28 July 2015). For a counter-narrative of the festival's origins and legacy, see Richard Paul Knowles, "From Nationalist to Multinational: The Stratford Festival, Free Trade, and the Discourses of Intercultural Tourism," *Theatre Journal*, 47 (1995): 19–41.
2 J. Kelly Nestruck mentions the rumour in conversation with Chris Abraham and Peter Sellars, "A Midsummer Night's Dream: One Dream, Two Productions," *Globe and Mail*, 22 July 2014.
3 "Stratford Festival Extends Two Shakespeares | Venue Set for Peter Sellars's A Midsummer Night's Dream," *Stratford Festival Press Release*, 24 February 2014.
4 Nestruck, "A Midsummer Night's Dream." Sellars comments early in the same interview that "anything that liberates Shakespeare from the idea of monoculture is to be applauded." He was speaking specifically of the Abraham production, but it is a politics at the heart of his own artistic priorities, in *A Chamber Dream* and elsewhere.
5 Details of the dimensions and physical layout of the Masonic Concert Hall are taken from its website (smch.ca), accessed 28 July 2015.

6   Abigail DeVille, "Midsummer Event Horizon" (2014), stage/set installation, as posted by the Rema Hort Mann Foundation at http://www.remahortmannfoundation.org/project/abigail-deville/ (accessed 28 July 2015). Two photographs of the installation unlit by theatrical lighting are available on this website.
7   This festival connection was mentioned by Richard Ouzounian in his review "Shakespeare's *A Midsummer Night's Dream* in Stratford: Like You've Never Seen Before," *Toronto Star*, 25 July 2014.
8   Jill L. Levenson, "*A Midsummer Night's Dream: A Chamber Play* (Stratford Festival) @ Stratford, Ontario, Canada (27 July 2014)," bloggingshakespeare.com (accessed 1 August 2015). Nestruck offers an extended discussion of the sound, concluding that "whole new passages opened up for me in different ways simply because I could listen to them whispered rather than wailed" ("A Dream Fulfilled: You Have to See Stratford's Radical Rethink of Shakespeare," *The Globe and Mail*, 25 July 2014).
9   Ouzounian, "Shakespeare's *A Midsummer Night's Dream* in Stratford."
10 The warning in the Stage Manager's book fell at 48, line 16. I am grateful to the Stage Manager, Janine Ralph, for sharing the rehearsal script with me (version V5.5, 27 July 2014), and for letting me take notes in the sound booth during one performance.
11 Charles Isherwood, "Beyond Shakespeare's Wildest Dreams," *The New York Times*, 12 August 2014. The lighting terminology draws on Jenn Stephenson's review, "*A Midsummer Night's Dream* by Stratford Festival, and *A Midsummer Night's Dream: A Chamber Play* by Stratford Festival," *Shakespeare Bulletin*, 33, no. 1 (March 2015): 168–74, 172.
12 Isherwood, "Beyond Shakespeare's Wildest Dreams," Nestruck, "A Dream Fulfilled," Ouzounian, "Shakespeare's *A Midsummer Night's Dream* in Stratford."
13 "Bottom's Dream," Ideas with Paul Kennedy (aired 17 December 2014). The participants were Peter Sellars, Sarah Afful, Dion Johnstone, Trish Lindström, and Mike Nadajewski. Episode available at http://www.cbc.ca/radio/ideas/bottom-s-dream-1.2914226 (accessed 28 July 2015). I am grateful to Philip Coulter for sharing with me the uncut interview recordings. All quotations from the CBC's interviews with director and cast are from the uncut files.
14 Personal interview with Sarah Afful, Dion Johnstone, and Mike Nadajewski (Masonic Concert Hall, 12 September 2014). I am immensely grateful to them all for agreeing to discuss the production with me, and to Shira Ginsler for facilitating the meeting.
15 Personal interview.
16 Lindström, CBC interview.
17 Personal interview.
18 Peter Sellars, "Cosmos for a Quartet of Voices: Director's Notes," *A Midsummer Night's Dream: A Chamber Play*, 24 July–20 September 2014, Program, 9; Nestruck, "A Midsummer Night's Dream."
19 August Strindberg, *Letters to the Intimate Theatre (1911–21)*, quoted in Levenson, "*A Midsummer Night's Dream*."
20 Nadajewski and Johnstone, personal interview.
21 CBC interview.
22 Nadajewski, in personal interview, continues, "The metaphors have become the plot, and what's left of the plot, like the proper names, *they* have become the metaphors."
23 CBC interview.
24 W. B. Worthen, *Shakespeare and the Authority of Performance* (Cambridge: Cambridge UP, 1997).
25 CBC interview.

26 Nestruck, "A Dream Fulfilled."
27 Djanet Sears, *Harlem Duet* (Toronto: Scirocco Drama, 1997). First performed by Nightwood Theatre (20 April–18 May 1997), and revived at the Stratford Festival in 2006.
28 Personal interview.
29 Sellars, "Director's Notes," 9.
30 *A Midsummer Night's Dream: A Chamber Play*, dir. Peter Sellars, 24 July–20 September 2014, Sound Cue Sheet (SEL SX Qs v11.1), dated 16 July 2014. I am grateful to Janine Ralph for sharing this with me.
31 Johnstone, personal interview. The actors noted that despite Sellars' direction not to play to the audience, they were very conscious of spectators adjusting their expectations of the play as a comedy; Johnstone explains that at the beginning of every performance, "there's a little bit of wrangling to be done to send a message that, 'No, this is not the play.'" Lauren Gienow acknowledges, however, the otherwise clear disconnect between stage and auditorium, writing, "It truly feels like these four performers are alone in a room acting out this intimate, bizarre and exciting dream" ("Stratford Festival's *A Midsummer Night's Dream: A Chamber Play*," *Broadway World*, 2 August 2014, accessed 2 August 2015). Carol Mejia LaPerle argues that by disrupting the expectations of seasoned spectators, this staging "transformed" patrons, allowing them to experience Shakespeare "without the crutch of recognition, without the rewards of familiarity" ("'Thou art Translated': Peter Sellars's Midsummer Chamber Play", forthcoming in *Borrowers and Lenders*).

3 The site of burial in two Korean *Hamlet*s

Yu Jin Ko

When it comes to global Shakespeare, the rhetoric of universality remains stubbornly universal, especially among theatre practitioners. Even as "foreign" practitioners appropriate Shakespeare in intercultural productions that go far beyond merely reproducing the Shakespearean original, many continue to view Shakespeare as the vehicle that enables access to the universal. The history of *Hamlet* in Korea is representative in this regard. Since the so-called Shakespeare boom began in the 1990s in Korea, Koreans have performed *Hamlet* more often than any other Shakespeare play.[1] Many reasons can account for this fact, but one clearly stands out: with its meditations on life and death, *Hamlet* exemplifies more than any other play for Koreans what Youn-taek Lee, the founding artistic director of the company Yonhuidan Gureepae, calls a "universal text."[2] The way in which Lee talks about his aspirations for the series of *Hamlet* productions that he directed is further telling. On the one hand, mutuality underpins his vision of universality in intercultural encounters, as seen in his desire to "universalize the culture of East and West in a comprehensive . . . way" (195); thus he emphasizes the need to preserve "Yonhuidan Gureepae's unique theatrical grammar" (195) and its "own contemporary Korean theatre style" (202) in its productions of Western drama. On the other hand, however, he clearly positions Shakespeare as the source of the universal when he talks of "learning how to incorporate the contemporaneity and Korean uniqueness that we have pursued . . . into the dimension of the universal" (195) through Shakespeare; he further adds that interpreting *Hamlet* in Yonhuidan's theatrical grammar "was possible thanks to the archetypal theatre form in Shakespeare plays that transcends the barrier of East and West and allows cultures to be interchangeable."[3] One can see why Yeeyon Im would say of Lee's *Hamlet* that "Shakespeare presides in the cultural encounter between Korea and the West not as a participant, but as a governing agent [who] guarantees the delivery of universality."[4] After all, as Sonia Massai has pointed out, even radical reworkings of Shakespeare can reinforce "the omnipresent image of the dominant other as its ultimate point of origin."[5]

For Youn-taek Lee's company in particular, the idea of using Shakespeare as a vehicle to "achieve"[6] universality can be even more fraught: the company's mission is indicated in its name (Yonhuidan Gureepae), which the company conveniently translates as Street Theatre Troupe, but which refers more specifically in Korean to *traveling* troupes of street players (like minstrels). For Lee's theatre, travel is both metaphorical and literal; the company seeks to traverse cultures while producing works that travel domestically and abroad. And in fact the company's *Hamlet* has traveled abroad extensively over a period of years. Shakespeare acts a vehicle indeed for this company, though this carries the danger that their unique "contemporary Korean theatre style" could become merely local trappings to what lies within – the supposedly universal soul of Shakespeare's play. Something similar might be said of a *Hamlet* production by another Korean theatre company that has received international recognition, the Yohangza, or "Traveller," Theatre Company. This company's founder (Jung-ung Yang) similarly speaks of harmonizing the "universal" with uniquely "Korean aesthetics" in intercultural productions while including international travel in the company's mission.[7] True to form, its production of *Hamlet* has also traveled abroad (though Westerners may be more familiar with the company's *A Midsummer Night's Dream*, which was performed at the Globe in London as part of the World Shakespeare Festival in 2012). With the possibility that "Korean aesthetics" function merely as ornamental dress for the universal core that makes Hamlet's plight "our story" (4), Yohangza's *Hamlet* also risks engaging in what has been called "complicit colonialism,"[8] as the local strengthens the global brand by corroborating and reinforcing the brand's universality. The center could simply grow stronger as an increasingly wider periphery circulates around it.

However, in thinking about intercultural productions, one should recognize that a gap often exists between practitioners' rhetoric and their actual productions. As this chapter argues, the theatrical practices of the two productions noted above transcend the rhetoric in ways that – intentionally or not – challenge traditionally post-colonial critiques. Of particular focus will be the ways in which both productions foreground burial grounds that come to define the local *place* – the local hamlet (with a lowercase "h") – and serve, by means of shamanistic rituals, as gateways to other, sacred worlds. Those other worlds that are accessed only through, and intersect with, distinctly local or Korean spaces, come to stand, I will argue, for the universal. That is, the local and the universal undergo reconfigurations and reversals as the ground underneath the play shifts, as it were, and in the process repositions the center.

The opposition between the local and the universal that I deploy here aligns of course with related binaries like familiar and foreign, target and source, local and global, adaptation and original, even East and West, among others. However, these terms, and the positions that they occupy in the polar oppositions, are relative, as many have pointed out. One may certainly agree enthusiastically with Li Lan Yong and Dennis Kennedy that intercultural revisions produce a "new text, a third text, which is neither the original nor the estranging device but the result of their performative interaction."[9] However, one should remember that Yong also emphasizes, not only the degree to which "perceptions" of an intercultural production's "meaningfulness"[10] depend on one's relative cultural position, but also how individual, fluid, complicated and even "performative" (532) one's location is in the range of cultural "positionalities" (531). With productions traveling abroad and spectators occupying an array of culturally hybrid positions, an intercultural production's "project of bridging cultures involves a spectator in intermingling, partial identifications and alienations that are porous to one another" (539). The vexed issue of authenticity can also be considered in this light. As Eleine Ng has pointed out, the rhetoric of authenticity that continues to permeate discussions of Shakespearean performance often intensifies in the case of intercultural productions as the authenticity of local theatrical traditions enters the field of assessment. However, the perception of authenticity is complicated by not only the "performativity of the authentic" – as a performance tradition is cited through dislocated performances – but also "spectatorial positionality."[11] This is all to say that any argument like mine about the disruptive force of an intercultural production will inevitably be inflected by the particular spectatorial position underlying the argument.

Hence, though I have to apologize in advance for taking pains to situate myself in some detail, it seems to me necessary to explain where I am coming from. I should first note that I will be writing about the two *Hamlet* productions as they exist in digital form in the Asian Shakespeare Internet Archive (A-S-I-A-web.org). Practical reasons as well as theoretical motivations account for this. I live in the United States, to which neither company has yet traveled, and during my recent visits to Korea, unfortunately neither company performed the play. Still, accessing the performances digitally, especially with the features (like subtitles) available through the A|S|I|A portal, does offer its advantages. Although I am conversationally competent in Korean (having lived in Korea until I was nine), some of the dialogue – especially at moments when the Korean, though modern, becomes dense, poetic, and heightened – would be inaccessible without subtitles, much as some Shakespearean dialogue in performance can go by in a blur for even native English speakers. On the other hand, my training in Shakespeare has made me pretty familiar with the text, which makes the Korean resonate with additional nuances, as chimes and dissonances echo in continual interplay. In this respect and in my case, watching a recorded performance can, as Li Lan Yong has written, "strengthen the definition and depth of an intercultural engagement with the performance," because "both interculturality and mediatization" are "aspects of the globalization of performance."[12] The productions travel to me digitally, in other words, and create a particular intercultural encounter.

Even more important, however, is how my idea of Korea filters the image of Korea that the performances assume and to which the discourse surrounding the performances (e.g., in Program Notes) directly alludes. Hyonu Lee has suggested that the popularity of *Hamlet* in Korea has to do with the play's capacity to express what Koreans call *han*.[13] Some near equivalents of the word *han* are "heartbreak," "pain," "sorrow," but it is the kind of deep heartbreak that issues from generational history and even defines a fatalistic world view. Having suffered colonial conquest, civil war, the division of the country, military coups, and dictatorships – all in one century – *han* remains a pervasive presence for Koreans, both abstractly and deep within people. Lee has further suggested that the presence of shamanistic exorcism rituals in so many Korean *Hamlet*s attests to the desire to exorcise *han* by means of the play (106). And indeed the Program Notes for Yohangza's *Hamlet* use the word *han* explicitly and repeatedly, while numerous essays by the Street Theatre Troupe's director evoke the concept. Yohangza's Jung-ung Yang, for example, calls Hamlet a "being stuffed and bruised with *han*," who, therefore, shows us "our form" in "our own time" – in modern-day Korea, that is, with the word "our" meaning Korean, which is how Koreans routinely use the word.[14] Yang further notes that he chose to incorporate the exorcism ritual of *gut* into his production because of his conviction that "we" need, as we live in "conflict and the loneliness born of turmoil," to "comfort" and to "release" *han* (4). Similarly, in relation to the scenes of madness that motivate gestures of exorcism in his production, Street Theatre's Youn-taek Lee speaks of the "loss of self" while living in a "chaotic reality."[15]

Although *han* may be considered Korea's "national sentiment,"[16] what it means specifically differs for individuals, and thus that individual understanding partly defines the spectator's position when watching *Hamlet*. For me, dynamic discord defines Korea. Most obviously, as a walk through nearly any part of Seoul today reveals, tradition and globalized modernity come crashing together in every aspect of life. Surrounding a Buddhist temple or even ramshackle homes with ceramic tile roofs will be gleaming skyscrapers with pulsating LED displays that advertise the latest electronic gadgets in the mongrel language that has become ubiquitous (especially in marketing) but which has been a source of national embarrassment for some: Konglish, which often takes the form of simply but awkwardly transliterating an English word phonetically into Korean (not just, say, common words of global commerce like "computer" but even terms for which there are perfectly adequate Korean terms, such as "flower shop" – transliterated into something like "pooh-rah-wuh shap"). A part of what gives the country its hectic energy is the extraordinary pace of change, which is exhilarating, dizzying, but also cruel. The race to keep pace in an overcrowded nation of 50 million packed into an area about the size of Maine (one of the smaller states in the US) can be seen not only in ferocious economic competition but also in groups of the elderly on subways with their heads buried in their Samsung smartphones. From one perspective, this energy keeps the country's spirit buoyant, especially as a communitarian ethic with a shared cultural memory reinforces a sense of a nation's being in it all together. People above a certain age – including the vast majority of those who have prospered economically from the country's boom – still remember, for example, when they and the country were poor. No one thinks twice about stepping out of a luxury department store and sitting down at a rickety food stall to eat a poor man's lunch (say, what's called "barracks stew," made originally from the scraps scavenged from trash bins outside US military barracks during the Korean War).

On the other hand, and paradoxically, extreme status consciousness (a legacy of Confucianism) combined with rampant consumerism (the consequence and engine of global capitalism) fuels a cutthroat competition for survival and success in which losers far outnumber winners. The win – or simply survive – at-all-costs mentality can thus be corrosive and does lead to regularly recurring national traumas that shake the country. One recent, devastating, and tragic example is the Sewol ferry disaster of April 2014, when a ferry capsized while carrying mostly high school students from one small city, 304 of whom died. From top to bottom, at each level at which personal responsibility and integrity were required, a categorical failure occurred that the public experienced as a profound betrayal. The ferry was illegally overladen with cargo at the instruction of the shipping company's corrupt owner, who routinely bribed maritime inspectors and government officials; the captain abandoned ship with the passengers still trapped inside; the crew was untrained in disaster response and thus, before themselves abandoning ship, gave the trapped students the wrong instruction to remain below deck. The Sewol ferry disaster reminded Koreans that, despite all the progress, suffering remains existentially insurmountable and fundamentally inseparable from even the current condition of relative prosperity. The moral breakdown that was perceived as betrayal clearly issued, as the country collectively acknowledged, from a modern, globalized socio-economic reality that motivates an unhinged form of excess desire. The word *han* sums up for Koreans the searing emotional pain associated with this tragedy.

Such events in modern Korea are not rare, however, which accounts in part for the presence of shamanistic exorcism rituals in the two productions of *Hamlet* under discussion. The ritual that most permeates both productions is *gut*, the name for a broad category of rites that involve communication, mediated by a shaman or *mudang*, between inhabitants of this world and of the afterlife or the invisible spiritual world. In one particular kind of *gut*, which both productions make use of, the spirit of a dead ancestor possesses either the shaman or a living relative to communicate its suffering (its continuing experience of *han*) and to appeal for appeasement or release. For the directors, *gut* clearly opens up possibilities for intercultural transposition: the ghost of Hamlet's father returns, after all, to expose betrayal and corruption beneath the new reality to inspire his son to revenge. Nonetheless, Yeeyon Im, for example, has argued that "many westernized Koreans" – principally, Koreans living in Korea with westernized sensibilities, rather than Koreans living in the West – "would have found" the shamanistic rituals in Youn-taek Lee's *Hamlet* to be "archaic and superstitious – more foreign than Shakespeare's *Hamlet*."[17] I suspect she would argue the same for Yohangza's *Hamlet*. I find her assertion misdirected for two specific reasons. First, as historians of shamanism and religious practices in Korea have pointed out, shamanism is syncretic in its outlook and therefore has evolved over centuries through its contact with "official" religions and philosophies like Buddhism and Confucianism. This means that shamanism has absorbed elements of other practices, but its own elements have also been integrated into other practices. Hence, although many do regard shamans as charlatans who trade in disreputable superstition, most still recognize some overlap between shamanism and other creeds and thus regard it as being part of a continuum of sacred practices.[18] The vast majority of Koreans, including Christians, still practice the Confucian ancestor-worship ritual of *che-sa*, for example, which has continuities (and vast differences) with shamanistic rituals.[19] Many shamans also engage in the continually popular practice of divination (for a fee), though they sometimes disguise their status as shamans while signaling it as an open secret with coded professional pseudonyms.[20] My late uncle, an evangelical minister in Korea, would say of shamans that you cannot underestimate their occult powers.

Perhaps more importantly, many shamanistic rituals intersect, as Jung-ung Yang emphatically underscores, with communal folk activities like song, dance, feasting, drinking (lots of it), and even "theatre," and hence hold significance "beyond the religious dimension."[21] This near-Rabelaisian but at the same time distinctly Korean mingling of the sacred with the physical in a communal rite of cheer, release, and consolation is regarded by Yang as an essential element of *gut* and an answer to *han*. At the same time, Yang links the exorcism of *gut* with festive play and theatre in an interestingly self-conscious way. He ends his Director's Notes with a phrase that translates literally as something like "Let's play *Hamlet* as a *gut*" (4), but which has a particular resonance in Korean: the verb phrase recalls the English phrase "Let the good times roll," or better yet the Cajun expression "Laissez les bon temps rouler." Let *Hamlet rouler* as a *gut*! is essentially what is said, though without the awkward phrasing. If there is one thing one can say about Koreans, it is that they pursue *les bon temps* with the same intensity as they pursue survival and success in the global marketplace. Yang tries with his *Hamlet* to create a tragic theatrical form that harnesses the intensity of ritual play to release *han*. Somewhat similarly, Street Theatre Troupe's Youn-taek Lee speaks of incorporating *gut* rituals into his production to enact "purification" or "release" and to realize the theatre's potential for "catharsis."[22] In this respect, though the two productions differ significantly, including in their uses of the *gut* ritual, the two can be said to originate from a similar vision of Shakespeare's play; namely, that Hamlet the character remains fundamentally incomplete in his spiritual journey and *Hamlet* the play remains incomplete as a vehicle of release. By means of a distinctly Korean version of shamanism, the productions envision how completion might become more possible.

To trace the ways in which *gut* lays the foundation for release to be enacted, we can return to the ground on which the play is set. I will begin with Street Theatre Troupe's production, because it is chronologically earlier, having started its continuing series of revivals and revisions in 1996, though the video recording I am using is of a 2009 production at the Nunbit Theatre in Seoul. This *Hamlet* begins with a funeral procession onto a dark stage that has at the rear a scrim onto which is projected the image of a large horse, more specifically, the mythical flying horse Chunma, which the wall of a historic earthen royal tomb in Korea called Chunma-chong depicts. While the audience is not to confuse the fictional setting in Denmark with Chunma-chong, the image conveys the sense immediately, as Youn-taek Lee has written, that the world is "a huge grave."[23] The sound of loud ritual wailing, which we discover comes from Gertrude as the lights come on, thus feels entirely appropriate for the sweeping funereal atmosphere of the setting. After the pallbearers lay Old Hamlet's body into the grave, Claudius launches into his speech from 1.2 ("Though yet of Hamlet our dear brother's death"[24]); however, upon announcing that he has taken his sister-in-law to wife, he and Gertrude engage in a long, romantic kiss, which leads Hamlet to look in astonishment at the audience and walk downstage. The royal couple, along with the mourners and courtiers who take their cue from them, then throw off their black cloaks of mourning, revealing more courtly regalia of an unspecific but modern period, and begin to dance as Renaissance music plays in the background.

Because Gertrude's shift from mourning to erotic festivity occurs so abruptly, and punctuates a sudden change in the scene's momentum, it clearly stands out as something remarkable and raises questions about her emotional authenticity and the authenticity of stylized rituals of mourning in traditional Korean funerals.

I am reminded here of a story that circulated about my cousin in Korea, whom we idolized in fear when we were children because of his tendency towards rebellious waywardness. At the funeral of an uncle, my cousin is said to have surprised everyone by the intensity of his mourning, engaging in the form of ritual wailing that goes by the name of *koksori*. Then suddenly, the story goes, he turned to his mother and very ostentatiously asked in front of all the gathered mourners, "Was that enough?" In exposing how insincerely theatrical mourning rites can be (and how he was forced into performing them as simply a social obligation), he appears to have wanted to expose hypocrisy and moral fraudulence more broadly. Because Gertrude's behavior itself exposes her mourning to be insincere, Hamlet is left to distinguish himself from the court and to articulate his disgust and disillusion, as he does in the immediately following exchange (while drunk) that leads to the "I know not seems" (1.2.76) speech. The Korean departs subtly from Shakespeare here to emphasize how the issues of authenticity and individuality come together. Lee's Hamlet dresses like the others, but demands of Gertrude what he might do or wear to express a sorrow that goes beyond both seeming and conventional expression: "No shape of grief can truly show my sadness. What do you want to see? Inky cloak of mourning? . . . Fruitful river in the eye?" The questions indicate that he is searching for a unique vocabulary – whether in language or other signs – that is at once self-authenticating in its expression of sorrow and expressive of what he uniquely, as an individual beyond conventional signs, can feel.

At the same time, and metadramatically, the scene – whether intentionally or not – raises the question of authenticity with regard to intercultural Shakespeare productions. How can a production be "faithful to the original,"[25] as Lee himself asks, while retaining the unique theatrical grammar of the company's particular contemporary Korean style? In this connection, one might be tempted to say that the court attire in Lee's production is western, especially since a character dressed in a semblance of Renaissance motley appears, but of course the pervasive style of contemporary Asian attire is very much global western. In fact, within the production at large, an eclectic mix of periods, cultural styles, imagistic and auditory allusions, protocols of mourning, and more resists binaries like east and west or domestic and foreign or traditional and modern. What's at issue is not simply Koreanizing Shakespeare. As Jan Creutzenberg has rightly pointed out, Youn-taek Lee seeks a Korean element for his *Hamlet* that is unique to his company: "an individual interpretation of *Hamlet* rather than a mere localisation based on national culture."[26] For Lee, the question is: What kind of distinctly Korean theatrical grammar can be authentic to Shakespeare while also being self-authenticating?

The next sequence in the opening scene suggests a possible but troubling answer. After Gertrude flirtatiously and rather seductively convinces Hamlet to stay in Denmark, and the courtiers leave the stage, Hamlet delivers a short version of his soliloquy from 1.2 ("Frailty, thy Name Is Woman," 146). Afterwards, as a bell chimes midnight, the doors of the grave open and a hand slowly reaches up from it. Eventually, the body – or rather the ghost – of the Old King emerges and an encounter follows that takes the form, as Lee has pointed out and many have commented on, of a *gut* in which *jeop-shin*, or the possession of one's spirit by the spirit of an ancestor, takes place.[27] More specifically, after Hamlet addresses the ghost, an elaborately choreographed mime follows that indicates the onset of possession, after which a one-sided dialogue takes place in which only Hamlet delivers lines – "Murder?" "My uncle?" – in response to mimed actions and gestures by the ghost. One is to understand that the ghost communicates directly to Hamlet and resides therefore as much inside as outside of him. Koreans would also recognize that the ghost returns because he remains "perturbed" (2.1.182), or afflicted by some form of *han*. In possessing the son's spirit, that perturbation also passes to the son, whose mission it then becomes to appease the ghost. For Lee, the incorporation of *jeop-shin* is central to developing a "unique narrative structure"[28] that enables Street Theatre to harmonize his company's individual Korean aesthetics with Shakespeare's original. For Hamlet the character, the fact of possession becomes the ground that accommodates and authenticates a range of actions that variously have elements of, or are interpreted by others as, madness, crafty madness, play-acting, melodramatic over-acting, or simply outrageous rudeness. It should be noted that Hamlet's lines about putting "an antic disposition on" (1.5.172) are entirely cut: his often maniacally antic disposition becomes an outcome and expression of possession. *Jeop-shin* produces, to borrow Jan Creutzenberg's vocabulary, a productive "semiotic ambiguity" in this production.[29] Neither Ophelia nor we know precisely whether Hamlet is mad, pretending to be so, in the throes of a manic passion, or is experiencing possession when he approaches her in her closet and affrights her (a scene that gets staged here). When he engages in caustic sarcasm with Polonius in the equivalent of 2.2 ("fishmonger"), we don't know whether possession empowers him to defy decorum, or whether he simply exploits his perceived lunacy as license – in the manner of a court jester – to heap unmitigated scorn on the court and its betrayals and corruption. Though possession remains the foundation that drives Hamlet's actions in Lee's production, that foundation accommodates a constellation of other extraordinary "wild and whirling words" (1.5.133) and behavior. At the same time, the question of authenticity with regard to human action gets absorbed into this foundation of possession. One might further say that Lee's choice to employ *jeop-shin* provides the objective correlative that T. S. Eliot famously lamented the absence of in this play.

However, the first scene of ghostly possession noted above creates a spectatorial position that is decidedly curious and potentially disturbing. Though one might guess at the ghost's words through his actions and Hamlet's responses, the silence surely echoes loudly with Shakespeare's text – for those who are familiar with it. The ghost delivers the truth that will drive the action forward, and yet the text remains conspicuously absent, which thus requires a prior, and rather intimate, knowledge of Shakespeare for the fullest understanding. The A|S|I|A website takes the extraordinary step of providing that text, in brackets, so that the viewer can have access to that absent presence. Metadramatically speaking, one might say that the ghost acts as a figure for Shakespeare, and, by requiring prior knowledge of the text, reinforces the essential primacy of the Shakespearean text. In this respect, it is as though through the portal of the grave – the gateway to the eternal and the universal – Shakespeare appeared, bearing silently the absent text as a secret "eternal blazon [that] must not be / To ears" (1.5.21–22) untrained in his text. Only we in the know can "list" (1.5.22), only we who have prior access to Shakespeare. And that "we" is more likely to be western than Korean.

The importance of access to that absent text gets reinforced as the play goes on, especially in relation to the process of *jeop-shin*. As with Hamlet's manic behavior, Ophelia's madness has its origins in possession, though as a viewer can see, and as Lee reaffirms, the madness has many sources: her "painful" love for Hamlet, her brother's departure, her father's death, and, in this production, as hinted at briefly in a scene of hurried dressing, an "improper affair" with Claudius.[30] These causes collectively define the "chaotic" and morally unmoored world that she experiences and which leads her to "lose" herself (197–98). However, the words and songs she gives voice to in madness are simultaneously meant to be understood as flowing from possession, as when a possessed shaman delivers the words of the possessing spirit in dialogue and ritual song. Further, the production highlights a specific moment as crucial to the process of *jeop-shin* – the interpolated scene in her closet when Hamlet comes to her, and speaks lines to her from the ghost's absent text: "But that I am forbid / To tell the secrets of my prison-house. . . . To ears of flesh and blood" (1.5.13–22). For someone familiar with the text, this is a chilling moment that resonates in numerous ways, literalizing Ophelia's description of Hamlet in this scene as a ghost just "loosed out of hell" (2.1.80). More importantly, as Dong-wook Kim, the dramaturg for the production, confirms, this "repetition" of the ghost's silent lines enacts the first moment of possession, as possession passes as if infectiously from Hamlet to Ophelia.[31] But how is an audience member who is not familiar with the text to understand all this? The structural reworking of the narrative with *jeop-shin* as the spine extends the experience of possession to others and even lends more dramatic plausibility to some of the actions, but the sense of Shakespeare as the source of a ghostly master text that possesses the production also intensifies.

A counter-action can also be sensed, though it remains unclear whether it was intended or not. This centers again on the grave, though the setting is the play-within-the-play. In Lee's production, Horatio is a female character who leads the players. During the first movement of the play-within-the-play, Horatio acts almost as a narrator in the Korean folk genre of *pansori*, in which a single narrator/singer (or *sori-kkun*) provides the narrative while also enacting and voicing the characters to the accompaniment of a percussionist. In this particular instance, the Player King and Queen, both in traditional masks, mime their actions in a manner reminiscent of folk drama, or *madang-guk*, while Horatio gives voice very dramatically and beautifully to the characters. I would add that the evocation of older traditions here clearly befits the linguistic mode of the play-within-the-play in Shakespeare. However, the feel of the aesthetic rightness of this scene ultimately derives from the fact that the style does not try simply to replicate traditional modes, but integrates those modes into a still recognizably modern aesthetic. The costumes and music, for example, evoke traditional forms but depart from them. Here, authenticity is indeed "performative"; aesthetic fitness to a moment of performance, not fidelity to a tradition, defines authenticity in a way that is inevitably tautological, as anything that is self-authenticating can only be. In the event, after the first sequence, Hamlet plays the role of Lucianus and speaks his own lines, though in a mask, and violently kills the Player King by stabbing him with a knife in the ear. The Player King writhes but continues now as the ghost of the Player King, and, with Hamlet, re-enacts the scene of their encounter that we saw at the beginning of the play itself. However, the grave remains closed throughout it all: the dead Player King simply transitions into the ghost, while Hamlet, having shed the mask of Lucianus, essentially plays himself. Further, after Hamlet mimes the process of possession, he again speaks the lines he had earlier spoken, but Horatio, again as narrator, gives voice to the words of the ghost – to the authentic absent text. At this point, the necessary information gets revealed and shared, if retroactively, and thus different spectatorial perspectives align. Because the grave remains closed, however, it is as though, at least in this dramatic representation, Horatio usurps the ghostly figure of Shakespeare in the guise of a *sori-kkun*, the narrator bard of *pansori*. Put another way, a contemporary figure rooted in Korean history takes over the narrative function from the ghost of Shakespeare.

Tellingly, Youn-taek Lee gives special attention to Horatio as a central figure in the drama. Taking a cue from Hamlet's admiration for Horatio for not being "passion's slave" (3.2.72), Lee highlights Horatio's special ability to maintain a "distance"[32] from the action, in both the plays s/he enacts and within the fiction. This posture affiliates her with a "court jester" and a "poet" (199), both of whom use their distance to tell the truth about their worlds. In this, s/he also resembles a shaman in that a shaman experiences possession and gives full dramatic voice to the spirit, but remains unperturbed after the possession passes. Hence, though Lee traces the roots of Horatio-like narrators back, for example, to a Greek chorus, it is clear that Horatio also stands as a figure for Lee himself – the Korean dramatist who can be possessed by Shakespeare but who can also remain authentic to himself.

The figure of Horatio can be contrasted with those who die from different forms of possession. After the play-within-the-play, Hamlet becomes more and more unhinged. Not only does he kill Polonius unwittingly in a manic fit, but he also kills, in this production, both Rosencrantz and Guildenstern on the way to England, one by repeated stabbing (which recalls the killing of the Player King by Lucianus) and the other by strangulation. In his continual attempt to appease the ghost, Hamlet becomes even more discomposed and in need of purification. Of course Ophelia goes mad and drowns. Possession by the force that comes through the grave leads, in this production, to madness and destruction. But that is not the only possession in this production. As Lee notes himself, characters are also possessed by something in this world – "worldly desire" (198). Indeed, this more mundane and figurative possession leads to torment in the afterlife and the inability to complete the journey to the other world. Worldly desire initiates, that is to say, the perturbation that afflicts the afterlife and motivates the perturbed spirit to possess the living. This desire most visibly afflicts Claudius, of course, who murders his brother for power and seeks to possess the bodies of not only Gertrude but also Ophelia. Gertrude herself is portrayed as overcome with desire, often but not exclusively figured in some way as sensual in nature. The desire for vengeance undoes Laertes. Fortinbras, whose voice booms overhead as he claims his "rights" in the kingdom (5.2.389) at the play's end, will simply perpetuate, the production seems to suggest, the cycle of possession.

Thus it is that after the play proper, a white hemp cloth that resembles a cerement covers the entire stage, and the dead emerge again through the grave to break through a slit in the cloth to "wander"[33] in a ghostly dance in their continuing state of *jeop-shin* on their long and uncertain way to the other world. As a requiem continues to be sung from offstage, Hamlet emerges, and as he makes his way upstage to exit, he turns around and stares at the audience as the lights fade. That stare presumably reminds the audience that the "sad" ghosts of all these souls, as Lee tells us, continue to keep this world "dizzy" (198). One spotlight does remain on, however, and focuses on Horatio, who, by one wing of the stage (which is the space that folk and shaman musicians occupy), sings the final notes of the requiem that has been playing throughout the dance of ghosts. Horatio acts as the final voice of propitiation, underscoring in the end the effort to offer release and catharsis through drama.

Lee's allusion to Horatio as a "clown" might be considered again in this light. Among the characters who enter the grave during the play, two stand out: the gravediggers, or clowns. As the lights come up in 5.1, we hear singing and see two skulls being held up by two homespun, and very Korean, bumpkins who stand in the grave. Curiously, the A|S|I|A site gives Shakespeare's song from the scene ("In youth when I did love," 5.1.61), which the gravediggers sing later in the scene. Their song at the outset is as follows (in my inelegant translation):

> So sad, the ways of the world, like a dream
> If you go now, when will you come back?
> Everything of the world comes to nothing
> Love, romance, comes to nothing
> Pretty girls, ugly girls, not much difference
> Strip them down and the skulls are the same
> Beautiful, ugly, who can tell?

What's exhilarating as well as poignant is that the gravediggers sing the song in the style of music that accompanies folk play and communal, drunken cheer – the kind of play that might begin with the Korean equivalent of "Laissez les bon temps rouler." As it is in Shakespeare's play, this yoking of oppositions in the gravediggers represents an attitude or even philosophy towards life and death. This attitude contemplates the emptiness that death induces, but also embraces it with cheer. As Lee writes about the gravediggers, death "materializes the tragedy of living," and yet in "*our* people" (my emphasis), an "optimism" survives that accepts with "playfulness" this "craziness in life" (199). These clowns, as well as the "clown" that is Horatio, are hopeful representations of Koreans. The clowns are the only characters in the production who remove actual soil – red soil that looks fertile – from the grave. This red soil has special meaning for Lee, as seen in what he writes of the stage design that keeps the earthen tomb of Chunmachong continually in mind. He notes that "as Alexander can become a stopper for a beer barrel, love, truth, and all human feelings become materialized" (201) in their return to earth through death; thus he asks where he can find solace in "living" (201). His answer: "our beautiful soil" itself, for it gives him a sense of "familiarity, peace, and even a warm despair" that makes him want to "love the world even more" (201). That soil embodies not despair and nihilistic pessimism, but the kind of peace that comes with accepting the pain of finitude with cheer and philosophical distance. In this, there is the suggestion that the gravediggers' acceptance of finitude contrasts with the excessive desire that ultimately initiates the cycle of worldly possession and chaos that produces *han*. Finitude here does not mean absolute finality, however, for the grave always remains a permeable portal between this world and the afterworld. In their cheerful attitude towards the grave, the gravediggers illustrate the attitude that looks to "our" soil, laden with the spirituality of shamanistic theosophy, for consolation for the universal condition of mortality that afflicts even Alexander. That attitude also contains the posture of distance in the production's stand-in for Lee himself – Horatio, the Korean bard who has the philosophical distance to materialize Shakespeare in and on Korean soil, and make drama an authentic vehicle of consolation and release.

* * *

Jung-ung Yang's 2009 *Hamlet* for Yohangza (Myeongdong Theatre, Seoul) picks up where Lee's left off. Yang similarly incorporates *gut* rituals into the production, most visibly in the three sequences listed in the Program Notes: Hamlet's encounter with the ghost, dramatized as a *jinogigut*, which seeks appeasement for a spirit; Ophelia's burial, during which a ritual for those who died by drowning, *sumangut*, is performed; and the end, when a ritual that prepares a person for the afterlife before his death, *sanjinogigut*, is performed for Hamlet as he nears death after the duel. However, as Hyonu Lee has demonstrated, Yohangza's production might be thought of as an extended *gut* that incorporates different varieties of *gut* rather than a play that incorporates *gut* at discrete moments.[34] Indeed, at many other moments, shamanistic elements enter the dramatization. When the players enter the play for the first time, they play music from a *gut* that is offered to the guardian spirit of a village. The play-within-the-play is similarly staged as a *gut* with shaman musicians playing. At the start of the closet scene, Gertrude appears with a basin filled with water to perform a ritual in honor of the dead. And this list does not exhaust the ways in which the production comes across as a *gut* performance that happens to follow the narrative thread of *Hamlet*. It is almost as if the production were declaring that it will seek to provide the release that neither the original play nor even Youn-taek Lee's production provides.

I should say at the outset that, compelling as Yohangza's production is, I do not find it as powerful as Street Theatre Troupe's for a simple reason. The production never quite sufficiently establishes the chaotic world of corruption and emptiness evoked in Yang's Notes in the Program, even as a certain excess theatricality in this Hamlet makes his suffering seem too much the result of his own predisposition. The production begins, for example, with a somewhat manic version of the "To be or not to be" speech (with Hamlet's white warm-up track suit befitting the feverish delivery) before we have any chance to understand the context in which it is delivered. As the scene continues, Gertrude and Claudius enter in mourning dress, carrying a table to perform a ritual in honor of the 49th day after King Hamlet's death. They end up not speaking any words at all during the scene, however; Claudius's unctuously effective speech ("Though yet of Hamlet"), his political dealings, the exchange between Hamlet and Gertrude – all get cut in favor of Hamlet launching another soliloquy ("Frailty, thy name is woman") from upstage with ferocious indignation as the ritual gets performed. Given the narrative details about the hasty marriage that the soliloquy provides, we are presumably to distrust what seems a pious and sincere show. Because the scene gets so compressed, we are continually left without a concrete enough sense of the social reality and the ruptured relationships behind Hamlet's extreme state of anger.

A recognizable method to this cutting and compression does exist, however. Opening with "to be or not to be" establishes an emotional crisis in Hamlet without clearly revealing a cause, and thus initiates a process whereby the cause reveals itself through shamanistic logic. In this logic, the false mourning performed by Gertrude and Claudius raises the possibility that Hamlet's deep perturbation is not only a response to hypocrisy, but is also induced (though unawares to Hamlet) by Old Hamlet's continuing suffering as a ghost because of something rotten in the state of Denmark. It thus follows that immediately after Gertrude and Claudius exit the first scene, shamans in traditionally bright colors enter to perform the *jinogigut* for Hamlet's father, which begins with a festive dance as the shamans chant a song to call back the "poor soul." The shamans then alternately speak in the voice of the departed, intoning, chanting and singing lines that express hope in jubilant and earthy tones and rhythms: "I see you'll release all my *han*," or, embodying the syncretic nature of shamanism, "Buddha, be merciful." However, as one shaman enacts the ghost's journey in the afterlife by slicing through a hemp cloth that's stretched out and held up, she abruptly stops and suffers a paroxysm of possession, symbolizing the ghost's inability to continue that journey towards release. She then delivers lines that echo the ghost's from the play, while other shamans deliver more information about the murder and issue an order of revenge. The *gut* thus partly explains Hamlet's preceding crisis (again, affliction issuing unawares from the ghost's perturbation) but equally importantly provides him with a dramatic motive and establishes the narrative direction for what follows. This entire opening sequence captures the dramatic logic and rhythm that persist through the entire play: a compressed, or distilled, textual moment (a soliloquy, a streamlined dialogue) becomes the occasional cause or motivation for a *gut* or some other shamanistic ritual, which in turn motivates or produces more textual moments in a mutually reinforcing or contrapuntal structure.

Indeed, immediately following the *gut*, Hamlet collapses and kneels in the throes of seeming uncertainty, but concludes by imploring Horatio, "Do not be too surprised if I do some crazy things." The phrase Hamlet uses, 미친짓, might be translated as "crazy acts," because "acts" captures some of the ambiguity in the Korean; the phrase in this context could refer not only to actions but to strategic play-acting. However, in the subsequent early scenes, Hamlet does not perform any crazy actions but simply acts crazy. Thus, these scenes lead, in the dramatic logic of Yang's production, to another *gut*, more specifically the Pyrrhus scene with the players. After a raucous and whirling entry (during which *gut* music is played), the players stage the speech about Pyrrhus as something resembling a *gut*, with actors alternately taking on the *sori-kkun* narrator's role, as if possessed by the voice of the characters, while others mime the actions with dramatic, stylized intensity. It is a commonplace of Shakespeare criticism that Pyrrhus serves as a foil to Hamlet in going from hesitation ("Did nothing," 2.2.482) to action ("Now falls on Priam," 2.2.492). In Yohangza's production, the narrative voices serve as a stand-in for the ghost, while the mimed actions reinforce the sense of the ghost's presence and his call for vengeance.

Fittingly for Hamlet, however, the action he chooses in response is another act – the play-within-the-play, which again gets staged as a *gut*: a *sori-kkun* narrator voices the characters in a manner reminiscent of shamans under possession, while the Player King and Queen mime their actions in (beautifully) stylized gestures. In response, both Claudius and Gertrude experience the kind of fear and possession appropriate to encountering a ghost. Claudius eventually prays in a shamanistic style while Gertrude, as noted earlier, appears in her closet performing a ritual in honor of the dead. In this way, once again, textual moments and shamanistic ritual revolve together, motivating and issuing from each other. Dramatically striking as some of the *gut* scenes are, they perform emotional and spiritual work at the expense, sometimes, of the dramatic work that the text performs in establishing the emotional needs that are addressed by those rituals. Put another way, the symbolic work of *gut* forms the spine of the production.

It is nonetheless in this symbolic dimension that I would like to consider the special value of this production. To return to the scene of the *jinogigut* for Old Hamlet, as Hamlet kneels on the ground after the *gut*, he picks up some soil and says, "O earth, help me stand straight." But the earth that he picks up is composed of rice. The stage design is remarkable in this respect. First, illustrations of shaman spirits, or *mushindo*, cover the walls on all sides. These are illustrations that furnish the walls inside the houses or halls of shamans, and thus the stage itself recalls a place of ritual. The stage is a low, rectangular platform covered with straw mats, but a broad border of rice several meters wide surrounds the entire perimeter of the stage. It has been pointed out in connection with this production that rice – Korea's staple food – is Korea's symbol of life as well as a talisman against misfortune.[35] Hence, the earth represented on stage becomes both burial ground and a space (like a rice paddy) of regeneration. Even more importantly, given the setting of a ritual space, the combination of a rectangular platform and rice evokes a *che-sa* or other ritual table with rice as an offering.[36] What this ultimately suggests is that the play itself – its enactment as a *gut* – serves as a kind of offering to the spirits.

The place evoked by the stage is both an abstract and highly material realization of Korea and its indigenous forms of spirituality. Shakespeare gets transformed into a radically different form and becomes an instrument – akin to food on a *che-sa* table – of appeasing or releasing the *han* of those souls who live in the eternal or universal dimension envisioned by the indigenous religion of shamanism. As Hamlet lies dying at the play's end, shamans enter and, along with both the dead and living characters, sit Hamlet up and perform a *sanjinogigut*, a ritual for those approaching death to release their sorrow and prepare their way for a state of peace in the afterlife. The living and the spirits of the dead wander together as a community, offering consolation through their participation in the *gut* in a way they were not able to in the chaos of a social reality filled with *han*. It is as though they can now offer each other compassion as they are linked by a shared memory of the hectic reality they experienced together. They all seem to remember that they were at some point filled with corrupt desires and engaged in betrayal. The space in which this occurs is a liminal space, neither here nor there, but somewhere in between two worlds, and permeable to both. This space, once again, is accessible through a ground that acts at once as a burial ground, a fertile field, a yard for play, and a portal to a place of rest. This is the ground where the universal resides. In the production, rice literally composes the ground, defining it as uniquely, authentically Korean.

* * *

In both *Hamlet* productions, the drama of releasing *han* takes place in an eclectically contemporary world that reflects the evolving, hybrid character of social reality in Korea. Even Konglish makes an appearance in Youn-taek Lee's production when Hamlet asks a player (Horatio) for a taste of his quality: "What *repertory* did you bring today," Hamlet actually asks in the Korean, phonetically sounding out the word "repertory." When Jung-ung Yang's Hamlet says to Ophelia, after explaining the "paradox" (3.1.113) of beauty transforming honesty into a bawd, "Such is the world now," he uses an often-repeated phrase among contemporary Koreans to refer with resigned lament to the state of the world today. Shakespeare in translation itself reflects this world: Shakespeare still remains decidedly foreign in today's Korea, and yet that foreignness paradoxically marks it as a part of the cultural fabric of contemporary life. Ironically, then, Shakespeare in translation exemplifies the kind of world that the productions seek spiritual delivery from. In this respect, the effort to locate something authentically and fundamentally Korean in Shakespeare does not so much signal complicit subjugation to Western cultural hegemony as it reveals a desire to recover balance and a deeper center that both productions figure as *our soil*. To continue with the figurative ideas that both productions materialize, only when Shakespeare has been grounded in *our soil* can it offer access to the universal – that spiritual dimension in which the unique history of a national culture exists as a living story.

Notes

1. The phrase "Shakespeare boom" comes from Hyon-u Lee, "Introduction," *Glocalizing Shakespeare in Korea and Beyond* (Seoul: Dongin Publishing, 2009), 3. For the popularity of *Hamlet* in Korea, see Hyon-u Lee, "Shamanism in Korean *Hamlets*: Exorcising *Han*," *Asian Theatre Journal*, 28, no. 1 (2011): 104–28.
2. Youn-taek Lee, "The Director's Note: Facing Hamlet," in *Facing Hamlet*, ed. Youn-taek Lee (Kimhae: Doyo Art Books, 2010), 202. The quotation comes from the English translation of Lee's Korean text, which is also included in the volume. At other points, I will use my own translations, or combine it with variations from other translations that differ slightly, in part because Lee's text in Korean evolved over the years and thus exists in several different versions.
3. Lee, *Hamlet Il-ki* (Miryang: Urigeuk Yeonkooso, 2001), 20, translation quoted from Yeeyon Im, "The Location of Shakespeare in Korea and the Mirage of Interculturality," *Theatre Journal*, 60, no. 2 (May 2008): 273.
4. Im, "The Location of Shakespeare in Korea," 274.
5. Massai, "Defining Local Shakespeares," in *World-wide Shakespeares: Local Appropriations in Film and Performance*, ed. Sonia Massai (New York: Routledge, 2005), 5.
6. Lee, *Facing Hamlet*, 195.
7. Program for *Hamlet* (Myeongdong Theatre, Seoul: October 30–November 11, 2009), 5.
8. Im, "The Location of Shakespeare in Korea," 273, quoting Vijay Mishra and Bob Hodge, "What is Post(-)colonialism?" *Textual Practice*, 5, no. 3 (1991): 407.
9. "Introduction: Why Shakespeare?" in *Shakespeare in Asia: Contemporary Performance*, eds. Dennis Kennedy and Li Lan Yong (New York: Cambridge UP, 2010), 10.
10. L.L. Yong, "Shakespeare and the Fiction of the Intercultural," in *A Companion to Shakespeare in Performance*, eds. W. B. Worthen and Barbara Hodgdon (Hoboken: Wiley, 2008), 539.
11. E. Ng, "Performing Shakespeares: (Dis)locating the Authentic in a Korean Intercultural *Dream*," *Shakespeare*, 10, no. 4 (2014), 429.
12. L.L. Yong, "Of Spirits and Sundry Other Phenomena in Intercultural Shakespeare: Text and Performance," *Anglistica*, 15, no. 2 (2011), 48.
13. See Lee, "Shamanism," esp. 104–6.
14. *Hamlet* program, 4.
15. Lee, *Facing Hamlet*, 198.
16. Lee, "Shamanism," 124.
17. Im, "The Location of Shakespeare in Korea," 269–70.
18. For succinct accounts of shamanism in Korea, see Chai-shin Yu and Richard Guisso, eds. *Shamanism: The Spirit World of Korea* (N.p.: Asian Humanities Press, 1988), esp. "An Introduction to Korean Shamanism" and "Shamanism and the Korean World-View."
19. See James Huntley Grayson, *Korea: A Religious History* (New York: RoutledgeCurzon, 2002), esp. "Confucianism: The Residue of a Great Tradition" and "*Musok-kyo*: Folk Religion in Modern Society."
20. See Maria K. Seo, *Hanyang Kut: Korean Shaman Ritual Music from Seoul* (New York and London: Routledge, 2002), 52–3.
21. *Hamlet* program, 4.
22. Lee, *Facing Hamlet*, 201.
23. Lee, *Facing Hamlet*, 207.
24. G. Blakemore Evans, ed. *The Riverside Shakespeare* (Boston: Houghton Mifflin, 1974). All references to Shakespeare will be to this text.

25 Lee, *Facing Hamlet*, 195.
26 J. Creutzenberg, "To Be or Not to Be (Korean): Lee Youn-taek's *Hamlet* and the Reception of Shakespeare in Korea," *Shakespeare Seminar*, 7 (2009): 29.
27 Lee, *Facing Hamlet*, 197–8.
28 Lee, *Facing Hamlet*, 197.
29 Creutzenberg, "To Be or Not to Be (Korean)," 33.
30 Lee, *Facing Hamlet*, 197–8.
31 Kim, "Glocalizing Hamlet – A Study of Youn-taek Lee's productions from 1996 to 2005," in *Facing Hamlet*, 101.
32 Lee, *Facing Hamlet*, 199.
33 Lee, *Facing Hamlet*, 198.
34 Hyonu Lee, "Gut and Korean Shakespeare" (in Korean), *Shakespeare Review*, 49, no. 2 (2013): 251.
35 Lee, "Gut," 252.
36 Lee, "Gut," 252.

4 The merchant of Ashland: the confusing case of an organized minority response at the Oregon Shakespeare Festival

Jason Demeter and Ayanna Thompson

Introduction: "Too unkind a cause of grief"

In February 1991 the Oregon Shakespeare Festival (OSF) premiered what was to become one of the most controversial productions in the company's then-56-year history. A modernized staging of Shakespeare's *The Merchant of Venice* directed by Libby Appel and starring Richard Elmore as Shylock, the production almost immediately sparked claims of anti-Semitism by the local and regional Jewish community. Throughout the spring and summer of 1991, complaint letters from festival attendees and other interested parties flooded company offices. Although the festival had presented Shakespeare's divisive comedy ten times since its inaugural season in 1935, negative responses to the 1991 production were unique in terms of both their prevalence and intensity: the vehemence of the complaints was unlike anything the festival had experienced before from their primarily white, upper-class audience base.[1]

What follows is an exploration of the external outrage that greeted the 1991 production as well as a look at the company's public response to these objections, and we treat OSF, Ashland, Oregon, and the northwest United States as unique sites for this socio-religious controversy. Because the demographics of the northwestern United States include a much smaller Jewish population (both in terms of raw numbers and relative percentages) than in the Northeast, the specificity of the organized protests against OSF's 1991 *Merchant* and the company's response present a fascinating case study in the power of organized minority responses.

Furthermore, we discuss how the festival successfully assuaged the concerns of the local Jewish community through concerted efforts at community engagement and educational outreach. Beginning with an investigation of the nature and tenor of opposition to the 1991 staging as manifest within complaint letters and within the local and regional press, we explore how the company managed to turn some of its most vocal critics into powerful allies while maintaining its artistic integrity by ardently resisting calls for what those associated with the festival deemed censorship. In order to reach a greater understanding regarding the company's continued relationship with Ashland's relatively small Jewish community, we then turn our attention to the reactions that greeted subsequent productions of *Merchant* by the festival in 2001 and 2010. While still serving as a source of significant ethno-religious tension, we consider how these later stagings were able to negotiate the festival's commitment to multicultural engagement while refusing to sanitize the discriminatory tenor of Shakespeare's play to comport with the pluralistic sensibilities of modern playgoers.

"I ACQUAINTED HIM WITH THE CAUSE IN CONTROVERSY"

Located in the bucolic foothills of the Siskiyou and Cascade Mountains in southern Oregon's Jackson County, Ashland's local character and economy have been inexorably linked to the Oregon Shakespeare Festival since its early days. When founder and longtime artistic director Angus L. Bowmer mounted the festival's initial productions during the July 4th weekend in 1935, he drew upon two plays that he had recently directed while on faculty at Ashland's Southern Oregon State College (then Southern Oregon State Normal School): *Twelfth Night* and *Merchant of Venice*.[2] An early fixture of what was then simply called the Annual Shakespeare Festival, *Merchant* was produced again in 1936 and once more in 1938. The success of these productions is made plain by the fact that festival attendance increased steadily over this four-year-span from about 500 spectators in 1935 to over 2,000 by 1938.[3] While festival activities were suspended from 1941 to 1946 due to World War II, they resumed in 1947 with productions of four Shakespeare plays, including yet another staging of *Merchant*. Remarkably, this production would be revived yet again during the subsequent 1948 season. In all, five out of the festival's first ten seasons would feature productions of *Merchant*, making it the most frequently performed play in the company's early years. As the festival continued to make significant gains in both attendance and prestige throughout the postwar period, *Merchant* would remain a fixture, with productions being mounted about once every seven or eight years.[4]

Despite being among the most frequently performed plays throughout the festival's history, *Merchant* never inspired any significant controversy until the aforementioned 1991 production. One way of accounting for such a strong reaction is to consider the changing demographics of Ashland in the period. As already noted, the racial and ethnic composition of OSF audiences has always been consistently white and upper-class. Yet despite internal attempts from the late 1980s forward to better apprehend the cultural identities of their constituents, internal OSF data reveal nothing of the religious affiliations of theatregoers. While it is thus impossible to accurately account for the number of Jewish audience members who might have witnessed the 1991 production, it is the case that religious Jews were an increasingly visible part of the community in the years leading up to the controversy.[5] In 1973 the Rogue Valley Jewish Community was established in Jackson County. After operating for nearly ten years from its adopted home at the First Presbyterian Church in nearby Medford, the congregation eventually moved to its own dedicated space in Ashland and adopted a new name: Temple Emek Shalom.[6] In 1980, the first year for which such data is available, Jackson County's single Jewish congregation consisted of 109 adherents.[7] Just ten years later, this population had blossomed to include 500 congregants. While Jackson County's religious character was still dominated by Catholic and Protestant Christians, its Jewish population was now a sizable minority.[8] And it was at this point when controversy erupted.

Among the first complaints to arrive was a letter addressed to Jerry Turner, the festival's artistic director from 1971 to 1991. The writer, who describes himself as "a practicing Jew" who is well aware of *Merchant*'s "antisemitic strain," begins by noting his familiarity with the text, claiming to have "read and studied the play in the past," as well as having seen it in production "on numerous occasions."[9] "This time," he continues, "I saw this play and was appalled, uncomfortable and deeply and personally offended." He describes his initial excitement at being able to share what he had hoped would be a "positive cultural experience" with his sixteen-year-old daughter, who, due to her discomfort at feeling stereotyped, left the theatre "devastated and in tears."

The author of the letter, the vice president of a local business, goes on to highlight the reaction of his business partner, a "devout Christian," who had also attended the production and responded with a similar degree of distress: "He . . . was shocked and felt embarrassed for me and for himself and left with his wife at the intermission." After expressing his concern once more with the way that the production reinforced "preconceived stereotypes," the letter writer underscores his intense displeasure by announcing the revocation of his business's longstanding material support for the company. "I am sorry to say," he writes by way of conclusion, "but *at this point in time*, we must deny your . . . request for any corporate funds from our Company that has supported the festival for many years."

Within five days, Turner had composed a response. While giving assent to the sincerity of the writer's apparent offense, he expresses a significant degree of puzzlement as to its specific cause. "Your certified letter of March 15 rather astonished me," he begins. "It was never our intent to offend anyone personally with our production." Acknowledging the author's pain and outrage, Turner nevertheless puzzles about what exactly was so offensive. Indeed, other than two rather nonspecific references to the play's use of stereotypes, the specifics of the writer's objections remain fairly ambiguous. Turner makes this clear, noting his "confusion" as to the exact cause of offense. "Since you were familiar with the play," he writes, ". . . I can only assume that something in Mr. Elmore's performance must have been objectionable." After noting the "goodly amount of anti-Semitic abuse in Shakespeare's text" along with the festival's reluctance "to tamper with [it] in any fundamental way," he arrives finally at an issue that, while unarticulated by this particular writer, would inform a large majority of critiques that would be levied against the production: its contemporary *mise-en-scène*. Turner writes:

> It was Libby Appel's conceit that such "racial" feelings exist in any society at least as a kind of undercurrent. So, despite some hesitancy, she opted to place the play in modern times to bring out the universality of such themes. Was it this immediacy that personally offended you? Did it seem slanderous because it was so contemporary?

Turner concludes his letter by apologizing for the inadvertent distress the production may have caused, and notes that, while he respects the author's decision to deny the festival corporate funds, the company's "artistic standards and integrity" will not be influenced by monetary pressure.

Unfortunately for Turner, this missive would be only the first in a series of complaint letters targeting the production for its putative anti-Semitism. In the letters that followed, his early suspicions regarding the play's modernized setting as the primary cause for uneasiness were confirmed.[10] In a letter from May 13, 1999, another complainant makes her objections painfully clear. "I feel compelled to write to you about my reactions to *Merchant of Venice* because I was shocked and offended by the play and production," she begins. "Its modern dress version accentuates its anti-Semitic message, making it current instead of a tale set centuries ago. The depiction of Shylock as an orthodox Jew wearing a yarmulke and Tubal a prayer shawl is shocking. What is particularly ugly and repellent is the velvet fringed Tallis cover with the star of David covering the knife and sharpener (to exact the pound of flesh)." Here, the immediacy of the production's *mise-en-scène* takes center stage as the cause of offense, and the complainant's discomfort is centered directly on the production's use of recognizable signifiers from contemporary Orthodox Judaism. This critique would be echoed and expanded in a series of articles that would appear within various print media later that summer.

Composed by the erstwhile rabbinical student David Zaslow, these critiques left no ambiguity regarding the author's perception that Appel's modernized American setting was the root cause of the offense. Indeed, so incensed by the production was Zaslow that he would issue no fewer than four separate critiques within various local and regional media outlets, three of which are publications aimed at a specifically Jewish readership. Writing first in *The Jewish Journal*, self-described as "the largest Jewish weekly newspaper in the United States outside of New York City," Zaslow makes clear the source of his annoyance:

> This year the Oregon Shakespearean Festival's production of *The Merchant of Venice* in Ashland opened with a bang; actually it was a bell – a stockmarket [sic] bell rings in New York's financial district. . . . For a moment, I thought I was in the wrong theatre. But no, alas, this was the updated version and I was soon to meet the modern Shylock.
>
> The play has been modernized, with the actors wearing contemporary clothing. What stunned me was that Shylock wore a somewhat unpressed and slightly oversized suit; he was dressed as a modern Orthodox Jew! The director, Libby Appel, a Jew, rather than playing down Shylock's "tribe," made the decision to emphasize and update his religious affiliation. Throughout the play, it became clear how offensive the director's choices were.[11]

Zaslow expands upon these critiques in a subsequent piece that appeared in San Francisco's *Jewish Bulletin* (whose circulation was 22,000 in 1991), this time describing explicitly the pain and embarrassment the production's "modern dress and setting" caused for him because of the audience's reaction.[12] "The current production is already bringing strong responses to the festival by theatregoers," he writes, before recounting a particularly troublesome incident in which "a group of about five local teenagers was seen . . . yelling 'Jew, Jew, Jew' in the lobby during intermission as one of their friends pretended to be Shylock." To make matters worse, he reports, "They were pretending to spit on him – as the production had so graphically demonstrated." Implicit in Zaslow's critique is the fact that audiences completely unfamiliar with Judaism, or audiences who do not know any Jewish people, might adopt the play's anti-Semitic stances all too easily.[13] Indeed, it is easy to imagine members of Ashland's minority Jewish community reacting with justifiable alarm after witnessing such a display.

Rather than simply adumbrating his grievances related to the staging in his theatre commentary in *The Jewish Bulletin*, Zaslow recounts his attempts to reach out to the festival in order to find a mutually acceptable solution. He describes a conversation he had with Turner, whom he says "tried to convince [him] that [he] may have 'missed the point' of the production." And according to Zaslow, he was not alone in his efforts to persuade the festival to rethink its approach to *Merchant*: "Several members of the local Jewish community, including myself, have made a series of requests to the festival for production modifications and making educational materials available for young theatre-goers." The possibility of a pedagogical means of ameliorating the perceived slight to modern Judaism is once again referenced in his essay's conclusion. Zaslow claims, "At least Shakespeare's Shylock can be relegated as a stereotype out of the past. The play can be regarded as a 'period piece' worthy for its brilliant language and ripe for educational examination." In contrast, he argues, Appel's modern production is framed as "a grotesque, stereotypical mockery of Jewry itself.... It is an insult."

Zaslow would go on later that summer to publish a virtually identical essay in Seattle's *Jewish Transcript* as well as a response to an editorial by Jerry Turner in a regional newspaper, *The Daily Tidings*. While Turner ardently defended the production as well as the artistic integrity of OSF, Zaslow rejects accusations by Turner that critics of the production are attempting to censor the festival's production. "No one has even asked 'to change' the play," he notes.[14] More important for our purposes, however, are Zaslow's repeated calls in his response to Turner for the festival to create educational paratexts that would contextualize the objectionable material within Shakespeare's play and Appel's production. Zaslow first requests that the festival "address the educational needs of elementary school-age children who will come to see the play with some kind of handout written by the festival." His particular concern with young children's reactions is given credence by the fact that, as Zaslow goes on to note, the production was slated to be performed no fewer than ten times before audiences comprised largely of local and regional students. "Why is the Festival so reluctant to make educational handouts available?" he questions. "If kids are going to be in the audience throughout the summer ... then the Festival should ... place the play and production in proper context for the audience."[15]

Significantly, the prospect of young people who may not be aware of the long and horrific global history of anti-Semitic ideology and violence bearing witness to the production was a prominent feature of several of the complaint letters addressed to the festival. In addition to the aforementioned high school student who was reduced to tears by the staging, the author of an April 12, 1991, letter to William Moffat, then president of OSF's board of directors, notes specifically that, despite having been disturbed by *Merchant* before, it was the presence of "several young people seated in front of [him]" in addition to his "judgment of the effect of the play on these young people" that caused him particular distress. Another letter from April 21 of that year, presumably from an educator, recounts attending the production with 43 other people, 32 of whom were junior high students. The author expresses particular consternation at the fact that, in light of the generally high quality of the festival's offerings, "the lessons that students take away with them are ones that leave deep impressions upon them." For this writer, the fact that the production so profoundly resonated with members of its student audience was precisely the problem. His distress was only compounded when "members of the cast . . . visited with people after the performance." Describing what appears to be a talkback, the author expresses a particular distaste for the way that many performers seemed reluctant to even admit to the text's problematic ideological content. "Whereas I found them very engaging when speaking on how they prepared for the part . . . I found, with a few exceptions, their analysis of the play and Shakespeare nothing short of a rendering of company policy." Especially problematic for this commentator was the cast's generally uncritical veneration for Shakespeare. In a particularly insightful critique, he notes that the performers seem to "have brought into forum discussion a dangerous glorification of Shakespeare as a God of all literature, defending him at all costs." The writer pointedly advises, "One does not have to diminish greatness when finding fault with a particular play or part of a play, [just as] one does not have to project schools of thought and approaches that were not part of his time [onto Shakespeare's text], placing him above and beyond the pale of the epoch."[16] Implicit to the author's argument, then, is the notion that context matters, and that an audience's response to *Merchant* can only be enhanced by the addition of contextual subtlety, honest reflection, and, above all, sophisticated educational outreach that refuses to pander to audiences by looking past the very real problems embedded within Shakespeare's text.

Though the festival's 1991 production remained saturated in controversy throughout its run, those involved with the festival seemed to resist calls for the creation of contextual paratexts that would accompany the stagings. Significantly, though Jerry Turner and, less frequently, William Patton responded dutifully and with polite deference to the complaints they received, the festival never shied away from vociferously defending its artistic choices. With that being stated, it is clear that the company had been affected by the controversy, and the play would not be staged again for another ten years, the longest gap between productions of *Merchant* in OSF history. Even with such distance, the company approached its subsequent staging of the play with an eye toward the controversies that might arise.

"I HAVE SPOKE THUS MUCH TO MITIGATE THE JUSTICE OF THY PLEA"

In June 2001 OSF opened what was to be its thirteenth staging of *Merchant*, this time under the direction of Michael Donald Edwards, then a Los Angeles-based freelancer who had grown up in Australia. An account appearing in the *Seattle Post-Intelligencer* just days after the production's premiere makes clear the degree to which the 1991 controversy remained within the regional community's memory. After describing the earlier production as "extraordinary," theater critic Joel Adcock goes on to admit that "the most remarkable thing about it was the uproar it caused."[17] Libby Appel, now in an elevated role as the festival's artistic director, was once again asked to account publicly for the company's decision to stage the notoriously divisive play. "I was the target of a lot of egg throwing and rotten-tomato throwing 10 years ago," she recounts. "As you can see, I've cleaned myself up. But I felt like, 'Oh, gosh, I never want to go near that play again!' And when the idea of doing *Merchant* this season came up, I was a little bit gun shy," she admits finally.[18] Spurred in part by encouragement from the festival's artistic staff, Appel says that she approached the 2001 staging with a strategy for defusing controversy already in hand. As Adcock's article notes, "to avoid shocks and misunderstandings, both Appel and Edwards have been reaching out to and keeping in touch with the (albeit tiny) Southern Oregon Jewish community."[19]

While it may have been relatively small by some standards, the Jewish population in Jackson County had actually doubled to include close to 1,000 individuals in the ten years since the initial 1991 controversy.[20] And Appel's strategy this time was to enlist the affected community in an open and honest dialogue before another controversy had time to ripen. One of her first priorities in this regard was to reach out specifically to one of the most vocal critics of the 1991 production. An undated letter from Appel sent to both Rabbi Marc Sirinsky, the spiritual leader of Ashland's Temple Emek Shalom, and David Zaslow, by then an ordained rabbi operating as "the spiritual leader of Havurah Shir Hadash, a Jewish Renewal congregation in Ashland, Oregon," outlines the festival's efforts at community engagement.[21] "Dear Rabbi," she begins; "I wanted to take a moment to reconnect with you in these final days before our production of *The Merchant of Venice* opens." She goes on to thank them for providing the company with "the opportunity to speak with members of [their] congregation[s] earlier this year," noting that "the exchange of ideas and opinions was extremely valuable for all of us from the festival who participated." Clearly then, Appel had moved preemptively to solicit advice from local Jewish leaders about steps that might be taken to mitigate potential discomfort and fear regarding the play's potential to spark or reinforce strains of anti-Semitism.

Although it is impossible to know exactly what suggestions might have been proffered in meetings between festival representatives and members of the local Jewish community, Appel's missive suggests that, as before, increased efforts at educating the broader public about the play's troublesome ideological content were among the community's chief concerns. "I wanted to bring you up to date on the plans we have to encourage dialogue and education around this year's production," she writes, going on to describe the festival's considerable efforts to contextualize the production for audiences in such a way as to make clear their patent disavowal of Shakespeare's anti-Semitism:

> We have currently scheduled six lectures in Carpenter Hall [a property adjacent to the theatres on OSF's campus], fifteen Prefaces (thirty minutes of

preparation prior to the performance), sixteen post-show discussions which will take place once a week during the afternoon, thirteen screenings of the *Shylock* documentary [a 1999 film by director Pierre Lasry that contextualizes *Merchant* within a larger history of European anti-Semitism], as well as one sign-interpreted performance.

In addition to these events, Appel notes the availability of *In Focus*, "[a] publication . . . designed to provide a forum to explore the play in greater depth."

An eight-page publication available for sale that season in theatre lobbies and at other locations on festival grounds, *In Focus* bills itself as "a new dramaturgical supplement of the Oregon Shakespeare Festival intended to augment our existing play publications . . . and provide a forum to explore certain plays in even greater depth."[22] Opening with a short interview with Edwards conducted by Douglas Langworthy, the production's dramaturge, the director is questioned directly about the play's many "ambiguities." Perhaps unsurprisingly, Edwards endeavors to emphasize the positive aspects of Shakespeare's characterization of Shylock. "Did [Shakespeare] include some basic anti-Semitic attitudes in his configuration of Shylock?" he asks himself, before concluding, "absolutely – he knew nothing else." Nevertheless, he contends, "[Shakespeare] couldn't help but write a human being, and that's why [*Merchant*] has become such a problem." Edwards goes on to emphasize that, like Shylock, the play's Christian characters are all compromised morally as well, and thus no one comes out looking entirely good or bad. When questioned finally about his approach to directing *Merchant* in the face of the play's manifold complexities, Edwards admits that the Shakespeare we have inherited is not always the one we might have wanted. "As a director, I would love to do a production that challenges every bit of anti-Semitic behavior in the world and puts Shakespeare on the side of those who believe in equal rights for everybody." "Unfortunately," he concludes, "the play isn't a political tract and you'd have to change it profoundly to make it into one."

The interview seems to accomplish several important things. First, it acknowledges immediately that Shakespeare's portrayal of Shylock is rooted in painful anti-Semitic stereotypes and thereby faces the play's problematic ideological content head-on in an unequivocal manner. Quite simply, it refuses to make excuses for Shakespeare. At the same time, Edwards rightfully acknowledges the degree to which the playwright had imbued his creation with a degree of humanity and, indeed, the attendant potential for sympathy. Thus Edwards contrasts Shylock specifically with his Marlovian progenitor, "[the] villainous Barabas," who exists strictly as an embodiment of everything early modern European Christians would have feared about Jews. In acknowledging Shylock's essential humanity, Edwards argues against the idea put forth by some that *Merchant* should be retired outright. And he does this not by shielding himself behind the ultimate authority of Shakespeare, arguing for inclusion simply as a function of the play's unimpeachable imprimatur, but instead by immersing himself in the play's "moral ambiguity," celebrating its propensity to be received as "stimulating and provocative for some audience members [while remaining] infuriating for others."

The remainder of *In Focus* is comprised primarily of quotations on *Merchant* from prominent critics such as W. H. Auden, Harold Bloom, C. L. Barber, and William Hazlitt, in addition to musings by theologian Karen Armstrong and director Jonathan Miller. These excerpts are organized around prominent dichotomies within the play (interest/thrift, villain/victim, revenge/mercy, etc.) and each excerpt seems to have been chosen for either the relative sympathy that it might elicit toward Shylock or the ambivalence it might inspire toward the play's Christian characters. Characteristic of both tendencies, for example, is a page featuring the Edwardian poet and scholar Walter Raleigh's well-known appropriative quip that "Shylock is a man, and a man more sinned against than sinning." Equally prominent is a substantial quotation taken from James Shapiro's *Shakespeare and the Jews* (1985):

> Much of the play's vitality can be attributed to the ways in which it scrapes against a bedrock of beliefs about the racial, national, sexual, and religious difference of others. I can think of no other literary work that does so as unrelentingly and as honestly. To avert our gaze from what the play reveals about the relationship between cultural myths and peoples' [sic] identities will not make exclusionary attitudes disappear. Indeed, these darker impulses remain so elusive, so hard to identify in the normal course of things, that only in instances like the production of this play do we get to glimpse these cultural faultlines. This is why censoring the play is *always* more dangerous than staging it.[23]

For Shapiro, *Merchant* is worth preserving precisely because of its unflinching engagement with patently offensive tropes and traditions. His spirited defense of the play is premised largely on the idea that its continued ability to shock and offend is exactly why it must continue to be reckoned with by modern theatergoers. Given the prominent position the quotation occupies in the publication, appearing directly after the interview with Edwards, as well as the degree to which Shapiro's contentions seem directly to refute earlier criticisms leveled against the 1991 production, it seems likely that its inclusion was intended specifically to address what many associated with the festival viewed as calls for censorship. While working as a principled affirmation of the company's decision to continue to stage *Merchant*, Shapiro's claim is effective in addressing the controversy because it also recognizes outright the play's ability to wound. While those who feel that *Merchant* should be retired from the repertoire might very well disagree with Shapiro and, by proxy, the festival's conclusions, so too are they assured that the decision to stage the play was not made lightly or without serious reflection on the political and personal implications of that decision.

While it is difficult to measure with any certainty the ultimate success of OSF's strategy of public outreach, educational engagement, and open dialogue, the 2001 production did manage on this occasion not to incite significant controversy within the local and regional press. Still, it cannot be said that the 2001 production was without its detractors. Indeed, the festival received a fair number of complaints due to the play's anti-Semitism once again that year (in addition to at least one letter championing their steadfast resistance to censorship). Yet even among those who raised objections, it is important to note that this time it was the play itself, rather than the specific tenor of OSF's production, that was the primary object of debate. While *Merchant* was still deemed by some as an affront to communal harmony, many appreciated the festival's efforts to address the play's problematic content head on. Even more, despite a few complainants who were just as strident in their opposition as those who objected to the 1991 staging, Appel, in her role as artistic director, was now in a much better position to respond. Rather than simply upholding the festival's commitment to an antiracist agenda and reaffirming the necessity for artists to maintain their freedom of expression, she could now assert confidently, and with ample evidence, that the festival did not take lightly the responsibility of staging the incendiary play. Even among those who remained unpersuaded regarding the value of staging *Merchant*, one gets the sense that they valued somewhat the effort and sensitivity the festival had shown. This is perhaps most apparent in a letter from a patron who pleads to Appel that "you cannot escape the fact that the play is anti-Semitic," and that there is no excuse for "spreading and reinforcing anti-Semitism with great art." Even in spite of the intensity of this correspondent's appeal, it is telling that her letter opens with a heartfelt note of gratitude: "Dear Ms. Appel," writes the correspondent, "I would like to thank you for your talk last night at the Temple Emek Shalom about *The Merchant of Venice*." Though the writer and artist do not agree on whether the play has a place within the modern repertoire, they both seem to welcome the resultant dialogue that it has inspired, resting assured that, while their options still diverge sharply, each party has endeavored to recognize and respect the other's position in a way that the contending religious factions represented within *Merchant* cannot.

CODA: "HE IS WELL PAID THAT IS WELL SATISFIED"

"With *The Merchant of Venice* being staged at OSF this summer," reads a June 2010 listing on a local online community bulletin board, "a detailed study of this Shakespearean play is timely" ("Merchant of Venice"). In commemoration of the festival's 75th anniversary, artistic director Bill Rauch chose to present versions of the two plays that had opened its inaugural season in 1935, meaning that, once again, *Merchant* would be on the bill in Ashland. Given the play's recent record at inciting local controversy, elements of the Jewish community prepared themselves to address the play's problematic history, this time by way of a series of classes held at the Havurah Shir Hadash, Ashland's Jewish Renewal temple. What is perhaps most surprising about the series of lectures is the identity of the individual who would preside over them. "Join Rabbi David Zaslow, spiritual leader of the Havurah, for a two-session course on this brilliantly written, but tragically flawed play" reads the announcement, before delving into the play's troublesome history:

> Using all the available stereotypes and libels against Jews (they love money more than people, they are less than human, they are driven by the devil, they seek the flesh and blood of Christians) the play was beloved in Nazi Germany. Rabbi David will analyze the roots of the play along with the history of anti-Semitism that is rooted in the distorted interpretation of Christian Scriptures.

Clearly, the once-contentious relationship between Zaslow and the festival had softened into one of mutual cooperation, as the rabbi who had once objected so vociferously to the festival's lack of adequate contextualization and sensitivity surrounding the play now worked within the community to provide such context himself. From the festival's perspective, these interventions seemed to pay off since the 2010 production met with comparatively little objection within Ashland's Jewish population.

We have focused on the impact this small Jewish community in this specific northwestern town in the United States had on the Oregon Shakespeare Festival to highlight the ways organized minority responses can effect real change. OSF altered its production practices in order to forestall the mounted resistance their productions of *Merchant* faced. In many ways, this can be read as David's (a very small Jewish community in Oregon) victory over Goliath (a very wealthy and successful theatre company).

Yet there is another way to read this narrative that is less generous and more troubling, especially when extrapolating arguments from the site specific, or micro, to the global, or macro. What if Goliath merely subsumed David, silencing his salient objections? Do we know that contextualizing *Merchant* through program notes, talkbacks, publications, educational paratexts, and so forth actually solves the problems described for OSF's 1991 production? We know that the Jewish community felt more at ease, but what about the majority of the audience? Did they experience something different because of the contextualization?

Indeed, a 2004 study conducted by Willmar Sauter and Yael Feiler for a production of *Merchant* at Stockholm's Royal Dramatic Theatre suggests that the play itself may be the problem. Presenting audience members with a two-part questionnaire that sought to measure an individual's implicit anti-Semitism both before and after a performance, Sauter and Feiler found that prejudice against Jews was generally more pronounced after the curtain had fallen. The researchers then repeated this experiment on a smaller scale for performances in Germany and Sweden and found similar results; though there were some differences in how the numbers broke down in terms of the age of respondents, each revealed at least a slight increase in anti-Semitism after respondents viewed performances of *Merchant*. As Sauter concludes, "Shakespeare's play in these cases always brought some slumbering anti-Semitism to the fore, irrespective of the concept of the production. . . . [While] the damage that the play may cause can be limited by the production to a certain degree . . . there is obviously a risk group in every audience that is willing to blame the Jews."[24] If we accept these findings, what remains to be considered is the degree to which outreach and frank discussion might work to mitigate this tendency. Can talkbacks and educational paratexts work effectively to combat the deleterious effects that a production of a discriminatory play exerts upon members of its audience? While there currently exists no easy answer to this question, it is clear that those interested in considering *Merchant*'s place within the contemporary world would do well to build upon Sauter's investigation, extending the questions asked therein in order to consider just how much good attempts at education, however well-intentioned they might be, are actually able to accomplish. And were we to find that such outreach is ultimately ineffective in combating the anti-Semitism that *Merchant* seems to exacerbate, would companies then feel compelled to remove the play from their repertories? Would the ubiquitous "complete works" cycles cease to exist? Or would most simply find new and novel ways of arguing for its inclusion?

While it is impossible to know the answer to these questions without further research, it seems clear that appealing to Shakespearean completists remains a dependable marketing strategy for theatre companies. It is thus unsurprising to find that in 2015, as a celebration of its 80th year in operation, OSF has once again committed itself to running through the entire Shakespearean canon, this time over the span of a single decade. Clearly intended to foster a lasting relationship between the festival and its attendees, the official OSF press release invites audience members to "tick off their plays in the Shakespeare canon by purchasing a Shakespeare Passport at the Tudor Guild Gift Shop."[25] Given the often-cited crisis in contemporary funding for the arts, it is hard to begrudge the festival for taking advantage of such opportunities to further cultivate a loyal and enthusiastic patronage. At the same time, Sauter and Feiler's study leads us to wonder if stagings of *Merchant* might not be particularly deleterious in communities such as Ashland, in which the Jewish population is so distinct a minority. For despite the increasing numbers making their homes within the community, it remains the case that Jewish culture in the Pacific Northwest lacks the visibility and prominence one might find within major East Coast metropolitan areas. And if the most visible public expression of Jewishness for many within the surrounding community is limited to performances of *Merchant* at least once every decade, it is difficult to imagine the problem of the play's anti-Semitism being solved through mere community outreach. Yet it is equally hard to envision companies such as OSF removing one of the poet's most performed and historically resonant plays from its "complete works" cycles.

While the above analysis shows how a small minority community within Ashland was able to provoke institutional change within the preeminent local cultural institution, what was being asked of OSF in this case were minor conceptual and paratextual revisions. Though the company was able to negotiate these controversies deftly by enlisting the help of its most ardent critics from within the Jewish community, it remains likely that, were the more radical step of retiring the play from the repertoire entirely considered, the attendant reverberations and recriminations that would erupt from free-speech absolutists and steadfast champions of artistic freedom would, once again, result in a controversy whose consequences would extend far beyond the site-specific conditions of the small northwestern community from which they arose.[26]

NOTES

1   While OSF began making efforts to collect demographic data on its patrons through audience surveys in 1957, much of the available information from these early years is limited to matters of geography, as the festival seemed interested primarily at this point in ascertaining the number of audience members drawn from outside of Ashland, Jackson County, and Oregon itself. Beginning in 1978, the festival began conducting more detailed demographic surveys about every three years in conjunction with the Southern Oregon Regional Services Institute of Southern Oregon University. The surveys increase slightly in their scope and sophistication over subsequent years, but it is at this point where information on the vocation, educational background, and household income of OSF patrons becomes available. While data from the 1978 study is not preserved in the archives, information aggregated by the survey conducted in 1981 points broadly to an audience comprised of highly educated, middle-aged individuals with household incomes almost double that of the year's national median of $17,495 (see "Census Report Says After-Tax-Income Fell in 1981." *The New York Times*. February 27, 1984, accessed January 31, 2015). The 1981 survey also reveals that 51% of respondents had completed at least some post-graduate education and that another 29% held college degrees. These numbers remain largely consistent in the data from 1985. Surveys were then expanded in 1988 to ask questions about race and ethnicity. Here, we see 97% of patrons describing themselves as "Caucasian," with 1% identifying respectively as Hispanic, Chinese, and "other Asian." Subsequent demographic

data remains remarkably stable in similar studies from 1991, 1994, 1997, 2000, and 2004, especially when patrons' income is adjusted for inflation and compared against the national median. By the time we reach 2007, the final year in which data was available, 87% of respondents reported having at least a four-year college degree while the median yearly income of ticketholders was reported to be $95,000, almost $40,000 more than that of the national median (see "Real Median Household Income in the United States." FRED Economic Data. Federal Reserve Bank of St. Louis, n.d., accessed January 31, 2015.). By that year, ethnic and racial diversity in festival attendees had also increased slightly, though self-identified whites still accounted for 93% of audiences. In short, despite the festival's admirable commitment to diversity within the company and staff as well as their good-faith efforts to appeal to individuals from a wide variety of ethnic, racial, economic, religious, educational, and class backgrounds, OSF's audiences still remain comprised primarily of wealthy, well-educated, white playgoers.

2 Edward Brubaker and Mary Brubaker, *Golden Fire: The Anniversary Book of the Oregon Shakespeare Festival* (Ashland: Oregon Shakespeare Festival Association, 1985), 47.
3 Brubaker and Brubaker, "*Golden Fire*," 113.
4 The festival presented *The Merchant of Venice* subsequently in 1953, 1958, 1964, 1970, 1977, 1985, 1991, 2001, and 2010.
5 Interpreting the available data regarding the Jewish population in the U.S. is especially tricky. For one, the Census Bureau has been legally prohibited since 1976 by Public Law 94–521 from asking respondents mandatory questions regarding religious identification. Even if this were not the case, however, Judaism's status as an ethnoreligious category whose boundaries and divisions are often contentious among Jews themselves makes identification exceedingly problematic. The best available data, which is cited herein, comes from the Association of Religious Data Archives, a privately funded consortium run out of the Department of Sociology at Pennsylvania State University that aggregates self-reported data from over 236 religious groups in the United States. Given the ARDA's methodologies, only practicing Jews who are currently affiliated with a local synagogue are represented in the data.
6 See "A Short History of Temple Emek Shalom." Temple Emek Shalom of Ashland, Oregon, accessed January 31, 2015, emekshalom.org.
7 Clifford Grammich, Kirk Hadaway, Richard Houseal, Dale E. Jones, Alexei Krindatch, Richie Stanley, and Richard H. Taylor, "County Membership Report: Jackson County Oregon." *The Association of Religion Data Archives*, 2010, accessed January 31, 2015, TheARDA.com.
8 In 1991, according to ARDA figures, the Catholic Church could claim the highest number of adherents in the county, with nearly 14,000 parishioners distributed throughout five congregations. The same year, there were eleven strains of Protestantism represented in the data, each of which was able to boast more than 1,000 adherents. The 1991 survey also shows that almost 5,000 Mormons belonged to temples based in Jackson County, making the Latter-Day Saints a significant influence on the religious character of the local community.
9 All quotations from letters of complaint come from the Oregon Shakespeare Festival's archive. To ensure anonymity, we do not include the letter writers' names. We only list the letter's date and the author's gender.
10 The festival's archives hold copies of seven separate letters of complaint regarding this production, many of which were written by authors who self-identified as Jews.

Significantly, only one other production up to that point in the festival's history, a 1988 staging of *Romeo and Juliet*, seems to have courted such vocal and negative responses from audience members. For more on that production see Ayanna Thompson, "(How) Should We Listen to Audiences?: Race, Reception, and the Audience Survey," *The Oxford Handbook for Shakespeare and Performance*, ed. James Bulman (Oxford: Oxford University Press, 2016).

11 David Zaslow, "Mistaking the Bard: Oregon's Shakespeare Festival Opens with a Controversial Shylock in *Merchant of Venice*," *The Jewish Journal*, April 26–May 2 (1991):21.
12 David Zaslow, "Oregon's Mocking *Merchant of Venice* Insults Jews." *The Jewish Bulletin*, July 12, 1991. N.p. Due to gaps in OSF's archives, the specific page numbers for Zaslow's articles in *The Jewish Bulletin*, *The Jewish Transcript*, and *The Daily Tidings* are unavailable.
13 Zaslow's fears are not unfounded. As Wilmar Sauter's research has shown, many audiences of *The Merchant of Venice* leave the play feeling justified in any anti-Semitic feelings they had prior to the show. See Sauter's "Thirty Years of Reception Studies: Empirical, Methodological and Theoretical Advances," *About Performance* 10 (2010): 241–63.
14 See Zaslow, "Room for Compromise in OSF's 'Merchant' Play," *The Daily Tidings*, 22 May 22 1991, n.p. Zaslow makes clear in this piece that he is not in favor of censorship, noting that "Freedom, both religious and artistic, has been one of the pillars of Jewish social consciousness and expression from biblical times to the present" ("Room for Compromise"). Nonetheless, both of his essays in *The Jewish Journal* and *The Jewish Transcript* recount requests by him and other members of the local Jewish community for "production modifications" (Zaslow, "Mistaking," 21; Zaslow, "OSF's *Merchant of Venice*: Anti-Semitism from the Script to the Stage," *The Jewish Transcript*, 28 June, 1991, n.p.).
15 Zaslow and members of the regional Jewish community were not alone in their desire for the production to be accompanied by additional contextual materials. Indeed, Zaslow's piece for *The Daily Tidings* notes that "A letter was recently mailed to the festival by the B'nai B'rith Anti-Defamation League requesting that some sort of handout describing the historical aspects of Anti-Semitism regarding 'The Merchant' be inserted into Playbills, or at least be available in the theater lobby."
16 This particular letter was addressed broadly to the "Ashland thespians."
17 Joel Adcock, "Bard Times in Ashland," *Seattle Post-Intelligencer*, 20 June, 2001, accessed February 1, 2015. Seattlepi.com.
18 Quoted in Adcock, "Bard Times."
19 Adcock, "Bard Times."
20 Grammich et al., "County Membership."
21 "Bio." N.p., n.d. Accessed February 1, 2015, Rabbidavidzaslow.com.
22 Douglas Langworthy, et al. *In Focus: Oregon Shakespeare Festival* (Ashland: The Oregon Shakespeare Festival, 2001).
23 Langworthy et al, *In Focus*, 3. The quotation originates in James Shapiro, *Shakespeare and the Jews* (New York: Columbia University Press, 1996), 228.
24 Sauter, "Thirty Years," 258.
25 "OSF Celebrates 80 Years as 2015 Season Opens." The Oregon Shakespeare Festival, January 6, 2015, accessed April 27, 2015, OSFAshland.org.
26 This project could not exist without the generous assistance of Debra Griffith and Maria DeWeerdt from OSF's archives.

5 Exhibiting the past: Globe replicas in Shakespearean exhibitions

Clara Calvo

Replicas of the Globe Theatre can be found in many locations around the world, and they are often connected to either theatre festivals or exhibitions where the best-known example is probably the Globe replica built for the 1934 Chicago World's Fair and rebuilt the following year at the California Pacific International Exposition in Balboa Park, San Diego.[1] After the closing of the exposition, Balboa Park became the venue for the San Diego National Shakespeare Festival until 1978, when it was, like the first Globe theatre in early modern London, consumed by fire. Other replicas built for a festival include the Adams Memorial Shakespeare Theatre in Cedar City, Utah (which opened in 1977), and the Globe in Neuss, Germany (1991). There are, of course, exceptions, as some replicas were not built for an exhibition or a festival, such as the 1987 Globe on London's South Bank, the 1988 Panasonic Globe designed by Arata Isozaki in Tokyo, the 2000 Schwäbisch Hall Globe in Baden-Württemberg, Germany, and the 1966 Globe of the Great Southwest in Odessa, Texas, to mention a few.[2] A Globe replica was planned in Rio Acima as part of a cultural complex for the 2016 Olympic Games in Brazil.

Why this culturally shared impulse to create replicas of the Globe all over the world? The impulse stems from a desire to move beyond imagining this particular theatre, that privileged site of Shakespeare's art, through the written word or two-dimensional representations. It is a desire to give this long-lost space what Duke Theseus calls a "local habitation", in order to provide a phenomenological encounter with a physical space familiar to Shakespeare. The drive for a space that one can inhabit, for a building where one can bodily re-create what can no longer be lived – that is, the experience of a performance in an early modern playhouse – is the product of modern nostalgia. David Lowenthal's conception of the past as a "foreign country" has been instrumental in promoting a view of the past as an unassailable "other", as a distant and different realm, which can only be reached through re-creation and invention.[3] Globe replicas, in their attempt to replicate a building which no longer exists, are a good example of this nostalgic impulse and, given the lack of an original to reproduce, they contribute to the series of "invented traditions" that permeate Western culture.[4]

Globe replicas are thus an instance of the penchant modern societies have for projects that aim to construe the past. Historical reconstruction, according to Paul Connerton, differs from social memory, as the historian deals with traces of human activity which extend beyond individual or collective recollection and remembrance. Historical reconstruction is not dependent on social memory but it can give shape to, or at least guide, the collective memory of social groups.[5] In this respect, the function of Globe replicas in exhibitions has an added dimension to the function of Globe replicas built to serve, primarily, as performance spaces. In exhibitions, Globe replicas go beyond a desire for authenticity and the nostalgia for original conditions. In particular, when the Globe replicas are part of exhibitions, world's fairs, or, as the incipient Globe in Brazil suggests, Olympic Games, they acquire a function beyond their use as stages for performance and become repositories of cultural memory. The relation between memory and history is thus inverted. Collective memory is not the source of the representation of the past as history; instead, historical reconstruction shapes contemporary collective memory. In this essay, I explore some Globe replicas that were conceived not as self-standing buildings but as parts of exhibitions. As organized attempts to reconstruct the past, these exhibitions, I argue, exemplify an interaction between historical intervention and social memory. The Globe replicas within these exhibitions contribute in distinctive ways to processes whereby the British past is reinvented in a global context.

Approaching the past as constituted by sites of collective memory, in the tradition of Pierre Nora's sites of memory (*lieux de mémoire*), my aim is to explore how Globe replicas contribute to the projection of the past onto contemporary space.[6] For Nora, sites of memory are created by the interaction of memory and history. The formation of sites of memory is a direct result, Nora suggests, of the "acceleration of history", the awareness of a break with the past that quickly turns the present into history. In sites of memory, memory is embodied: it 'crystallizes and secretes itself' because in memory 'a sense of historical continuity persists'.[7] Sites of memory are sometimes purely material sites that turn into sites of memory when collective imagination invests them with a symbolic aura or when they become part of a ritual.[8] Unlike the Pantheon or Westminster Abbey, which are *imposed* sites of memory – because they were originally conceived as monuments with a symbolic, national projection – the Globe is a *constructed* site of memory which acquired its symbolic function through 'unforeseen mechanisms, combination of circumstances, the passage of time, human effort and history itself'.[9] As a constructed site of memory, the Globe has become a symbol of English national identity through, amongst other things, its proliferated replicas which have added various layers to its function in contemporary processes of collective and cultural memory.

CELEBRATING THE PAST: 1916

In 1916 the city of Boston planned to erect a permanent Shakespeare Village to commemorate the tercentenary of Shakespeare's death. The village was never built, but a drawing published by *The New York Times* (Figure 5.1) shows an attempt to reconstruct an early modern village out of a few significant buildings in Shakespeare's life: the Guild chapel, the grammar school, New Place, the Birthplace (labelled "Shakespeare's house"), Anne Hathaway's cottage, and Mary Arden's cottage (the last is typically known as Mary Arden's House or

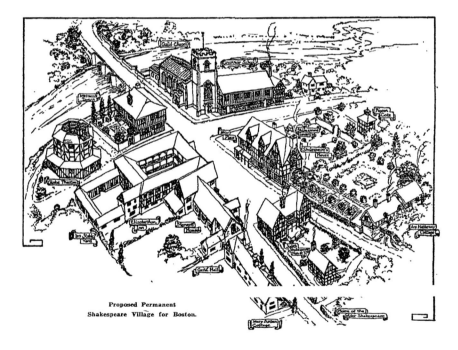

Figure 5.1   Proposed permanent Shakespeare Village for Boston. "Boston to Have Permanent Shakespeare Village," *The New York Times*, 25 June 1916. Public domain.

Farm). The Elizabethan village also sports an inn, with its own stable and yard, and there is a Judith Shakespeare's house, although the sign on the right bottom corner that reads "House of the Elder Shakespeare" is a plot of ground with no building attached to it. Whereas Trinity Church is missing from the plan published by *The New York Times*, Harvard House is awarded a central position, no doubt because of the resonances it would have for Boston citizens. Two other buildings included in the proposed plan, however, seem to sit oddly in this replica of an early modern English village: the Globe theatre and the Mermaid Tavern. The original playhouse and tavern were located in London, already in Shakespeare's time on its way to becoming the imperial metropolis it had become by 1916. As an Elizabethan village – and Shakespeare's Stratford in particular – would have had no public playhouse, the presence of a replica of the Globe in a project aiming to reconstruct a village by the river Charles points to the iconic force and characteristic Elizabethan associations prompted by the Southwark theatre. The Boston planners must have felt that the Globe playhouse unambiguously heralds Elizabethan England and projects a nostalgic vision of a distinct British past.

The presence of a Globe theatre in a plan for a Shakespeare village on the other side of the Atlantic raises questions concerning the nature of theatre replicas in world's fairs and exhibitions. How do these buildings negotiate their primary function as spaces for performance and their roles as exhibits? In what ways do they help to recreate the past? What do they tell us about the iconic force of Shakespeare's theatre today? By discussing some of these replicas in relation to their specific historical contexts, I aim to determine how these ephemeral theatres differ from other, more permanent reconstructions of the Globe. Although performances took place in some of them, replicas in Shakespearean exhibitions do not generally have the staging of plays as their sole or primary purpose. Often they transcend their function as spaces for performance, turning into a sort of archaeological item on display, an *objet pur* in Baudrillard's sense of the term – that is, an object devoid of function or use whose sole reason for existence is to exist and be looked at.[10] Replicas of buildings from the past, particularly if erected as part of a museum or exhibition, function as architectural relics to be gazed at both in isolation and as part of a re-created remote past. In the case of the Globe, its singularity as a building makes it stand out easily and this helps to convey a particular representation of the past as a foreign country, as a place different to the space inhabited by the present, in which, as L. P. Hartley put it in *The Go-Between*, 'they do things differently'. Given that neither of the two "original" Globe theatres survived, the replicas are simulacra of architectural relics and, as such, they become peculiar sites of social memory. What these replicas mobilize is nostalgia, a desire to re-create what no longer exists and by doing so to cope with a sense of loss – a loss of heritage and a loss of historical national identity. At the same time, the presence of Globe replicas in exhibitions testifies to a sustained desire to establish a continuity with the past, to retrieve some lost umbilical cord that links us to Shakespeare's time. In this respect, erecting a replica of Shakespeare's theatre becomes an act of remembrance that relates to historically mediated cultures of commemoration.

DUPLICATING THE PAST: 1912

The projected Boston Shakespeare Village owed much, no doubt, to the Elizabethan village the British architect Edwin Landseer Lutyens built for "Shakespeare's England", an Earl's Court exhibition which ran for six months in 1912. The exhibition, arranged by Mrs. Cornwallis-West (formerly Lady Randolph Churchill), was a charity venture aimed at raising funds for the Shakespeare National Theatre Memorial Fund.[11] The architect behind the never-built Shakespeare Village and the Globe replica in Back Bay Fens was Frank Chouteau Brown, a Boston architect who had specialized, like Lutyens, in residential architecture in the Tudor Revival style. Brown was known for his interest in New England's historic buildings and Shakespearean drama.[12] As Figure 5.1 shows, his objective was to re-create not Shakespeare's England but rather Shakespeare's Stratford-upon-Avon. Brown's work was, then, probably inspired by the exhibition at Earl's Court. In particular, the drawing of the Globe Theatre, on the bank of the river Charles in the Boston Elizabethan village plan, closely resembles the Globe replica designed by Lutyens for Earl's Court (see Figures 5.1 to 5.4). Neither seems to follow either Claes Janszoon Visscher's 1616 view of London or Wenceslaus Hollar's 1647 panorama, but both share the timber-framed addition on the ground floor that encircles the building (see Figures 5.3 and 5.4).[13]

An anonymous reviewer of the Shakespeare Exhibition at Earl's Court, while acknowledging the interest of the building, remarked on this strange structure: 'The Globe particularly is bound to be the centre of attention. Exactly what authority there is for putting a covered lobby round it we do not know – in fact, we can say that there is no authority'.[14] As Marion O'Connor has shown, the Globe replica at Earl's Court did not offer full-text performances of the play but only half-hour-long excerpts of Elizabethan and Jacobean drama three times per day (at 3.30, 5.30 and 9.30).[15] Irish-born actor-manager Patrick Kirwan and his company the Idyllic Players had ample experience of outdoor playing in Regent's Park and at the Crystal Palace exhibition grounds in 1910. The intended audience for these performances was a popular one, probably familiar with the Shakespearean excerpts that had become standard as music hall numbers, particularly at the London Coliseum. Unlike Willliam Poel's productions, the Globe performances

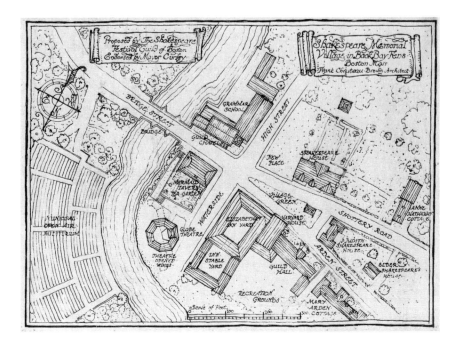

Figure 5.2 Frank Chouteau Brown. Plans for the Shakespeare Memorial Village in Back Bay Fens, Boston, Massachusetts. Proposed by the Shakespeare Festival Guild of Boston. Reverse brown print. Courtesy of Historic New England.

at Earl's Court were not antiquarian attempts at historical reconstruction. They aimed to offer what O'Connor has described as a 'spectacular "environmental" entertainment' in which the play on stage was not the only performance.[16] At Earl's Court, the reinvention of the Globe went beyond the architectural replica and extended to the pit and galleries, where actors in Elizabethan costume impersonated apprentices and orange girls. It is quite possible that many visitors did not have the chance or the inclination to attend these performances, but because of the way the exhibition had been laid out, they could hardly miss seeing the Globe, at least from the outside. The entrance to the exhibition led in a straight line to Drake's ship the *Revenge*, and whether visitors took the left or the right path after visiting the ship in its quay, a view of the Globe would present itself on their right hand (Figure 5.5). Most visitors probably went round the building, which was centrally displayed, and for those who had been to Earl's Court before, it had the attraction of being one of the few entirely new buildings in the exhibition.

Figure 5.3   Frank Chouteau Brown. Elevation of Shakespeare's Old "Globe" Theatre. Reverse brown print. Courtesy of Historic New England.

Lutyens's recreation of the Globe theatre was the result of a combination of factors: (a) his experience as cottage and 'country house' architect for the English upper classes; (b) Mrs. Cornwallis-West's interest in a commercial venture that in the interest of profit (whether for charity or private benefit is not entirely clear) placed, in the midst of an Elizabethan village, retail units selling modern products; and (c) a drive to link England's glorious early modern past as an emerging nation with its Edwardian present as imperial world power. O'Connor looked into how these three factors intersect and how the Globe stands in close companionship with Francis Drake's flagship *Revenge*, but Lutyens's replica also stood in a dialogue with the other Elizabethan buildings in the exhibition, built on a much smaller scale (see Figure 5.5).[17]

Figure 5.4   The Globe Theatre, Shakespeare's England, Earl's Court, 1912. Author's collection.

'The past', as David Lowenthal has argued, 'is always altered for motives that reflect present needs'.[18] Lutyens's timber-framed lower ground is a significant addition in a building that looks as if it owes more to Edwardian than Elizabethan technology. It scaled down the size of the original building, disguising its height and making it look more like other "Elizabethan" buildings in the exhibition: 'We reshape our heritage to make it attractive in modern terms; we seek to make it part of ourselves, and ourselves part of it; we conform it to our self-images and aspirations . . . history is continually altered in our private interests or on behalf of our community or country'.[19] Reshaping heritage, then, is possible thanks to the existence of imagined communities which share, as Connerton argues, a collective social memory shaped by historical reconstruction. Timber-framed houses could be found everywhere in the exhibition – in fact, what Lutyens did was to hide the permanent buildings in the Earl's Court site with wood and plaster so that they resembled Elizabethan townhouses. At Earl's Court, the Globe's timber-framed structure acquired the status of a site of national identity, linking the Elizabethan past and the Edwardian present. Lutyens's "Shakespeare's England" turned the timber-framed architecture which defines both Shakespeare's Globe and the English cottage into a means of re-imagining the past in terms of national identity. The exhibition also included a replica of Shakespeare's birthplace, which in 1912 had already become a site of memory as the natal house of the national

Figure 5.5   Bird's-Eye View of "Shakespeare's England," *The New York Times*, 23 June 1912. Public domain.

bard.[20] The birthplace was also a symbol of national pride, since attempts to buy the house at the 1847 auction that would have put it into private hands were averted and it was 'secured for the nation'.[21] Lutyens's replica of the birthplace reinvents it as the quintessential English cottage, with slanted roof and bow windows, but standing isolated, unlike its original in Stratford-upon-Avon, as a detached house (compare the example shown in Figure 5.6).

For his Globe replica, Lutyens may have consulted, as O'Connor suggests, Poel's small models (scale 1:24) of the Globe and the Fortune.[22] Both miniature replicas had been displayed in a previous Shakespeare exhibition held at the Whitechapel Art Gallery in 1910, also in aid of the Shakespeare National Theatre Memorial Fund. A few days before the opening, *The Sunday Times* announced the exhibition, drawing specific attention to the replicas:

> October 11 has been chosen as the date for the opening, in the Whitechapel Art Gallery, of the Shakespeare Exhibition, which will furnish a wonderfully complete collection of Shakespearean relics. Among others who have promised to lend pictures are Lord Northbrook (John Philip Kemble as "Hamlet," by

Figure 5.6   Postcard showing timber-framed and gabled houses by Edward Lutyens in the Earl's Court exhibition "Shakespeare's England." Author's collection.

Sir Thomas Lawrence), the Duke of Portland (Shakespearean miniatures), Mr. George Alexander (Gainsborough's David Garrick), the Duke of Newcastle (Reynolds's portrait of Foote), Lord Lansdowne (Hogarth's Peg Woffington), and the Shakespeare Memorial Theatre, Stratford-on-Avon. A feature of the exhibition will be the miniature reproductions of theatres, including Mr. William Poel's reconstruction of the Globe, which has been lent by Lady Mond.[23]

At the Whitechapel Art Gallery, Poel's model of the Globe shared location with a multiplicity of Shakespeareana in *wunderkammer* fashion. The theatre, no longer functional, an *objet pur*, occupied here a space next to relics of questionable authenticity and portraits of actors by famous eighteenth- and nineteenth-century painters. An image of the past was successfully assembled though objects which had no archeological relation to the period under reconstruction. For Lowenthal, 'The copy reflects the past no less than the original', thus Poel's model of the Globe, serving as inspiration for Lutyens, not only reflects the past but actively helps to re-create it.[24] 'Almost nothing displayed in museums was made to be seen in them', argues Susan Vogel,[25] but Poel's Globe model is different in this respect since it was created for the purpose of exhibition. Throughout its social life as an object, the Globe model mediated between a desire to know the past and a contemporary wish to reconstrue Elizabethan modes of stage performance.

EMULATING THE PAST: 1964

Unlike other reconstructions in world's fairs and exhibitions, the Globe replica included in Richard Buckle's 1964 Shakespeare Exhibition for the Stratford-upon-Avon celebrations of the quatercentenary of the poet's birth was never meant to serve as a theatre for live performance. In this respect, Buckle's Globe differs from transatlantic reconstructions such as one designed for the 1934 Chicago World's Fair or the Old Globe Theatre in the California Pacific International Exposition at Balboa Park in San Diego.[26] An advertisement for Buckle's Shakespeare exhibition in the *Sunday Times* gave considerable prominence to the Globe replica (Figure 5.7), but the information it contained might have been felt at the time to be slightly misleading: 'The Exhibition includes the great Globe theatre with voices of the most eminent living actors'.[27]

The Shakespeare Exhibition took place at a time when, according to Douglas Lanier, audio Shakespeare was enjoying a burst of interest.[28] In this context, the 1964 Globe treated its visitors to a *son et lumière* installation with the recorded voices of well-known Royal Shakespeare Company actors briefly heard on an

Figure 5.7   Postcard showing timber-framed and gabled houses by Edward Luytens in the Earl's Court exhibition "Shakespeare England." Author's collection.

empty stage: 'About 260 people can fit into the theatre for *son et lumière*. They'll be shunted along after six minutes of *son*, which will include Gielgud, Evans, Richardson and other leading actors who did the job for a case of champagne'.[29] Buckle had entrusted the recreation of the Globe to stage designer Alan Tagg, who had recently done the set for a production of *Peter Grimes* for Sadler's Wells. The description in the *Sunday Times* suggests that archeological accuracy was pursued only up to a point, as it was sacrificed for effect when convenient (see Figure 5.8): 'Tagg used a scale near to the original Globe for the ground space, but distorted the uprights, pulling them away from the audience to give the illusion of height. At one stage the theatre fades out to reveal a cyclorama of moving shapes'.[30] Once again, we see how knowledge of the past suffers alteration to accommodate the present.

With his *son et lumière* installation, Buckle's exhibition turned the Globe into a white cube, a gallery space in which, as Brian O'Doherty has argued, the artwork is displayed in a sacralized space.[31] The 1964 Globe was both a temple in which the words of Shakespeare were heard, if briefly, and a museum of voices, displaying, as in art galleries, the work of "masters" – here, the most highly regarded voices from contemporary British actors: John Gielgud, Tony Evans, and Ralph Richardson. Like O'Doherty's "white cube", the Globe was steeped in its "original" period, but was outside time, eternal.

As tourist attractions capitalising on the Shakespeare trade, both the Shakespeare's England exhibition at Earl's Court in 1912 and Buckle's Shakespeare Exhibition for the 1964 quatercentenary were commercial failures. The Shakespeare Memorial Fund, to which the Shakespeare's England exhibition at Earl's Court was supposed to contribute, had to cover the losses. At a meeting in Mansion House in May 1913, the *New York Times* reported, 'It was announced that from the $40,000

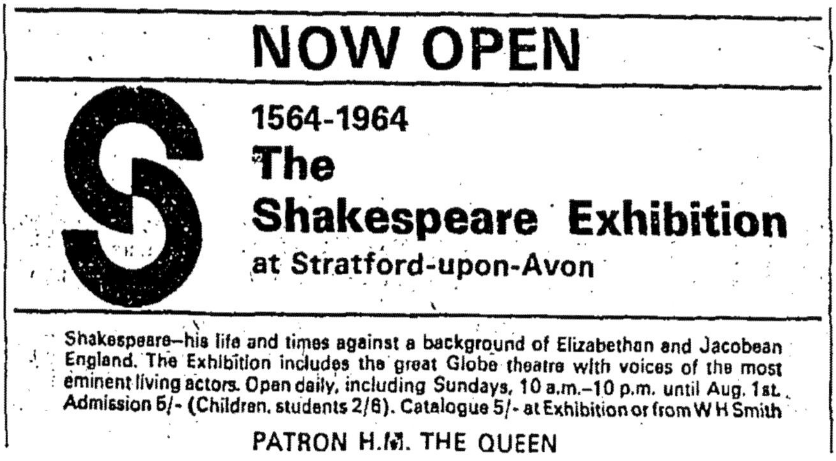

Figure 5.8   Advertisement for the Shakespeare Exhibition. *The Sunday Times*, 26 April 1964, p. 33. By permission of News Syndication.

Figure 5.9   The replica of the Globe interior under construction, showing the sloping uprights. The Shakespeare Exhibition. *The Birmingham Post*, 9 April 1964. Author's collection.

profits from various entertainments in London on behalf of the fund, $16,330 had to be deducted as losses on the Earl's Court Shakespeare's England Exhibition'.[32] Buckle's Shakespeare Exhibition ended up costing £250,000 and never managed to break even. The exhibition was later divided up, half being sent to Edinburgh and the other half to London, and the original artwork commissioned for the exhibition was eventually auctioned by Christie's. Even so, the exhibition sponsors had to meet a substantial part of the costs.[33]

One of the reasons behind its economic failure was that the exhibition was extremely expensive to produce, as much of the exhibition's newly commissioned work was prepared in London and then had to be transported to Stratford. Preceded by his success with his 1954 Edinburgh festival exhibition about Sergei Diaghilev (the founder of the Ballets Russes), Buckle prepared his Shakespeare show in a disused building at Alexandra Park in London which was then transferred to temporary exhibition space in Stratford, a series of white tents by the river Avon, on the bank opposite the Memorial Theatre and Trinity Church. The Globe replica was an expensive undertaking, costing £9,800, the biggest job ever undertaken by Edward Babbage, the theatrical scene-maker.[34] It was not the only building recreated for the exhibition: Nonesuch and Richmond Palaces along with Windsor Gates were also present through 'decorative suggestions of palaces superimposed' by the Greek artist Nicholas Georgiadis.[35] The exhibition was an ambitious project with a double purpose, according to Buckle himself: 'to present the evidence of Shakespeare's life and work and to offer a picture of his period'.[36] Its originality owes much to its then innovative design, as the visitor was invited to follow a predetermined path rather than wander among isolated items in individual cases. A contemporary critic, Erna Auerbach, described a visit to the exhibition as an unusual experience:

> The visitor to the exhibition travels back in time, to the Stratford-on-Avon of 1564. By a system of theatrical effects calculated to appeal to all his senses, he is led to witness (as an imaginary traveller) every phase of Shakespeare's life and career, to Oxford, London, the Court and back to Stratford. It takes some time to grow accustomed to the "Happening" technique, to the darkness, the music, the stage, the startling scenery, the mobiles; but slowly, guided by an instructive catalogue, one becomes absorbed. Incorporated in this general framework, contemporary books are displayed in cases; portraits of Elizabeth I and the great men of the later years of her reign are assembled in a "Long Gallery"; miniatures and jewellery are well exhibited in a small "gold room"; and in the "Jacobean Arcade" we find the images of James I, his family and the courtiers of his reign.[37]

In spite of their ideological differences and their variety of purpose, Shakespearean exhibitions rest on a conception of the past as something that can be reassembled out of objects and, in the case of the Globe playhouse, replicas. Buildings, by virtue of their peculiar nature as material entities meant to be inhabited by humans, enjoy a special status as objects to be lived, places where life unfolds. Replicas of buildings, without being deprived of this status, also become objects to be looked at. This is particularly so in the case of the Globe replicas in exhibitions where they are for the most part devoid of their original function – venues for theatrical performance – and become *objets purs*, objects whose function is to exist to be contemplated, not to be used.[38] Reassembled out of *objets purs*, the past becomes no longer a completely foreign land, thus replicas of the Globe promote familiarity with a place that no longer seems remote, erasing historical difference.

In *Shakespeare in the Present*, Terence Hawkes argued that the one thing replicas of the Globe cannot possibly re-create is the audience, 'the single most crucial element of the Elizabethan playhouse'.[39] Yet this is precisely what the "entertainments" at the Globe in Earl's Court aimed for, even if the result, according to witness reports, was the opposite, extending performance onto the pit and galleries and increasing the audience's awareness of its own contemporaneity.[40] At Buckle's Shakespeare exhibition, visitors were invited to imagine themselves as the Globe's original audience, encountering sound as the primary theatrical experience. It is difficult to imagine today how visitors to the 1964 exhibition reacted, although Buckle records that A. L. Rowse wrote to him and praised the exhibition and the replica Globe: 'it was the most wonderful evocation of the Elizabethan age and Shakespeare's career he could have imagined – Alan Tagg's Globe theatre with Richard Pilbrow's changing light and the voices of our most illustrious actors had moved him deeply'.[41] By not aiming for historical accuracy, the Globe of Buckle's exhibition transcended the desire for a facsimile of the lost original; instead, its "creative reworkings of earlier forms" successfully triggered an awareness of the past.[42] This awareness resulted from a fictionalized social memory whose function is, as Connerton has suggested, to establish continuity with the past. Of course, Buckle's Globe re-created the theatrical experience in Shakespeare's time through sound, but ignored the differences between the voice and delivery styles of twentieth-century actors and their Elizabethan counterparts.

Buckle's exhibition brought together objects from the past (such as Elizabethan and Jacobean portraits), artwork newly commissioned (such as Astrid Zydower's sculptures of larger-than-life Beefeaters, the Queen and courtiers, and "Young Shakespeare") and paintings by famous twentieth-century artists. Buckle reunited objects from the past with objects from the present in an "assembly of things" which, following Bruno Latour, both brings together the disparate and helps to display difference.[43] Past and present, old and new, intermingled in Buckle's installation to convey a sense of how much the past is remodelled by the present.

In this context, a Globe replica finds its natural space. Unlike Anne Hathaway's cottage, a Globe replica has no existing original to replicate, and by being displayed next to the Armada Portrait of Elizabeth I or Nicholas Hilliard's portrait miniatures, the lack of such an original becomes more evident.

CODA: 2012 AND 2016

The experimentation of Buckle's Shakespeare Exhibition contrasts with the archeologically driven nature of "Shakespeare: Staging the World", the British Museum exhibition which was part of the Cultural Olympiad arranged to accompany the 2012 Summer Olympics and Paralympics in London. In 1964 *National Geographic*'s issue for the Shakespeare quatercentenary included a map of Britain, closely linking the poet to the nation, but in 2012 the British Museum's webpage clearly avoided mentioning England – or for that matter, Britain. Instead the museum linked early modern London with the larger world:

> The exhibition provides a unique insight into the emerging role of London as a world city, seen through the innovative perspective of Shakespeare's plays. It also explores the pivotal role of the playhouse as a window to the world outside London, and the playwright's importance in shaping a new sense of national identity.
>
> London as it was around 400 years ago is brought to life through contemporary performance and amazing objects drawn from the Museum's collection and across Europe. Maps, prints, drawings and paintings, arms and armour, coins, medals and other intriguing objects are all examined through the lens of Shakespeare's plays.[44]

In spite of the "pivotal role" granted to playhouses on the webpage description, representations of the Globe or other early modern playhouses were practically absent from the British Museum exhibition. The only exception was Wenceslaus Hollar's panorama of London – which wrongly identifies the second Globe (1614) as the 'Beere bayting house'.[45] A visitor unfamiliar with either exterior or interior of an early modern playhouse was given no help in the task of imagining what the Globe might have looked like. Perhaps it was assumed that as the Globe replica on the South Bank has become such a well-known tourist destination that visitors would know. It is also possible that models or replicas of the Globe (which would have been easy to obtain) were not included since the exhibition mostly comprised items drawn from the British Museum's collection, or from other local museums, that the curators wanted to display for their value as artworks, or their capacity to arouse wonder. Playhouses of Shakespeare's time were simply evoked rather than reconstructed through the display of objects, many of which were archaeological finds from playhouse sites. Shakespeare's theatre was therefore present only through 'objects excavated from the sites of the Globe and Rose theatres, such as a sucket fork for sweetmeats and the skull of a bear', to suggest the proximity of the playhouses to 'bear-baiting arenas as well as brothels and pubs'.[46] In this exhibition, Shakespeare's playhouse was no longer seen as an object in a conversation with other objects from the past; rather, the Globe was an overarching, if spectral, presence. The archaeological objects displayed simply enhanced the sense of lost heritage and reminded visitors that no original early modern playhouse remains. London and its material culture, and not the theatrical experience or Shakespeare's texts, were the exhibition's main aim. Displaying London's genesis as world metropolis, and indirectly pointing at its current leading role in the global market and in globalized culture, was the exhibition's guiding thread, and the connection with Shakespeare or his plays often felt strained.

The archaeological gaze, in fact, was directed not at theatrical performance but at other activities that took place in the playhouses, such as eating, drinking, and bear-baiting. British Museum director Neil MacGregor (in *Shakespeare's Restless World*) and Jonathan Bate and Dora Thornton (in *Shakespeare: Staging the World*) look into the life of different period objects to reconstruct the theatrical experience in Shakespeare's time. When displayed, these objects acquired the nature of miniature sites of memory. An elegant sucket fork, oyster shells, and clay pipes proved that during performances audiences bought and consumed drinks and food and smoked tobacco, but they also suggested that the public playhouses were attended by a mix of social classes (although upper classes consumed different food and drink from that of the groundlings). A brown woollen cap was to remind us that performances were patronized by large numbers of apprentices who were, very often, loud and riotous, but it also signaled how dress codes displaying social class identity were enforced by law and divided individuals as effectively as the locations of the pit and the galleries. The plague proclamations illustrated that the London playhouses were on several occasions officially closed. MacGregor's history of Shakespeare's time in twenty objects and Bate and Thornton's exhibition catalogue suggest, perhaps in spite of themselves, that no matter how accurate a Globe replica may be, the experience of an early modern playhouse cannot be fully reproduced. In the modern theatre, food and drink are not sold during the performance and smoking is banned entirely. Modern audiences are far more homogeneous in social background and theatre seasons are not interrupted by the onset of contagious diseases. The absence of a lost original and the elusiveness of authenticity combine to confer on existing replicas of the Globe the function of sites of cultural memory. The role of *lieu de mémoire*, in fact, would have been the prerogative of the seventeenth-century Globe had it survived, or if a set of architectural remains could make a cultural pilgrimage possible. Paradoxically, the lack of the original Globe confers authenticity onto the simulacrum, awarding the Globe replica on South Bank the semblance of historical authority.

Visitors to the British Museum exhibition were likely to visit or to be previously acquainted with the replica on the South Bank, and so the absence of representations or models of the Globe playhouse probably went unnoticed. The existence of a replica of the first Globe on a site as close as possible to the land on which its original stood makes further replicas unnecessary, at least in London. The spectrality of the Globe in Danny Boyle's staging of national identity in his spectacle (entitled "Isles of Wonder") staged as the opening ceremonies to the 2012 Olympic Games is perhaps significant. The version of British history presented to the world on live television offered a seamless move from an idyllic and rural British landscape, symbolically re-created through sheep and the village common replete with Morris dancers, to the mills and chimneys of the industrial era, obliterating the development of urban Britain and bourgeois culture that took place during the early modern period. His was an abridged version of the historical development of the British Isles which consciously foregrounded the values of community and togetherness, on the one hand, and technological progress on the other. In this Britain, there was no room for Tudor England and Shakespeare's playhouse. The spectacle made use of literary celebrities such as Alice or Harry Potter, but in spite of the television popularity of *The Tudors* (Michael Hirst, *Showtime* TV series, 2007–2010), Hilary Mantel's award-winning and popular novels set in the period, and the status of William Shakespeare as national poet, there was no room in Boyle's history for the political and religious anxieties of the early modern subject, no allusion to the rise of London as world metropolis, no hint at colonialist ambitions and European wars. Shakespearean drama was present, though, in a de-contextualized form and through quotation and appropriation rather than performance, as Kenneth Branagh impersonated the Victorian engineer Isambard Kingdom Brunel reading one of Caliban's speeches from *The Tempest*. There was no need perhaps for a replica Globe theatre as Boyle's Britain was itself presented as a stage, a site in which a narrative of cohesive national identity was performed in a global exhibition for a world audience. By contrast, a replica of the Globe, absent from the 2012 Olympics, was intended to form part of the celebrations for the 2016 Olympics in Brazil.

Whether as duplication, emulation or ghostly presences, replicas of the Globe play a role in how nations understand British culture. For Connerton, 'societies are self-interpreting communities' and they are deft at presenting images of themselves as existing in a continuum, without fractures.[47] Most usually, Globe replicas help to construe an image of Britain, for both home and global consumption, as a community without ruptures from past to present. These replicas provide a space and a phenomenological experience that seek organically to link Elizabethan England with twenty-first-century Britain and, in this act, erase difference. The different ways in which the Globe has been reconstructed or exhibited also testify to the changing nature of modes of commemoration. These replicas show how remembering Shakespeare's theatre and reinventing the past are culturally and historically inflected, not only by technological transformations but also by political motivations in the present.

NOTES

1 Research for this essay has been made possible thanks to Research Project "Cultures of Commemoration II: Remembering Shakespeare" (FFI2011–24347). I would like to thank the Plan Nacional of I+D+i 2008–2011 (MICINN, MINECO) for providing funding to conduct research in libraries and archives. I also want to record my gratitude to Ton Hoenselaars for researching Frank Chouteau Brown with me in Boston and to the editor of this volume, Susan Bennett, whose suggestions for revision have been essential for the polishing of this piece.
2 A fuller overview of Globe replicas can be found in Marion O'Connor, "Reconstructive Shakespeare: Reproducing Elizabethan and Jacobean Stages," in *The Cambridge Companion to Shakespeare on Stage*, eds. Stanley Wells and Sarah Stanton (Cambridge: Cambridge University Press, 2001), 76–97. For a brief but inspired account of Globe replicas, see Ton Hoenselaars, "Shakespeare and the World," in *The Oxford Handbook of Shakespeare*, ed. Arthur F. Kinney (Oxford: Oxford University Press, 2012), 725–51.
3 David Lowenthal, *The Past Is a Foreign Country* (Cambridge: Cambridge University Press, 1985).
4 Eric Hobsbawm and Terence Ranger, eds., *The Invention of Tradition* (Cambridge: Cambridge University Press, 1983).
5 Paul Connerton, *How Societies Remember* (Cambridge: Cambridge University Press, 1989), 14.
6 Pierre Nora, "Between Memory and History: Les Lieux de Mémoire," *Representations*, 26 (1989): 7–24.
7 Nora, "Between Memory and History," 7.
8 Nora, "Between Memory and History," 19.
9 Pierre Nora, *Realms of Memory*, Vol. III (New York: Columbia University Press, 1992), x.
10 Jean Baudrillard, *Le système des objets* (Paris: Gallimard, 1968).
11 Although the official purpose of the exhibition was to raise funds for the Shakespeare Memorial National Theatre project, Marion O'Connor has suggested, on the evidence of a letter from Lutyens to his wife, that Mrs. Cornwallis-West also had personal profit in mind. See "Theatre of the Empire: 'Shakespeare's England' at Earl's Court, 1912," in *Shakespeare Reproduced: The Text in History and Ideology*, eds. Jean E. Howard and Marion F. O'Connor (London: Routledge, 1987), 78.
12 Frank Chouteau Brown designed several stage sets for productions of Shakespeare's plays.
13 Visscher's view of London (1616) is believed to reproduce the first Globe – the one that burnt during a performance of *Henry VIII* in 1613 – which was polygonal in shape.

Hollar's panorama, instead, reproduces the second Globe, bigger and circular in structure, like the bear-baiting house standing next to it. The labels for these two buildings in Hollar's engraving have been confusingly swapped.

14 "The Shakespeare Exhibition," *The Academy*, 25 May 1912.
15 O'Connor, "Theatre of the Empire," 86 and ff.
16 O'Connor, "Theatre of the Empire," 87.
17 O'Connor, "Theatre of the Empire," 82–6.
18 Lowenthal, *The Past Is a Foreign Country*, 348. The Globe replica built in the late 1980s on the South Bank, for instance, had to dispense with what we know about the past in order to accommodate staircases and fire exits to comply with today's safety regulations.
19 Lowenthal, *The Past Is a Foreign Country*, 348.
20 For accounts of how the two houses that John Shakespeare bought in 1556 and 1557 became "the birthplace," see Richard Schoch, "The Birth of Shakespeare's Birthplace," *Theatre Survey*, 53 (2012): 181–201, and Julia Thomas, *Shakespeare's Shrine: The Bard's Birthplace and the Invention of Stratford-upon-Avon* (Philadelphia: University of Pennsylvania Press, 2012).
21 Thomas, *Shakespeare's Shrine*, 43.
22 O'Connor, "Reconstructive Shakespeare," 76–97; 89.
23 *The Sunday Times*, 2 October 1910, 4.
24 Lowenthal, *The Past Is a Foreign Country*, 295.
25 Susan Vogel, "Always True to the Object, in Our Fashion," in *Exhibiting Cultures: The Poetics and Politics of Museum Display*, eds. Ivan Karp and Steven D. Lavine (Washington and London: Smithsonian Institute Press, 1991), 191–204; 191.
26 O'Connor, "Reconstructive Shakespeare," 89.
27 *The Sunday Times*, 26 April 1964, 33.
28 Douglas M. Lanier, "Shakespeare on the Record," in *The Blackwell Companion to Shakespeare and Performance*, eds. Barbara Hodgdon and William Worthen (New York: Blackwell Press, 2006), 415–36.
29 Kathleen Halton, "The Dicky Buckle Show," *The Sunday Times*, 19 April 1964, 42–4.
30 Halton, "Show," 43.
31 Brian O'Doherty, *Inside the White Cube: The Ideology of the Gallery Space* (Berkeley and Los Angeles: University of California Press, 1976, 1986).
32 *The New York Times*, 18 May 1913.
33 Anthony Cowdy, "Drama of Errors at Stratford," *Sunday Times*, 8 November 1964, 3.
34 Halton, "Show," 42.
35 Halton, "Show," 42.
36 Erna Auerbach, "Some Shakespeare Exhibitions," *Burlington Magazine*, 106 (1964): 333–4.
37 Auerbach, "Some Shakespeare Exhibitions," 333.
38 Baudrillard, *Le système des objets*.
39 Terence Hawkes, *Shakespeare in the Present* (London: Routledge, 2002), 140.
40 O'Connor, "Theater of the Empire," 88.
41 Buckle, "Trials," 14.
42 Lowenthal, *The Past Is a Foreign Country*, 309.
43 Bruno Latour, "From Realpolitik to Dingpolitik, or How to Make Things Public," in *Making Things Public: Atmospheres of Democracy*, eds. Bruno Latour and Peter Weibel. Catalogue of an exhibition at the ZKM, Center for Arts and Media Karlsruhe (Cambridge, MA, and London: The MIT Press, 2005), 34.

44 The webpage of the British Museum exhibition, "Shakespeare: Staging the World," http://www.britishmuseum.org/whats_on/exhibitions/shakespeare_staging_the_world/introduction.aspx (accessed 3 June 2015).
45 Bate, Jonathan and Dora Thornton, *Shakespeare: Staging the World* (Oxford: Oxford University Press, 2012), 21.
46 British Museum Press Release, http://www.britishmuseum.org/about_us/news_and_press/press_releases/2012/shakespeare_staging_the_world.aspx (accessed 3 June 2015).
47 Connerton, *How Societies Remember*, 12.

6 Spatial negotiations in the Brazilian street production *Sua Incelença, Ricardo III* by Clowns de Shakespeare

Anna Stegh Camati and Liana de Camargo Leão

The street spectacle *Sua Incelença, Ricardo III [His Excellency, Richard III]* (2011), by Clowns de Shakespeare, is a Brazilian intercultural production of *Richard III* framed in a specific context: the action of Shakespeare's play has been reset and re-contextualized to the region of the *cangaço* in northeast Brazil at the turn of the twentieth century and thus generates new expressive potentials and unusual communicative energies. In fact, when plays travel in this way across time and place, they aggregate hybrid specificities between the local and the global. In Brazil, Shakespeare's texts have, since the nineteenth century, been appropriated to serve multiple purposes in different times and socio-cultural contexts, in a movement of persistent interplay of past and present, demanding continual adjustment to new circumstances, ideologies and cultural imaginaries. Our discussion of *Sua Incelença, Ricardo III* illustrates the experimental tendencies typical to contemporary performance practices and considers the work of Clowns de Shakespeare as important to the historical trajectory of Shakespearean production in Brazil.

CONCISE HISTORY OF SHAKESPEAREAN PRODUCTIONS IN BRAZIL

To fully acknowledge the work of Clowns de Shakespeare as a specifically Brazilian site for Shakespearean production, we start with an historical overview that charts the shifts in the country's engagements with England's best-known playwright: back in the nineteenth century, the country's Shakespearean productions relied mainly on neo-classical adaptations by French dramatist Jean-François Ducis (1733–1816), who had adjusted Shakespeare's dramaturgy to eighteenth-century taste. This French mediation of Shakespeare predominated for a long time in Brazil, first initiated by European companies during the early nineteenth century, mainly after the arrival of Dom João VI and the Portuguese royal family in Rio de Janeiro in 1808. The transition from colony to empire in 1822 precipitated the development of a Brazilian national theatre and the establishment of local dramatic activities. The actor-manager João Caetano (1808–1863), considered the father of Brazilian theatre, is credited to be the first Brazilian star to incarnate Shakespearean characters. His Shakespeare productions were rendered by Brazilian actors in Brazilian Portuguese, differing from the performance traditions of Portuguese and Spanish companies touring in South America in the early nineteenth century, who tended to use Lisbon or Castilian accents when staging Shakespeare.[1]

According to data compiled by Celuta Moreira Gomes, published in 1959,[2] João Caetano mounted *Hamlet* in Rio de Janeiro in 1835, using a Brazilian Portuguese version by J. A. de Oliveira e Silva, probably translated directly from an English conflated edition of Shakespeare's text. Considering that this production was not well received by the public, in 1849 he performed Ducis' *Hamlet* translated by Oliveira e Silva. He had presented *Othello* in 1837, using a French version by Alfred de Vigny translated by J. C. Craveiro, before enacting, in 1838, Ducis' *Othello* translated by Gonçalves de Magalhães. The latter was received with great enthusiasm by audiences and critics, and his characterization of the Moor turned out to be his greatest achievement. He performed the role twenty-six times from 1837 to 1860. He played Shylock in an adaptation of *The Merchant of Venice* in 1838, the title role in a translated version of Ducis' *Macbeth* in 1843 and, from 1843 to 1844, he revisited *Hamlet* six more times.

In the latter half of the nineteenth century, the great Italian actors Tommaso Salvini (1829–1915) and Ernesto Rossi (1827–1896)[3] visited Rio de Janeiro and, on a lesser scale, São Paulo and Porto Alegre, during their transatlantic tours to North and South America. They excelled in Shakespearean roles, which constituted a major part of their repertoire, often performing "Shakespeare in heavily cut versions that stressed the importance of their own role at the expense of other parts in the play. Even outside Italy, the stars often acted in Italian, the rest of the cast being locals who used the audience's language."[4] The renowned Shakespearean scholar and theatre critic Barbara Heliodora (1923–2015)[5] reports that, in 1871, the company of Ernesto Rossi presented a large tragic repertoire at the Theatro Lyrico Fluminense, which included *Othello, Romeo and Juliet, Hamlet* and *Macbeth*, translated into Italian directly from English versions; in the same year, Salvini, an actor admired by Constantin Stanislavski, played the title role in *Othello* and *Hamlet*; and in 1882, Giacinta Pezzana Gualtieri (1841–1919) anticipated the acclaimed cross-dressed rendering of Prince Hamlet by Sarah Bernhardt (1844–1923), who also performed in Brazil in 1905. Heliodora mentions other productions staged by touring companies, such as Constant Conquelin Ainé's *The Taming of the Shrew* (1907), rendered in French, and Gabriel Trabulsi's *Hamlet* (1918) in Arabic. Shakespearean productions in the nineteenth century did not go unnoticed by Brazilian intellectuals and theatre critics, such as Gonçalves Dias, Álvares de Azevedo, Machado de Assis, Joaquim Nabuco and Martins Pena, among others. The well-known novelist Machado de Assis (1839–1908), besides making reference to Shakespeare's plays in most of his literary production, created a Brazilian Otelo in his novel *Dom Casmurro*, first published in 1899.

The flux of Shakespearean productions in Brazil, enacted in foreign languages, was interrupted by World War I, resumed in the mid-twenties, and intensified after the end of World War II. During the interwar period, Ermete Zacconi (1857–1948) presented *King Lear* and *Othello* in 1924, and *King Lear* in 1931; Jacob Ben-Ami (1890–1977) played *Hamlet* in 1947; and Madeleine Renaud (1900–1994) and Jean-Louis Barrault (1919–1994) enacted *Hamlet* in 1950.[6] Heliodora[7] mentions *Julius Caesar* staged by the Piccolo Teatro de Milano in 1954, and *Measure for Measure* by the Teatro Stabile di Genoa in 1958. After João Caetano's death in 1863, Shakespeare productions, performed with local casts, reappeared on Brazilian stages only in the 1930s. In 1938 the diplomat Paschoal Carlos Magno (1906–1980) founded the Teatro do Estudante do Brasil (TEB). The troupe's first Shakespearean production was *Romeu e Julieta*, directed by Itália Fausta, who resumed the practice, introduced by João Caetano, of using Brazilian Portuguese translations. The TEB also presented *Macbeth* and *A Midsummer Night's Dream*, but their most illustrious staging was the 1948 *Hamlet*, in Rio de Janeiro, directed by Wolfgang Hoffman Harnish, a German director "who lent to the production a strong element of German Romanticism."[8] In one of her reviews of the spectacle, Heliodora wrote that the 1948 *Hamlet* "took over the city, it became the main topic of conversation, it even influenced fashion."[9] The individual performance as Hamlet of Sérgio Cardoso, then only 22 years old, was responsible for the tremendous success. He founded his own company in 1956, when he directed *Hamlet* and played the title role again. After the revival of the interest in Shakespeare, promoted by Paschoal Carlos Magno and the TEB, a great number of professional Brazilian theatrical companies started mounting the plays, not only in Rio and São Paulo, but in almost all the regions of the vast Brazilian territory.

The celebrations in 1964 for the 400th anniversary of Shakespeare's birth coincided with the military coup in Brazil. The military authorities thoroughly supported the bard's festivities, because they considered Shakespeare's dramaturgy safe ground, not directly related to politics. Hence, a great number of events, press publications and local productions of Shakespeare's plays were made financially viable, and for the first time an English professional company was invited to perform in Brazil, headed by Barbara Jefford (1930–) and Ralph Richardson (1902–1983), who brought *The Merchant of Venice* and *A Midsummer Night's Dream* to the Teatro Municipal in São Paulo.[10] Many memorable productions in English followed, among them *Antony and Cleopatra*, in the 1990s, with a multiracial cast headed by Vanessa Redgrave; several productions by Cheek by Jowl such as *A Midsummer Night's Dream* (1986), *As You Like It* (1991) and *Twelfth Night* (2006); the *Ur-Hamlet* by the Odin Theatre in 2006; Peter Brook's *Hamlet* (2002); *The Rape of Lucrece* (2014) by Royal Shakespeare Company; and the Globe to Globe World Tour of *Hamlet* (2015).

During the dictatorship period (1964–1985), permanent vigilance and severe censorship haunted the Brazilian theatre: play-texts were cut, prohibited and cancelled, actors were imprisoned and police officers had reserved seats in theatres for controlling performances. By the end of the 1960s and the beginning of the 1970s, provocative leftist-oriented plays by Bertolt Brecht and Augusto Boal were staged on a larger scale than Shakespeare's to express indignation against the repressive power of the state. However, during the period of re-democratization and after, politicized renderings of Shakespeare's plays predominated to challenge the status quo. The Shakespearean productions that failed to meet their proposed critical intent during military dictatorship were *Júlio César* (1966), directed by Antunes Filho, one of the most respected Brazilian theatre practitioners; Fauzi Arap's *Macbeth* (1970), starring Paulo Autran, Brazil's most distinguished actor; and *Coriolano* (1974), directed by Celso Nunes, with Paulo Autran as producer and protagonist. Nunes' production was supposed to suggest a parallel between the popular discontent and class struggle in early Republican Rome and the Brazilian sociopolitical realities of the 1970s. However, as Roberto Rocha[11] explains, instead of showing the protagonist as a villain, Paulo Autran's charismatic figure and his heroic presentation of the character ended up by glorifying Coriolanus.

In face of these failures, Augusto Boal's "cannibalized version" of Shakespeare's *The Tempest* – titled *A tempestade* (1979), which ran in Rio de Janeiro from December 1981 to February 1982 – constituted the first Shakespearean production that effectively denounced the harsh measures of the military rule. In spite of Boal's Manichaean approach, the wider implications of his project, which included a reflection on colonialism and neocolonialism and their different mechanisms of oppression, were extensively recognized; he exposed the predicament of Latin American nations forced "to fight against the old and new colonizers, Europeans and North Americans."[12] Near the end of the dictatorship regime, another successful production emerged: in his 1984 *Romeu e Julieta*, Antunes Filho borrowed Roland

Barthes' anti-dogmatic love discourse to undermine the authoritarian postures of the military government.[13]

Shakespeare's popularity in Brazil increased in the 1980s, when two politicized TV Globo miniseries brought him close to the masses. *Romeu e Julieta* (1980) adapted by Walter George Durst, and *Otelo de Oliveira* (1983) by Aguinaldo Silva – both directed by Paulo Afonso Grisolli – combined Shakespearean themes with Brazilian social realities and problems, such as poverty, violence and issues of class, race and gender. In the last three decades, Brazil has witnessed a considerable expansion of Shakespearean performances in traditional and alternative theatre spaces. Besides politically engaged productions, a wide range of other genres have emerged – among them musicals, intercultural readings and street theatre.

After the restoration of the civilian government, Shakespeare's tragedies, mainly *Hamlet* and *Macbeth*, were successfully appropriated to denounce political corruption, urban violence and abuse of power. In Curitiba, Marcelo Marchioro's *Hamlet* coincidentally premièred on 20 August 1992, one month before Fernando Collor de Mello, the first president elected directly by the people after dictatorship, was forced to resign during the impeachment proceedings against him. Ulysses Cruz' production of *Macbeth* and Antunes Filho's *Trono de sangue [Throne of Blood]* also emerged out of the ferment of popular riots in the streets against President Collor's administration in 1992.

One of the most important Shakespearean productions of the post-dictatorship period, mixed with Brazilian matter, was *Ham-let* (1993), directed by José Celso Martinez Correa for the Teatro Oficina. He relied on Oswald de Andrade's concept of creative cannibalism to liberate Brazilian theatre from colonial ideology and aesthetic dependency. In 2004 Enrique Diaz's production for the Cia. dos Atores *[Company of Actors]*, titled *Ensaio. Hamlet [Rehearsal. Hamlet]*, explored current problems surfacing after the election of Luiz Inácio Lula da Silva, the first candidate the Workers' Party (PT) elected for president in Brazil. And in 2006 two Shakespearean productions of *Richard III* protested against the turmoil and scandals that were current near the end of the first term (2003–2006) of President Lula's administration: *Ricardo III*, adapted and directed by Jô Soares, and *Ricardo III*, adapted by Celso Frateschi and directed by Roberto Lage.

Musical adaptations of Shakespeare's plays, combining theatre, music and dance, also extended Shakespeare's popularity in Brazil. The production of *Sonho de uma noite de verão [A Midsummer Night's Dream]*, in 1991, staged, in Portuguese, by Teatro do Ornitorrinco [Duckbilled Platypus Theatre] in Central Park, under Cacá Rosset's direction and José de Anchieta's design, was originally commissioned by the New York Shakespeare Festival and later also presented in Brazil and Mexico. Another successful Brazilian musical version of *A Midsummer Night's Dream* is Patricia Fagundes' *Sonho de uma noite de verão* (2006), "in which new meanings are generated though the interplay of different medial codes and conventions."[14] The director fused theatre, dance, music and cinematic devices adapted for the theatre in a fresh and new way, relocating the action of the spectacle from the sixteenth-century forest of Arden to a twentieth-century cabaret or nightclub. And in *Otelo da Mangueira* (2006), rescripted by Gustavo Gasparani and directed by Daniel Herz, the Shakespearean universe is transposed to the lively world of the Mangueira Samba School in Rio de Janeiro in 1940. Although a series of radical alterations were made, the plot and themes of the show remain close to Shakespeare's *Othello*. Nós do Morro [We from the Hillside], a theatre group from the Vidigal *favela* [shantytown] in Rio de Janeiro, directed by Guti Fraga, and Caixa-Preta [Black-Box], a group of African-Brazilian actors, based in Porto Alegre, Rio Grande do Sul, directed by Jessé Oliveira, are two of the many Brazilian theatre ensembles that tend to approach Shakespeare from an intercultural perspective, subordinating the Shakespearean universe to local issues and values. In Caixa Preta's *Hamlet sincrético* [*Syncretic Hamlet*, 2005], for example, Shakespeare's *Hamlet* is appropriated and transposed to the Afro-Brazilian context and the dialogues are translated into Afro-Brazilian parlance.

Since the 1990s theatre groups from different Brazilian regions have tended to perform Shakespeare's plays in the streets, squares, parks, marketplaces and other venues of great public circulation and easy access, providing a socially liberating experience to people of all ranks of life who democratically come together as a community. In Brazilian street theatre, Shakespeare has assumed a similar function to Free Shakespeare in the Park, the legendary summer open-air season at the Delacorte Theatre in New York's Central Park, founded originally by Joseph Papp in 1962 and "famous for its long-term ambition to desacralize Shakespeare and make the plays accessible to non-elite audiences."[15] A vital role was played by Grupo Galpão, a southeastern street company founded in 1982, whose prolific participation in national and international festival circuits proved decisive for the shaping of their performance aesthetics and identity. The troupe's groundbreaking *Romeu e Julieta*, directed by Gabriel Villela, premièred in 1992, in front of the baroque church São Francisco de Assis, in the historical city of Ouro Preto, Minas Gerais, receiving immediate popular and critical acclaim. The most rigorous Brazilian critic, Barbara Heliodora, in her review of the spectacle, titled "Perfection in Infidelity," wrote that she believed Shakespeare "would perfectly understand the aim of this company, and feel delighted to be so much loved and treated with such intimacy."[16]

It is worth mentioning that while this intercultural spectacle was initially designed for the streets and amalgamated the Shakespearean narrative with popular culture traditions of Minas Gerais, much later it was adapted for indoor venues and was twice successfully presented at London's Globe Theatre in 2000 and 2012, garnering an international reputation for the company. It was also successfully presented, either indoors or outdoors, in more than 60 Brazilian cities and in a great number of foreign countries, such as Spain, England, Portugal, Holland, Germany, Uruguay, USA, Venezuela, Colombia and Costa Rica, among others. In the context of the 2000 Globe-to-Globe season, Mark Rylance, then artistic director of Shakespeare's Globe, remarked that the Brazilian company's carnivalized blending of tragedy and comedy was closer to Shakespeare than were many native Shakespeare productions in Britain.[17] And although Michael Billington, in his review of the spectacle, claimed that the Brazilian company never gets to grips with the tragic elements of the play, he surprisingly situated the production in the context of contemporary international theatre, when he stated that "Grupo Galpão's participation in the globalization of theatre practice today dramatizes the parochial force of intercultural performance at the Globe."[18]

Although there are many other Brazilian street theatre groups experimenting with Shakespeare's plays – among them the Ueba Troupe, settled in Caxias do Sul (Rio Grande do Sul), whose presentation of *A megera domada* (2009), a free adaptation of Shakespeare's *The Taming of the Shrew* (1592) – can be related to rough theatre as defined by Peter Brook, we look specifically at the *potiguar*[19] company Clowns de Shakespeare, based in Natal (Rio Grande do Norte), one of the most prolific street theatre ensembles in Brazil. The choice of the troupe's name, Shakespeare's Clowns, was inspired by the poem "Poética" [Poetics] by Manuel Bandeira, in which the lyric "I" manifests the desire for total freedom of expression, a privilege allowed to clowns in Shakespeare's plays.

Shakespearean comedies have been part of the company's repertoire since its foundation in the early 1990s, including *Sonho de uma noite de verão* [*A Midsummer Night's Dream*, 1993]; *Noite de Reis* [*Twelfth Night*, 1994]; *A megera do nada* [*The Taming of the Shrew*, retitled *The Shrew of Nothingness*, 1996]; and *Muito barulho por quase nada* [*Much Ado about Nothing*, retitled *Much Ado about Almost Nothing*, 2003]. In 2010 the troupe embraced a risky enterprise when it decided to adapt *Richard III* for outdoor performances, a play reputed to be unpalatable to popular Brazilian audiences. The production, retitled *Sua Incelença, Ricardo III* [*His Excellency, Richard III*],[20] and directed by Gabriel Villela, however, has been immensely successful, providing national and international recognition to the company.

The spectacle premièred in Rio Grande do Norte in 2010, where it was presented in several cities, among them Natal, Santa Cruz, Assu and Currais Novos. The national première took place in front of the Igreja da Ordem (Church of the Order), located in the historic center in Curitiba, marking the official start of the twentieth edition of the Theatre Festival in 2011. From there, the company toured the production in five Brazilian regions and participated in the main festivals in Brazil in 2012, such as the International Festival in Londrina (FILO), the International Festival in São José do Rio Preto (FIT), the International Festival of University Theatre in Blumenau (FITUB), Porto Alegre em Cena, Cena Contemporânea in Brasília, Tempo Festival in Rio de Janeiro (where they performed at the *favela* Complexo do Alemão), among others. The group also participated in the Festival Internacional de Santiago a Mil, in Chile in 2012, in the Montevideo Latin America Capital of Culture 2013, at Blanes Museum Gardens, in Uruguay, and in the Festival Internacional de Expressão Ibérica (FITEI), in Porto/Portugal in 2013. Although the production was acclaimed and favorably reviewed when touring abroad, Livia Segurado's review of the performance in Porto provided evidence that foreign audiences tend to lose the impact of regional concerns. She asserts that even though the "Northeastern Brazilian production seduces the audience to a great extent, some of the strongest regional references pass unacknowledged by the Lusitanian public."[21]

A hybrid performance aesthetics – influenced by Oswald de Andrade's "Cannibalist Manifesto" (1928)[22] and by Silviano Santiago's notion of hybridity or "space in-between" (1970)[23] – marks the Clowns' street performances. Andrade is a Brazilian modernist writer who anticipated theoretical perspectives on adaptation and appropriation later embraced by poststructuralist and postcolonial critics when, in his 1928 manifesto, he conferred legitimacy to "creative cannibalism" (a term he coined), grounded upon the productive borrowing of foreign cultural capital while affirming indigenous literary or cultural sources. Santiago is one of the first scholars to deconstruct binary oppositions, such as "center" and "periphery" and "original" and "copy." Fernando Yamamoto, the leader of Clowns de Shakespeare, working on a collective basis with his company, used Anna Amélia Carneiro de Mendonça's Brazilian Portuguese verse translation of *Richard III* to construct the performance script. Although whole scenes were cut, many lines syncopated and some speeches translated into indigenous idioms, a large part of the translated Shakespearean text was preserved. Yamamoto reported that one of the most serious challenges was reducing the number of speaking characters (fifty-two in Shakespeare's text), so that only eight actors[24] would be able to perform and/or double the main roles. He added that another difficulty consisted in devising an appropriate acting space, which would allow the use of the disparate formal and stylistic elements that integrate the group's hybrid performance practice.

As this panorama on Shakespeare in Brazil illustrates, from the 1980s onwards, Brazilian theatre practitioners have appropriated or adapted Shakespeare's plays in a multiplicity of styles and forms, thus turning away from "the cultural authority of the official English Shakespeare"[25] and establishing a tradition of their own. Hereinafter, we aim to explore the notion of space and site-specificity in *Sua Incelença, Ricardo III*.

SITE-SPECIFICITY AND SPATIAL ORGANIZATION IN *SUA INCELENÇA, RICARDO III*

The performance space envisaged by the Clowns for *Sua Incelença*, a circus ring built in public venues wherever the production is presented, with three gypsy wagons also used as acting spaces, tiered seats in front of the ring and open space for groundlings (Figure 6.1), is not site-specific in the strict sense, since the semantic referents of the different locations where the ring is constructed are not incorporated into the fictional universe of the performance text. However, the spatial configuration of the circus arena allowed the company to take a series of liberties with Shakespeare's play and make use of folk songs, dance rhythms, clowning, masking, physical acting techniques inherited from *commedia dell'arte*, mime and puppetry.

On the other hand, the dramatic space of *Sua Incelença* is site-specific, because the ambience of the production was conceived "about and for a particular community, in a particular place."[26] The setting of the dramatic narrative of Shakespeare's history play was translated into the northeastern universe of the *cangaço* (social banditry), where a backward, almost feudal political organization continued to flourish until the 1940s. The region of the *cangaço*, which included

Figure 6.1   The circus ring used as performance space. *Sua Incelença, Ricardo III* (2011), by Shakespeare's Clowns.

parts of seven northeastern states, among them Alagoas, Bahia, Pernambuco, Rio Grande do Norte, Sergipe, Ceará and Piauí, has ironically been denominated *sertão medieval* (medieval backlands)[27] by historians and anthropologists, because of the untimely maintenance of feudal privileges by the rich landowners called *coronéis* or colonels.

In these remote feuds, violent conflicts and confrontations among the *coronéis*, *cangaceiros* (social bandits) and *volantes* (police forces) were part of the daily routine. The *coronéis* oppressed and explored the poor peasants, imposing slavery-like labor conditions on them, and the *cangaceiros* claimed to fight against the *status quo*. The rich landowners were empowered by the Brazilian central administration, because they sponsored high-ranking politicians in election campaigns in return of political favors, a vicious practice which continues to prevail in contemporary Brazil and elsewhere in Latin America. Revisionist historians, among them Eric Hobsbawm (2000) and Luiz Bernardo Pericás (2010), claim that the phenomenon of the *cangaço* is complex and presents multiple contradictions. They argue that although the *cangaceiros* proposed to fight against the corrupt political establishment, they frequently changed sides and allegiances, supporting the landed oligarchy in return for material profit. The troupe explores the contradictions of the *cangaço* – specifically the fact that some landowners used to hire the services of *cangaceiros* to get rid of their enemies. Along these lines, Shakespeare's Richard is translated into a despotic, corrupt *coronel*, hiring a ruthless *cangaceiro* to eliminate all those who are in his way. This ingenuous cultural translation provided a link between issues foregrounded in the appropriated classic text and the local circumstances,[28] constituting the target of the company's critical intent.

The director Gabriel Villela reported that when *Sua Incelença* was presented in the northeastern village of Acari in Rio Grande do Norte, in the *sertão* (remote backlands) of Seridó, which served as site and source of inspiration for the production, the local audience felt as if they were watching episodes of their own lives, since violent acts, such as hiring professional killers to assassinate whole inimical families, continue to be commonplace in the backlands in our time. When a vendor of vegetables, after watching the performance, remarked: "Here we are aware of what it means to be embraced today as a friend, and be killed tomorrow. What happens in the play is very close to our own reality,"[29] the group realized that they had achieved their critical purpose.

The acting space established the right mood and tone for the production, since the spatial configuration, shaped like a circus ring, was entirely appropriate for the "circus of horrors" engendered by the ringmaster Ricardo. The protagonist can be seen as a perverse ringleader, because instead of providing joy and excitement as does a master of ceremonies in the ring, he causes revolt and disgust by masterminding lives and ordering a succession of monstrous acts. He enters the ring grunting, making obscene gestures and wearing a wild boar mask, a reference and homage to Richard Loncraine's film *Richard III* (1995). The wild boar, an emblem shown on the coat of arms of the historical Richard III, relates to his repulsive and violent nature, symbolizing the casting off of civilized identity and return to barbarism.[30] Furthermore, Ricardo's quick removal of the mask foreshadowed his penchant for masquerade and dissimulation.

To enhance the flow of energy from spectators to performers and back, the spectacle starts with a circus parade. The actors, wearing lavish costumes in rich colors and textures, some of them using facial paint and clownish red noses, enter the circus arena dancing, singing and playing musical instruments. After this festive entrance, one of the actors, who doubles as chorus,[31] delivered an interpolated prologue that summarizes the main plot of the rivalries between the houses of York and Lancaster, standing for the enmities involving rival families in the Northeast (in the past and now), and invites the audience to liberate the powers of their imagination, making a direct, brief reference to the prologue of *Henry V*.

The spatial code of the circus propitiated the combination of the lyricism of Shakespeare's pointed dialogue (albeit in translation) with music and dance. As mentioned before, music is announced in the very title of the spectacle. The traditional northeastern funeral songs, called *incelenças*, constitute the *leitmotif* of the production. They set the dramatic mood and tone of several scenes and dramatize acts of violence. Musical interpolations, which had already proved highly successful in the Clowns' previous aesthetic experiments with Shakespearean comedy, besides enhancing the festive atmosphere and the feeling of communal pleasure, assume important expressive and narrative functions in *Sua Incelença*. As most spectators watching a play in public venues are easily distracted and do not concentrate on dramatic dialogue for a long time, extensive sections from the Shakespeare source play were cut or translated into popular songs, among them Luiz Gonzaga's "Assum Preto" (blue-back grassquit), "Sabiá" (red-bellied thrush) and "Acauã" (bird of ill omen). The marriage of Brazilian rhythms with contemporary English pop rock music, by Queen and Supertramp, not only reinforced the dialogue between source and target culture but also served to provide a link between the scenes, since in the open-air arena it is impossible to mark the entrances and the exits of the actors by blackouts or sophisticated lighting.

In this context of short scenes linked by musical numbers, Ricardo, the ringmaster of the show, expresses himself, not only in Shakespearean verse translated into Brazilian Portuguese, but also in rhythms and rhymes of *cordel* literature (chapbooks) sold at fairs. These booklets (containing popular narratives, poems and songs) are also known as "string literature," because they were displayed on strings by street vendors to call the attention of potential clients. While in Shakespeare's play the character of Richard succeeds in manipulating everybody through puns and linguistic intricacies, in the tropics he seduces through music. Ricardo is, in fact, a hybrid character, neither solely Shakespearean nor Brazilian.

A Brazilian *ciranda* by Alceu Valença, titled "A rosa vermelha" (The Red Rose), marks the entrance of Lady Anna, played by a cross-dressed actor, into the circus ring. Her solitary chant and dance present an ironic contrast to the vibrancy of the *ciranda*, which is a communal round or circle dance. The lyrics of the song, referring to red and white roses as symbols of eternal love, are supposed to evoke a romantic atmosphere, but in the context of the performance, they remind the audience of the feuds of inimical families living in the northeastern backlands who, like the houses of York and Lancaster, also use roses as emblems. Lady Anna's mourning rites are interrupted by the entrance of the lascivious Ricardo, who is determined to woo her as part of his diabolical stratagems to gain power. The seduction scene, rendered in farcical style, culminates with Ricardo's vulgar gesture at the moment he asks her to wear his ring (Figure 6.2). After his cynical comment that he will have her, but will not keep her long, a melancholy atmosphere emerges when the chorus sings another *ciranda* that tells a story of lost love and death, because of the loss of a ring.

The circus ring, as acting space, not only allowed the Clowns to alternate scenes of parodic play with tragic moments charged with intensity, but also constituted an

Figure 6.2   Seduction scene. Ricardo's vulgar gesture when he asks Lady Anna to wear his ring. Pablo Pinheiro, photographer.

ideal frame for the transposition of the dramatic space of Shakespeare's play to the northeastern socio-cultural context of the *cangaço*. Patrice Pavis contends that an important aspect to be considered in intercultural performance practices is the two-way dialogue at the intersection of at least two different situations of enunciation. He also argues that the change of geographical context demands adjustments to new circumstances, ideologies and imaginaries.[32] In the Clowns' street production, the political intrigues of the Yorkists and the Lancastrians gain regional contours. Visual scenic elements, such as costumes and props, reinforced the intercultural dialogue. The costumes combined silks and brocades, inspired in the garments of the English nobility, with flowers, ribbons, leather, metal and rattan, elements that compose the outfits of the *cangaceiros*. Only Tyrrel – renamed Tyrrel Jararaca – was dressed as a typical *cangaceiro* (Figure 6.3), except for his "mirrored aviator glasses, a trait immediately recognizable by a Latin American audience as distinctive of the repressors of their former dictatorships".[33] The name Tyrrel Jararaca is a fusion of Shakespeare's Tyrrel with Jararaca, one of the most ferocious *cangaceiros* of Lampião's band.[34]

The assassinations of Rivers, Hastings, Buckingham and the young princes, which in Shakespeare occur at different moments, are assembled in a single act in which medial borders are crossed for specific purposes. This segment of the spectacle imitates the codes and conventions of the opera, combining dance choreographies, mime and musical renditions in *cordel*.

Figure 6.3   Tyrrel Jararaca dressed as a *cangaceiro*. Pablo Pinheiro, photographer.

The option for an operatic approach is part of the overall conception of the production, which also prioritizes stylization: the suffocation of the princes by Tyrrel, for instance, is represented by weaving pieces of straw around two coconuts which stand for the heads of the boys (Figure 6.4). In this operatic act, Shakespeare's dialogues are either entirely suppressed or translated into *cordel* tunes and rhythms. The company borrowed formal devices from Dona Militana's popular *romanceiros*[35] to capture the attention and emotion of the Brazilian spectators who are familiar with *cordel*'s syntactic, rhythmic and aural dimensions. To illustrate the inventive cultural translation of Shakespeare's dramatic verse into *cordel*, a small part of the dialogue between Richard and Tyrrel (4.2.66–81),[36] in which the former persuades the latter to kill the children, is transcribed below and translated into English:

Ricardo

(Canta) Tyrrel Jararaca	(Sings) Tyrrel Jararaca
Chegue logo cá	Will you hither come
Chegue logo cá	Will you hither come

Figure 6.4   Stylization of violence: the heads of the young princes are represented by two coconuts. Pablo Pinheiro, photographer.

Tenho um trabalhim	I have a little job
Pra tu executá!	Which has to be done!

Tyrrel

Querido patrão	My dear master
É só me dizer	Just say what it is
É só me dizer	Just say what it is
Fazer suas vontade	To do what you wish
É sempre um prazer.	Is always bliss.

Ricardo

Tem duas crianças	It's the little boys' fault
Que me tiram o sono	I can sleep no more
Que me tiram o sono	I can sleep no more
Mate os dois na Torre	Kill both in the tower
Me garanta o trono	I demand this chore.

Tyrrel

Isso que me pede	What you ask from me
É serviço suspeito	Is a suspect deed
É serviço suspeito	Is a suspect deed
Mas não se preocupe	But I say it's done
Considere feito!	Worry you don't need!

Ricardo

Mate as criancinha	Kill the little children
Não tenha pudor	Do not feel abashed
Não tenha pudor	Do not feel abashed
Serei teu amigo	I will be thy friend
E teu protetor![37]	And will love thee best!

When the series of murders comes to an end, Ricardo plays the accordion and sings original lyrics from *O Cabeleira*, which is part of Dona Militana's repertoire. This *cordel* narrative tells the story of José Gomes, one of the first *cangaceiros* roaming in the backlands and code-named Cabeleira – a bandit without a social purpose. He was introduced into the life of crime by his father Joaquim Gomes, who encouraged him to be fearless and cruel and taught him to kill:

Mamãe dei-me as contas que eu fosse rezar, que eu fosse rezar
Papai, dê-me as facas que eu fosse matar

Eu matei um homem, meu pai não gostou, meu pai não gostou.
Eu matei dois homem, meu pai me ajudou.
Eu matei quatr'homem, meu pai não gostou, meu pai não gostou.
Eu matei seis homem, meu pai me ajudou.
Eu matei nove homem, meu pai não gostou, meu pai não gostou.
Eu matei doze homem, meu pai me ajudou.[38]

Mom give me the rosary for me to pray, for me to pray
Dad give me knives for me to assassinate
I killed one man, my dad did not like it, my dad did not like it
I killed two men, my dad helped me
I killed four men, my dad did not like it, my dad did not like it
I killed six men, my dad helped me
I killed nine men, my dad did not like it, my dad did not like it
I killed twelve men, my dad helped me.

Ricardo's premonitory dream is preceded by a memorable visual moment. The chorus chants the song "Acauã," which refers to a bird called *acauã* whose song is considered a bad omen. While chanting, the cast manipulate curved bamboo stalks to represent birds' wings (Figure 6.5). Later on, the curved stalks are used as bows with which they shoot arrows into the air to simulate the bloody battle of Bosworth Field.

The closure of *Sua Incelença* moves away from Shakespeare's text completely. The performance does not end with Richmond's speech announcing the dawn of a new era, but with the chorus chanting an *incelença* to commend the soul of the deceased. Dorival Caymmi's *incelença* "Velório" (Funeral Wake), combined with lines from the long dramatic poem by João Cabral de Melo Neto titled *Morte e vida severina* (1954–1955), suggests that we all, King Ricardo included, will have to account for our deeds on Doomsday:

Uma incelença entrou no paraíso
Adeus, irmão, té o dia do juízo
Finado rei Ricardo, ao passares em Jordão
E os demônios te atalharem, perguntando que é que levas
Dize que levas cera, capuz e cordão mais a Virgem da Conceição.
Uma incelença, dizendo que a hora é hora
Ajunta os carregadores que o corpo quer ir embora.
Duas incelença, dizendo que a hora é hora
Ajunta os carregadores que o corpo quer ir embora.
Três incelença, dizendo que a hora é hora
Ajunta os carregadores que o corpo quer ir embora.[39]

Figure 6.5   The chorus chants "Acauã" (bird of ill omen). The curved bamboo stalks suggest birds' wings. Pablo Pinheiro, photographer.

An Excellency entered heaven
Farewell, brother, till doomsday
Deceased King Richard, when you cross the river Jordan
And demons stop you, asking you what you carry
Say you carry wax, hood and string plus the Virgin of Conception.
One Excellency, saying time has come
Gather the carriers, for the body wants to leave.
Two Excellencies, saying time has come

> Gather the carriers, for the body wants to leave.
> Three Excellencies, saying time has come
> Gather the carriers, for the body wants to leave.

The lyrics, borrowed from *Morte e vida severina*, draw on superstitions current in the backlands, among them the belief that the deceased must carry "wax, hood and string plus the Virgin of Conception" in order to trick the devil when crossing the river Jordan, which conducts to paradise: the hood to hide the face, the wax (candle) to illuminate the way and the mercy of the Virgin to gain forgiveness of sins.

CONCLUSION

Outdoor Shakespeare performance in Brazil follows contemporary trends in the popularization of the bard, as accomplished by the film industry, graphic novels, new media and other manifestations of popular and mass culture as by theatre. Although Shakespeare is not a major performance focus for open-air productions in Brazil, he has since the 1990s assumed a prominent place in the repertoire of important street theatre companies throughout the country. Professional street ensembles are representatives of a rich tradition not only in local and national terms, but also on a wider global scale, because they have successfully reframed and reinvested Shakespeare with the public character he used to hold in his time. They temporarily modify the cityscape, transforming urban sites where theatrical spectacle provides opportunities for reflection and entertainment for passers-by who interrupt their quotidian routine to become active spectators. *Sua Incelença, Ricardo III* is a cannibalistic version of *Richard III* that shifts meanings in the process of transculturation. Like Grupo Galpão, the company Clowns de Shakespeare is concerned with contemporary theatre's intercultural discourse, opting for a kind of expression that freely appropriates elements from high art and popular culture, at the same time as they incorporate the traditions of the region they represent, such as folk music, dance rhythms and *cordel* literature. Parallels between medieval England, the time of the *cangaço* and contemporary Brazil are ironically drawn in the production and, considering that the pernicious practice of sponsoring politicians to obtain political favors is still alive and strong in our time, it can be inferred that the troupe's critical exposure of past social and political maladies is a thinly disguised strategy to denounce endemic problems of corruption in Brazilian political affairs.

The investigation of site specificities in this essay, which highlights the interaction between acting space and dramatic space, has demonstrated the vital importance of spatiality in theatrical semiosis. The transposition of the fictional universe from medieval England to the Brazilian *cangaço* instated shared memories of the politics of *coronelismo* and its aftermaths in the local spectators' minds. On the other hand, the inventive spatial configuration of a circus ring allowed the company to use farcical devices and musical interludes, which altered perception, provided critical distance and liberated carnivalesque energy and subversive laughter among the audience.

Notes

1 José Roberto O'Shea, "Early Shakespearean Stars Performing in Brazilian Skies: João Caetano and the National Theatre," in *Latin American Shakespeares*, eds. Bernice W. Kliman and Rick J. Santos (Madison: Fairleigh Dickinson University Press, 2005), 25–7.
2 Celuta Moreira Gomes, "Shakespeare no Brasil: Bibliografia," in *Anais da Biblioteca Nacional*, v. 79 (Rio de Janeiro: Biblioteca Nacional, 1959), 29.
3 Marvin Carlson calls these two actors, along with Adelaide Ristori, "the Italian Shakespearians." See his book of the same name for a history of the roles and venues they played (London and Toronto: Associated University Presses, 1985).
4 O'Shea, "Early Shakespearean Stars in Brazilian Skies," 26.
5 Barbara Heliodora, "Shakespeare no Brasil," in *Shakespeare, sua época e sua obra*, eds. Liana de Camargo Leão and Marlene Soares dos Santos (Curitiba: Beatrice, 2008), 325–6.
6 Gomes, "Shakespeare no Brasil: Bibliografia," 186–8.
7 Heliodora, "Shakespeare no Brasil," 330.
8 David George, *The Modern Brazilian Stage* (Austin: University of Texas Press, 1992), 7–8.
9 Heliodora quoted by George, *The Modern Brazilian Stage*, 8.
10 Margarida Gandara Rauen, "Brazil," in *The Oxford Companion to Shakespeare*, eds. Michael Dobson and Stanley Wells (Oxford: Oxford University Press, 2001), 54.
11 Roberto Ferreira da Rocha, "Hero or Villain: A Brazilian *Coriolanus* during the Period of the Military Dictatorship," in *Latin American Shakespeares*, eds. Bernice W. Kliman and Rick J. Santos (Madison: Fairleigh Dickinson University Press, 2005), 49.
12 Marlene Soares dos Santos, "Theatre for the Oppressed: Augusto Boal's A Tempestade," in *Foreign Accents: Brazilian Readings of Shakespeare*, ed. Aimara da Cunha Resende (Newark: University of Delaware Press, 2002), 50–1.
13 George, *The Modern Brazilian Stage*, 115–6.
14 Anna Stegh Camati, "Intermedial Performance Aesthetics in Patricia Fagundes' 'A Midsummer Night's Dream,'" *Aletria: Revista de Estudos de Literatura*, 23, no. 3 (2013): 155.
15 Denise Albanese, *Extramural Shakespeare* (New York: Palgrave Macmillan, 2010), 40.
16 Barbara Heliodora, "A perfeição na infidelidade," in *Barbara Heliodora: Escritos sobre o teatro*, ed. Claudia Braga (São Paulo: Perspectiva, 2007), 880.
17 W. B. Worthen, *Shakespeare and the Force of Modern Performance* (Cambridge: Cambridge University Press, 2003), 149.
18 Billington quoted in Worthen, *Shakespeare and the Force of Modern Performance*, 159.

19 The adjective *potiguar* refers to people who are born or live in Rio Grande do Norte, a northeastern coastal state. The name derives from an indigenous tribe of the Tupi nation living there at the time of the discoveries.
20 The full video and additional scenes of the production *Sua Incelença, Ricardo III* are available on the Global Shakespeares open-access archive: http://globalshakespeares. mit.edu/ricardo-3-villela-gabriel-2011/. The first part of the title is constructed upon two figures of speech Shakespeare was fond of: the pun and the malapropism. It is a pun because it encloses two meanings: *Sua Excelência* (His Excellency) is an honorific title dating back to the time of the empire, and the traditional northeastern funeral songs are called *incelenças*. In the backland, "His Excellency" is mispronounced as *Sua Incelença*, thus it is a malapropism.
21 Livia Segurado, "Shakespeare à la Brasileira Colors Portugal. A review of *Sua Incelença, Ricardo III*, Produced by Clowns de Shakespeare. Porto, Praça D. João I, 09 June 2013," http://bloggingshakespeare.com/reviewing-shakespeare/sua-incelenca-ricardo-iii-clowns-de-shakespeare-porto-praca-d-joao-brazil-2013/
22 See Oswald de Andrade, "Cannibalist Manifesto," trans. Leslie Barie, *Latin American Literary Review*, 19, no. 38 (1991): 38–47.
23 Silviano Santiago, "Latin American Discourse: The Space In-Between," trans. Ana Lúcia Gazola and Gareth Williams, in *The Space In-Between: Essays on Latin American Culture*, ed. Ana Lúcia Gazzola (Durham and London: Duke University Press, 2001), 30.
24 The company uses a reduced number of actors to make tours financially viable.
25 Jyotsna Singh, "The Postcolonial/Postmodern Shakespeare," in *Shakespeare: World Views*, eds. Heather Kerr, Robin Eaden and Madge Mitton (Newark: University of Delaware Press, 1996), 39.
26 Susan Bennett and Mary Polito, "Thinking Site: An Introduction," in *Performing Environments: Site-Specificity in Medieval and Modern English Drama*, eds. Susan Bennett and Mary Polito (New York: Palgrave Macmillan, 2012), 1.
27 Ligia Vassalo, *O sertão medieval: as origens europeias do teatro de Ariano Suassuna* (Rio de Janeiro: Francisco Alves, 1993).
28 Peter Burke, *Cultural Hybridity* (Cambridge: Polity Press, 2009), 55–68.
29 Anna Stegh Camati and Liana de Camargo Leão, review of "*Sua Incelença, Ricardo III* (directed by Gabriel Villela for Clowns de Shakespeare) at Largo da Ordem, Curitiba PR, Brazil, 29 March 2011," *Shakespeare: Journal of the British Shakespeare Association. Special Issue: Global Shakespeare*, 9, no. 1 (2013): 340.
30 See Jack Jorgens, *Shakespeare on Film* (Bloomington: Indiana University Press, 1991), 323–4.
31 Throughout the performance, there are other narrative interventions delivered by different choric characters who provide the spectator with the necessary information for understanding the plot.
32 Patrice Pavis, *Theatre at the Crossroads of Culture* (London and New York: Routledge, 1992), 136–8.
33 Verónica D'Auria, review "Shakespeare's Clowns: An Irreverent and Magical Brazilian Version of Richard III," *Multicultural Shakespeare: Translation, Appropriation and Performance*, 10, no. 25 (2013): 137.
34 Lampião was the most famous bandit leader of the *cangaço*. He has become a folk hero, the Brazilian equivalent of Robin Hood.
35 Dona Militana, *Cantares* (sound recording, 2000), http://oser-taosoueu.blogspot.com.br/2013/01/dona-militana-cantares.html. The repertoire of Dona Militana is a fairly

recent discovery in the academy, though her songs have long been part of the folklore in the northeast. Although she is illiterate and as a woman was not allowed to sing in public, Militana committed to memory the songs she learned from her father, who had encountered old traditional folk songs in *folhetos de cordel* (loose sheets of paper sold in fairs and streets), also called *romanceiros*, which had been circulating in the northeast of Brazil since the eighteenth century. The folklorist Deífilo Gurgel, who discovered and recorded Militana's art in the 1990s, when she was already elderly, recovered this rich cultural tradition which otherwise would have been lost forever.

36 William Shakespeare, *King Richard III*, in *The Arden Shakespeare. Third Series*, ed. James R. Siemon (London: Methuen, 2009), 323–4.
37 Fernando Yamamoto, *Performance Script of Sua Incelença, Ricardo III* (Natal, 2011), 13–14. Translated into English by Anna Camati and Liana Leão.
38 Yamamoto, *Performance Script of Sua Incelença, Ricardo III*, 15.
39 Yamamoto, *Performance Script of Sua Incelença, Ricardo III*, 18.

7 Shakespeare going out here and now: travels in China on the 450th anniversary

Li Jun and Julie Sanders

"This may well be China's busiest Shakespearean year at least for a single venue since the 1st Shakespeare Festival was held in April 1986," declared *China Daily*'s columnist Raymond Zhou in April 2014.[1] He was referring to the programming for China's National Centre for the Performing Arts (NCPA) in Beijing's "Salute to Shakespeare" series, which witnessed eight productions of different Shakespeare plays or adaptations by production companies from different countries and in different languages, all highly divergent in performance style and methodology, which took place between April and November that year. His direct comparison of 2014 with the watershed moment of 1986 and the first Shakespeare Festival in post-Cultural Revolution China is a topic this chapter will address in its wider consideration of "Shakespeare" as it is being experienced on site in China at this particular moment in time.

The 2014 NCPA programme is instructive, providing an insight into a changing appreciation of Shakespeare's resonance, global and local, in contemporary Chinese culture. Alongside the National Theatre of Scotland's collaboration with the Royal Shakespeare Company, *Dunsinane*, written by David Grieg (2010), a sequel to *Macbeth* (a co-production with its own reconfigured place-related cultural and political meaning in a year when a referendum on Scottish independence was taking place in the UK), a Tim Robbins-directed *A Midsummer Night's Dream* from Los Angeles, an in-house production of Verdi's operatic interpretation of *Othello*, a Chinese-Japanese co-production of *Macbeth*, a physical theatre production of *Romeo and Juliet* by experimental Lecoq-influenced Beijing company SanTuoQi, Lin Zhaohua and Yi Liming's *Coriolanus*, a Shanghai Dramatic Arts Centre reworking of *The Taming of the Shrew* relocated to 1930s Shanghai, and another *Dream*, this time Dominic Dromgoole's Original Practices production from the Globe Theatre, London, featured. Many of these productions were not new commissions as such but specific revivals intended to speak to the 450th anniversary context. NCPA's own publicity was explicit about the influence it had taken from Dromgoole's 2012 Globe to Globe festival when 37 Shakespeare plays were staged in 37 languages as part of the London Cultural Olympiad.[2] The theatre also sponsored a world theatre forum as part of the year's events emphasising its desire to engage in a global academic debate about the Shakespeare brand as well as about performance studies more generally.

This essay will, then, explore the significance of this self-conscious act of programming by the NCPA and the wider "glocal" questions about Shakespeare in modern China that it reveals.[3] In the process it will strive to unpack new or changing attitudes to festival or "series" Shakespeare in 2014, comparing the NCPA event to several major previous festivals since 1986. The Chinese productions in "Salute to Shakespeare," directed by two young artists – Zhao Miao's physical *Romeo and Juliet* and Huang Ying's *Macbeth* (under the supervision and guidance of the famous Japanese director Suzuki Tadashi) will receive special attention because they represent the youngest generation of Chinese Shakespearean directors/adapters and, to some extent, present the visage of "Chinese-Shakespeare-to-come." In the 1980s and 1990s when the two large-scale Chinese Shakespeare festivals were held (1986 and 1994 respectively), Zhao and Huang were still in primary and secondary school (Huang was born in 1978; Zhao in 1979). We can confidently state that they were actively shaped by the existence of such influential festivals and the rise of other Shakespearean and theatrical activities after China's opening-up and reform under the leadership of Deng Xiaoping. Both directors began to dabble in drama in the late 1990s and matured in the 2000s, and are especially indebted to an annual University Students Drama Festival, later developed into the Beijing Youth Drama Festival in 2008.[4] It is meaningful, therefore, to find young artists such as Zhao and Huang taking a distinctive and important role in the 2014 Shakespearean event.

Much recent academic discussion of performance, as this special journal edition testifies, has been strongly inflected by theories of place, space, and mobility. Mike Pearson, seminal theorist of site-specific performance, has written in this regard about "an increasing appreciation of cultural specificities and social congregation."[5] What might it mean, then, to apply that thinking to productions of Shakespeare taking place in China today, both indigenous and co-conceived productions, alongside touring productions from other countries?[6] Certainly in this context we need to think as much about concepts of journeying and travelling as being "on site," and in turn we need to revisit generalized understandings of how ideas of repertoire, canon, and theatre programming circulate and operate in the Chinese context. Taking the 2014 NCPA "Salute to Shakespeare" series as our central focus, we aim in this chapter to interrogate how Shakespeare as "drama" and China as "site" co-inform each other in contemporary theatre practice and reveal subtle shifts in understanding since the first flourishing of Shakespeare productions that took place in China after the Cultural Revolution, in the 1980s and 1990s. In the process, we hope to nuance concepts of site or theatrical venue in China, building on the suggestions of Mimi Sheller and John Urry that "[p]laces are [. . .] not so much fixed as implicated within complex networks by which hosts, guests, buildings, objects, and machinery are contingently brought together to produce certain performances in certain places at certain times."[7] The implications of and for China in a host of Shakespearean festivals and productions in recent years will be the focus of reflection here.

SHASHIBIYA ZAI ZHONGGUO

Writing in 2003, Chinese theatre studies specialist Li Ruru reflected on the existence at that time of a Chinese Shakespeare firmly rooted in notions of canon and the West: "What attracts Chinese officials in Shakespeare are neither the rich images in his poetry, nor his deep understanding of the human condition, nor even his intriguing stories. Their touchstone is his canonical status in the Western culture."[8] Li was forming her argument in the wake of the initial decades of post-1976 Shakespeare performance when the Chinese authorities were actively supporting and endorsing international theatre festivals and a renewed engagement with Western culture following what had effectively been a ban on circulations of Western literature during the Mao era. In 1978 a new *Complete Works of Shakespeare* in translation was published, followed swiftly after by a Shanghai Youth Theatre production of *Much Ado About Nothing* later that year. In 1979 a touring production of *Hamlet* came to China from the UK's Old Vic Theatre directed by Toby Robertson with actor Derek Jacobi. This was the first professional drama production from the West to be staged in mainland China since 1949.[9]

The 1980s witnessed the founding in 1984 of the Shakespeare Society of China (SSC) and an emergent academic space for Chinese studies of Shakespeare, most notably Lu Gusin's 1980 Fudan University paper "*Hamlet* across Space and Time" and Fang Ping's 1983 collection of essays, *Let Us Make Friends with Shakespeare.*[10] Shakespeare research centres were founded both in Fudan and at the Central Academy of Drama Beijing at this time.[11] It was the SSC which oversaw the first Chinese Shakespeare festival in 1986. Between 10 April and 23 April of that year, 23 different companies from all over mainland China (including Beijing, Shanghai, Tianjin, Shaanxi, Liaoning, Jiangsu, Hubei, Anhui, and Zhejiang) mounted 18 plays in 12 different theatres and many parallel academic events and symposia.

This festival has rightly been understood as a watershed moment in the history of Shakespeare on site in China and as part of the greater cultural openness that followed in the wake of Premier Deng Xiaoping's policies of reform, but we must also recognize that the version of Shakespeare being presented to audiences in these 1986 productions and related events and publications was still very much one that was being read through the class struggle lens of the Cultural Revolution.[12] The companies performing in 1986 were state-sponsored and approved and included the Academy of the People's Liberation Army as well as workers' companies from mining and railway communities. As Li Ruru's 2003 comments highlight, Shakespeare in this context was useful as a symbol of increased openness and political and cultural engagement with the West, and productions reshaped the material to suit those overarching ends and aims. The notion of the "usefulness" or otherwise of Shakespeare to China is a point to which we will return as we chart the changes that have taken place in both cultural and performance-based approaches between this watershed festival and the 2014 NCPA programme.

Murray Levith has previously commented on how the Chinese have "happily appropriated and expropriated the Bard to serve their own particular ends," and this is not only true of the much-cited 1986 festival.[13] Several other Shakespeare festivals followed over the next two decades or more, including another high-profile international festival in 1994 and several held on university campuses throughout the late 1990s and up to 2008. That these events received both publicity and government-level funding and support may have galvanized the interest of some theatre practitioners to engage in Shakespeare in a manner akin to the impact of subsidized theatre in the UK. Li Jun, one of the co-authors of this chapter, has in another context gone so far as to identify particular productions whose intention was reshaped to accommodate Shakespeare so as to be included in the programming for such festivals. This is a powerful example of cultural capital in operation: "The Bard's cultural and political capital was exploited by ambitious Chinese officials [and] artists."[14] One key example of this utilitarian approach to Shakespearean content is the Beijing director Tian Qinxin's 2008 production of *Ming*.

Ming, Tian's debut in Shakespearean adaptation, was a high-budget and high-profile government-assigned and government-subsidized production for a large-scale festival, the Third International Drama Season held by the National Theatre of China in honour of Shakespeare in 2008.[15] The Third International Drama Season provides us with a helpful overall impression of Shakespeare in China in the earliest years of the twenty-first century for the purposes of this chapter. The organizers of this festival claimed to present "the best Shakespearian [sic] dramas [productions] from home and abroad, demonstrating the Chinese dramatists' interpretation of Shakespeare." The festival aimed to provide an encapsulation through its programme of the current situation of Shakespeare in China. Major productions included not only *Ming*, the opening presentation at the NCPA in Beijing described as an "adaptation" of *King Lear*, directed by Tian, but also three versions of *Hamlet* by the Lin Zhaohua Theatre Workshop, People's Art Theatre, and an Israeli theatre respectively, a musical rendition of *A Midsummer Night's Dream* by Tianjin People's Art Theatre, and several other plays by theatres from home and abroad.

Despite the fact that it cites no more than thirty lines from Shakespeare's tragedy of over 3,000 lines, *Ming* claimed to be a Chinese version of *King Lear*, relocating the play to the grand imperial court of the Ming Dynasty and telling a story of how the old emperor solves the problem of abdicating the throne and passing it on to one of his three sons. Tian laid bare the pragmatic starting point of this *tian jia* (astronomical price) production in an interview:[16] "the National Theatre allotted a sum of money (for the 2008 Shakespearean festival).... What we needed was an appealing proposal.... Then we thought of *King Lear*.... To put it straightforwardly, the theatre was [willing] to spend a sum of money on a Shakespeare play, [and we wanted the money]."[17] It seems that this considerable sum of public money was spent by the National Theatre of China not only "in honour of Shakespeare," but for the sake of asserting Chinese theatrical culture and attainment as well as contributing to the glory of the Beijing Olympics.

As was made clear in publicity for *Ming*, "in an age when China flexes her muscles to the world through the Beijing Olympics," Tian Qinxin sought to render such a view explicit onstage, expressing in the process a director's "deep affections to her mother land and the flourishing age."[18] Tian also demonstrated a somewhat unquestioning approach to China's recent achievements in an interview conducted at the time: "The opening ceremony of Beijing Olympics was so spectacular that it exhibited a 'grand nation's air.' In *Ming*, we just want to re-exhibit a like grandeur in China several centuries ago."[19] The conscious deployment of Shakespeare in an Olympic year to assert a host nation's cultural authority was to be repeated, of course, in the 2012 London Cultural Olympiad. The centrality of Shakespeare to that series of events, including the opening and closing ceremonies in the Olympic Stadium, has been the focus of considerable academic endeavour and might instructively be read alongside these earlier Chinese inflections of the Bard in an Olympian context.[20] The purpose here is not to point the finger at Tian Qinxin's pragmatism or even patriotism but to recognize the uses to which Shakespeare in performance is put and the ways in which this is often inflected, even dictated by the site-specific context.

Nevertheless, as Shakespeare became a more regular presence on Chinese stages as a result of this form of self-conscious, festival-located programming, so also a willingness to challenge previously held assumptions about canon and authority – and even about the "Western" identity of Shakespeare in China that may have been enshrined in earlier performances and commissions – started to surface. Tian herself, while still regarded by many as more or less a state-sanctioned director, has made a mark in recent years with a touring production of *Romeo and Juliet* that was first conceived as a Sino-Korean co-production but which has come increasingly to be adapted to and embedded in its local circumstances in both its Hong Kong and mainland Chinese performances. The aim appears to be to speak, as directly as possible, to local, predominantly youth, audiences, literally so in terms of the production's conscious use not only of culturally specific properties and references but also contemporary Chinese slang.[21]

Another of the 2008 festival production directors was Lin Zhaohua. It is his *Coriolanus*, first staged in the Chinese capital in 2007, rather than the *Hamlet* he staged then, which has come to speak volumes in recent years about the status and meaning of Shakespeare in and through the prism of China. This production, which adroitly deployed the analogy of ancient Rome to address conflict between elites and the masses in contemporary China much as Shakespeare has been seen to address contemporary seventeenth-century politics, garnered much attention when it used over 100 local migrant workers to perform the role of the citizenry in a grand-scale production. The migrant worker chorus was, sadly, not transported to Edinburgh in 2013 when the production was revived for the purposes of yet another key festival encounter there, although the two heavy metal bands which provided live music for the show did make the cultural crossover. The very audible presence onstage of Chinese heavy metal bands "Miserable Faith" and "Suffocated" became an easy means for the UK press to discuss the anti-authoritarian elements of this production, famed as "nu-metal" music is in China with challenging governmental and establishment norms since 1989.[22]

The journeying of Lin Zhaohua's *Coriolanus* to Scotland is an example of different kind of mobility in the context of Shakespeare and China. This is a production that has reached international audiences as part of a wider trend of the "going out" of Chinese culture and been redefined and reconfigured along the way as part of that experiential journey.[23] This new context of cultural traffic and exchange is an indicator in microcosm but also in lived practice of what Poonam Trivedi and Minami Ryuta have described as "a shift in intellectual property relations" between Asia and the West that is currently in process.[24] Arguing that this shift has introduced "more equitable and interrogative terms" into the field of global studies, they further observe the "increasing worldwide repertory of translated and localized Shakespeares" this particular cultural moment has produced.[25] Our considerations of site and place here have for this reason been quite deliberately inflected by other notions of journeying and travelling from new mobility paradigms. The "China" this offers to Shakespeare productions in 2014, we would argue, is a very different concept to that which shaped the 1986 festival productions.

As Lin's 2007 and 2013 *Coriolanus* in its plural manifestations evidences, more experimental productions and approaches have begun to come forth not least as Shakespeare in China began to be (as elsewhere in the world) absorbed and reproduced by a broader digital and remediated culture. Central to this effort within China has been a decisive move away from "original practices" productions – or "doublet and hose" productions as they are often referred to in the mainstream Chinese English-language press – to something distinctly more hybridized, contemporary, accessible, and rooted in local cultures and meanings. Li Jun writes elsewhere about this move to "recontextualisation" or cultural "proximation" in Chinese Shakespeare productions in the following terms: "Rendering Shakespeare in a contemporary (temporal) Chinese (spatial) context is the decisive device for actualizing 'accessibility' of popular Shakespeare."[26] There is a strong case being made here for a Shakespeare in China that speaks to the "here and now" of its audiences.

"Here and now" is the phrase utilized by Raymond Zhou in a 2012 piece ostensibly worrying that Shakespeare productions were losing relevance in a modern China.[27] Zhou was responding directly to a tour by UK all-male theatre company, Propeller, with Shakespearean plays less usually performed in a Chinese context, *Henry V* and *The Winter's Tale*. In the process of reflecting (positively) on the avant-garde and experimental approaches of this company, he recalled experiencing the 1986 festival and in particular productions of *A Midsummer Night's Dream* and *Timon of Athens*: "Like most Western plays," he notes, "Shakespeare was given the 'exotic' treatment in the early years by receiving the standard wig and foreign look"; and he worries, ahead of the Propeller tour, that "[t]he Bard is held in high esteem but he is more revered than loved," since he is seen as "out of touch with today's China." The solution for Zhou in 2012 was that productions should find contemporary cultural relevance and speak to the "here and now." The remainder of this essay, through analysis of two of its home-grown interpretations, will concentrate on unpacking and situating the ways in which the 2014 "Salute to Shakespeare" series spoke to the "here and now" of its moment of production in China and to its place on the "global-local axis" of Shakespeare studies more generally.[28]

The 2014 series

The 2014 series began, as already noted, with a *Macbeth* appropriation, itself a politically loaded collaborative production between the National Theatre of Scotland and the Royal Shakespeare Company in the year of the Scottish referendum on independence.[29] The Scottish play was a noticeably strong presence in the 2014 programme, with a second production bringing Shakespeare to the stage in a Sino-Japanese collaboration (a union not without its own tensions in 2014 in the wake of political disputes over Japanese President Abe's stance on wartime atrocities and Chinese assertions of rights to islands in the South China Seas). That production, a collaboration between Huang Ying and veteran Japanese director Suzuki Tadashi, will be discussed in more detail later.

Elsewhere in the programme, adaptation was equally strongly to the fore in the production of *Otello*, an in-house interpretation of Verdi's operatic *Othello*, further indicating the interest in China in hybridized and reinterpreted versions of the early modern texts. One of the two productions of *Dream*, a "doublet and hose" original practices production from the Globe Theatre, London, which the NCPA described tellingly in its marketing as "retro" Shakespeare, endorses the claims made earlier that China has shifted away from so-called authentic productions to an interest in something more experimental, culturally specific, and locally produced. A more sociological study might usefully map this change against a move towards creativity and innovation more generally in Chinese public policy, in science and technology as much as in a liberal arts and creative industries context. As stated in the introduction to this essay, however, our focus is somewhat more specific, zooming in on the two productions in the series that showcased the work of innovative young Chinese directors as a means to take the temperature of Shakespeare in modern China, in the "here and now."

Zhao Miao initiated the theatre company SanTuoQi when he was still a Year One senior high school student in Beijing in 1996. Over the past 18 years, SanTuoQi (the name means literally "three pioneer flag," suggesting "people pioneering together [in theatre] makes a difference") has grown from being an amateur high school drama society to a highly professional and in many ways remarkable company specializing in physical theatre, and Zhao is widely acclaimed as "one of the most promising young directors" in China, winning the "Asian Arts Awards: Best Directing" prize at the Edinburgh Fringe Festival in 2014 with his production of *Shi Ge [Hymne à la disparition]*.[30] Zhao's *Romeo and Juliet* by Theatre SanTuoQi was first created as a graduation performance in 2008, during his last postgraduate year at the Central Academy of Drama. It was a physical production with important lines spoken by the protagonists Romeo and Juliet retained. The same play was presented in a bolder version for the 2014 NCPA series, which "subverted" the earlier productions:[31] – while both the 2008 and 2011 versions retained some lines from Shakespeare's script, the 2014 version took an uncompromising approach to pure physicality with no lines remaining from the Shakespearean "original." Zhao Miao explained this significant departure from the past in the following terms:

> We kept a fraction of lines from the original script [Chinese translation] in the earlier versions due to two reasons: One is that there had been various "noises"

that stressed the "undeletability" of Shakespeare's canonical work; the other is that we feared that some people in the audience could not follow without lines. However, in the 2014 version, we cut all lines completely, because, in my view, Shakespeare's greatness lies in the hundreds and thousands of ways to interpret and express his works and audiences need different versions to understand and appreciate them; besides, the NCPA, as the highest domestic performing platform, should be big enough to tolerate the "guts" [ambition] of [companies like] us.[32]

To achieve this, the 2014 production basically adopted two sets of physical movement: a narrative one that served for plot development and characterization and a lyrical/expressive one that reflected the internal movements and psychologies of characters. In addition, some moments of stillness were created which proved as powerful as those gestures on the move. For example, when Romeo and Juliet meet for the first time, a notably long pause of stillness was deliberately used to create the spellbound moments of the two young people falling head over heels in love with each other at the first sight (achieved through a shared sonnet form in the Shakespearean text), which, in Zhao Miao's words, "leaves time for people in the audience to fill in the stillness with imagination of what Romeo and Juliet feel and with all kinds of beautiful words that naturally occur to them at such gripping moments."[33]

The popularity of *Romeo and Juliet* as a play in China is one common reason many directors or producers choose this play to stage.[34] It is a well-known story to ordinary Chinese people, often mentioned in association with the traditional national tragic folktale *The Butterfly Lovers*, and especially popular with young people previously exposed to this play in its various stage and screen adaptations, not least Baz Luhrmann's 1996 film *Romeo + Juliet*, starring Leonardo DiCaprio. This is certainly true for Zhao Miao, who finds Shakespeare both abundant in terms of cultural presence and accommodating enough to "allow all dramatists [adapters] to use their imagination and originality to present totally new Shakespeare," yet Shakespeare that is "familiar and accessible enough to guarantee itself against recognition difficulties for ordinary audiences."[35]

However, there are some more profound reasons than mere accessibility for Zhao Miao to select *Romeo and Juliet* as his Shakespearean debut in 2008 and then to reproduce it in 2011 and 2014. Unlike some other productions of the play mounted in the same period which seemed to be particularly keen to depict or release a "crazy" *zeitgeist* version,[36] Zhao Miao discerned some subtler relevance to the social and emotional vista in China today: "The love story of *Romeo and Juliet* serves as a mirror for contemporary Chinese young people who are [somewhat] at a loss with faith and love, because they are obsessed with material and utilitarian pursuits, so much so that even love and marriage are measured by standards like houses, cars and bank accounts."[37]

Yet Zhao Miao is not just a cynical critic of reality; he also succeeds in creating an inspiring poetic work by employing metaphorical and symbolic devices and to some extent the physical pantomime in SanTuoQi's 2014 version transcended the language of Shakespeare. In the 2014 telling, Zhao attempted to portray and foreground the "animal" nature of the two feuding Verona families: the Capulets, resembling clumsy wading birds, who must rely on two sticks when walking, otherwise they would fall down; the Montagues, on the other hand, always crawl upon the ground like lizards. Hatred and lack of love distorts the feuding families' humanity and metamorphoses them into avian and reptile species. In contrast, Romeo and Juliet, formerly identical to their parents and relatives in their display of animal traits, find themselves increasingly unleashed from these invisible chains and free again to walk and even run on foot after having been struck by the force of real love. The onstage spectacle of the two lovers running hand in hand – though wordless – extols the miraculous power and beauty of love, proving that for Zhao Miao and SanTuoQi this love folktale is not only a mirror of traditional Chinese stories or Western canonical culture but also a source of inspiration in the here and now to young audiences in China. (See Figure 7.1.)

Apart from the dual function of *Romeo and Juliet* as both a mirror and an inspiration, the influence of Western theatre practices, especially the domain of physical theatre, has also shaped and matured Zhao Miao's dramaturgy. The earliest direct influence may be traced back to Theatre O, a British physical theatre, and its visit to Beijing with *Three Dark Tales* in 2002. As Zhao Miao recalls,[38] he was enormously influenced by this eye-opening physical production from the UK, and as a consequence got to know about the work of the great French physical theatre artist and educator Jacques Lecoq, because the founder of Theatre O, Joseph Alford, and several other major actors in the company all graduated from Ecole Jacques Lecoq, the French international school specializing in physical performance training. This, in Zhao's words, marked the starting point of his continuous learning from European physical theatre. Furthermore, Zhao and his company took the opportunity of attending three consecutive Edinburgh Fringe Festivals from 2012 to 2014 and toured around Europe, benefitting immensely from witnessing performances and engaging in communicative activities with practitioners in various forms.

Zhao Miao's conscious absorption of Western theatre and culture is combined with a strong self-awareness of Chinese theatre and cultural forms. His dramaturgy embodies a well-balanced fusion of both European physical performing arts and traditional Chinese theatre which also features rich physical elements. In recent years, Zhao has directed his company to take more efforts to study indigenous

Figure 7.1   *Romeo and Juliet*, 2014: the transformative power of love. The protagonists develop from suppressed and twisted animal figures who can stand only with support to awakened and free-moving bodies. The iconic balcony scene is staged with a trampoline in a moment potentially influenced by the work of UK physical theatre company Kneehigh. Images courtesy of Zhao Miao and photographer Guo Xiaotian and integrated by Li Jun with their kind permission.

artistic and cultural forms, such as oriental masks, frescoes, puppet and shadow plays, and *t'ai chi chuan* (shadow boxing), to integrate these forms and elements in their intercultural performances, and to make the physical stylization in Chinese *xiqu* (traditional theatre) compare and interact with the physical elements in Western pantomime and other theatrical forms (see Figure 7.2).[39]

In an interview Zhao recalls that a professor from Paris-Sorbonne University once reminded him that it is essential for Chinese artists to study their own physical-performing system. Chinese bodily expression, though reserved, is tremendously rich and multiple in its semiotics; otherwise there would not have been *xiqu*, *t'ai chi chuan*, and kung fu (martial arts).[40] For Zhao Miao and other Chinese artists like him, the ultimate goal is, then, as the title of an article about his work suggests, that "Going out enables you to know yourself better."[41] In this article, Zhao Miao is

Figure 7.2　*Romeo and Juliet*, 2011, 2014: Chinese shadow puppetry reimagined in Zhao Miao and Theatre SanTuoQi's production melding ancient and modern approaches to theatre. Image courtesy of Theatre SanTuoQi.

reported to have made this statement when comparing producing a play to cooking a dish while reviewing his experiences at the Edinburgh festival: "While seeing a play [appreciating a dish], we should also see how the chef made it. [Someone] sees a green dish, and then manages to cook a green one as well; but the taste is quite different from the one made by the chef. Why so? Because the person hasn't gone to see how the [dish] is made." The author of the article further interprets Zhao's words as follows: "In the [contemporary] circle of Chinese theatre, some people always covet quick results and instant gains, striving to be an overnight success by '*shanzhai*' (copycat culture) [, borrowing] something well-made by other people instead of bothering to contemplate how the 'chef' has been trained [to make good dishes]. SanTuoQi is different, carrying their own 'cooking utensils' to the kitchen of the chef and learning how to cook 'Chinese dishes' there."[42]

A similarly intercultural and inclusive approach has been taken by Zhao Miao's peer Huang Ying, who has already been widely acclaimed as one of the leading directors of the new generation in China and enjoys an increasing fame beyond the domestic theatre.[43] Like Zhao Miao, Huang Ying started his theatrical experience as a schoolboy amateur. While still an undergraduate majoring in biology at China Agriculture University, he directed Molière's *Tartuffe*. Following this, the Western dramatic influence can be seen in his career via a series of European classics, including *Macbeth*, *The Taming of the Shrew*, *The Good Person of Setzuan*, *The Visit*, *The School for Scandal*, *El Cid*, and *The Misanthrope*.[44] Yet in recent years, Huang also became keen to tap into Chinese traditional theatre and culture, as demonstrated by such productions as *Xi you ji* [The Journey to the West] (2008), *Luzhu* [Pot-stewed] (2009), *Soushenji* [Tales of Gods] (2010), *Huangliangyimeng* [Cooking a Dream] (2011),[45] and *Zaushu* [Jujube Tree] (2014). It is, however, in *Macbeth* (2014), his latest major work, and the collaboration with Suzuki in the "Salute to Shakespeare" series, that Huang presents most fully an intercultural and hybridized theatre that celebrates the Bard from the perspective of the "here and now" (see Figure 7.3).

Huang's directorial creativity in the 2014 *Macbeth* was demonstrated in several ways. First, the set was a steel-structured scaffold resembling ancient Chinese or Japanese architecture. The cold greyish lustre of the steel provided a stark contrast to ancient buildings of coloured glaze. The scaffold also suggested a cage or snare or, indeed, a ward in a hospital, which further enhanced the adapters' interpretation of this tragedy.[46] Secondly, to fit with this hospital/asylum-like environment, a bold

Figure 7.3   *Macbeth*, 2014: 'A *Macbeth* adapted for the Chinese here and now': note the presence of the English text on stage. Image courtesy of Huang Ying.

casting decision was made to condense the three witches into one self-consciously seductive young lady acted by a Russian performer dressed in a nurse costume.[47] Quite unexpectedly, in a later part of the performance, four "stagehands" dressed in hospital uniform at the side of the stage, who had previously seemed to be controlling sound or other stage effects, turned out to be pivotal agents who had all the time been coolly observing and lurking, ready for the final tragic stroke: in the final fight scene, one "stagehand" in doctor's uniform stepped onto the stage abruptly to give some instructions to the nurse-costumed witch and then raised a rifle to shoot both Macbeth and Macduff.

In sequence with the asylum/hospital setting, the other characters, together with the desire-obsessed Macbeth and his wife, were depicted as either lunatic, socially transgressive, or disabled: Duncan was reduced to a lifeless flabby suit and pants with a hat and shoes sitting in a wheelchair, Malcolm portrayed on crutches, Banquo cross-dressed as woman for his flight, and Macduff was depicted as a funny guy in sunglasses who did kung fu stunts. All of them were guarded and manipulated by the "nurse"/witch, who, in turn, was directed by the "doctor"; thus the seemingly comic and absurd characterization was tinged with a sense of tragic fatalism. Thirdly, to further reinforce the hybrid style of this production, as embodied in the setting (Chinese and Japanese; ancient and modern) and characterization (Chinese, Japanese, and Russian in its references; comic and tragic), the music was a mixed assembly of genres and references, using a popular English song, "Stand by Me," as a leitmotif, a well-known Christmas song, "Little Drummer Boy," in a version by the commercially popular Three Tenors (thereby bringing both opera and popular music simultaneously into the frame), and a famous piece of Chinese traditional festive music, "Higher Step by Step." Such a musical blending or assemblage exhibits Huang's eclectic theatrical style, which is justified by the director himself as a reflection of contemporary society in China but which also evidences the strong influence of cinematic culture and film scores on this aspect of Shakespearean theatre production in the here and now.[48] The music also served to strengthen and underscore the black humor in this production. For example, "Stand by Me" sung by different characters at different points in the play could hold different meanings, sometimes reflecting inner loneliness and helplessness, while the joyful tone of "Higher Step by Step" on the one hand implied the Macbeths' insatiable desire and on the other hand stood in stark contrast to Macbeth's horror and hysteria (see Figure 7.4).

When asked why he mixed so many different elements, Huang stated that this was just a reflection of the kind of eclectic, diverse, and hybrid life Chinese people lead in this age, returning us to the idea of the convergence or mediated culture mentioned earlier.[49] This eclecticism reflects a noteworthy phenomenon in China that a more "relaxed" attitude makes it possible for emerging artists like Huang

Figure 7.4   *Macbeth*: Note the basin Lady Macbeth uses to wash her bloody hands: it is a red enamel basin painted with floral designs, typically used by Chinese people as an auspicious and festive household utensil before the period of opening-up and reform. Image courtesy of Huang Ying.

Ying and Zhao Miao to be less affected by various external factors superimposed on drama, and perhaps provides more space and freedom for artistic creation. Li Ruru has referenced a Chinese proverb to make this point: "*Tashanzhishi, keyiweicuokeyi gong yu* (它山之石，可以為錯，可以攻玉) [...] The stone from another mountain can be used as a file to work on jade." She notes that this "describes the ultimate goal of signified Shakespeare productions and their method of implementing intercultural performance on the stage."[50]

In a recent interview conducted for the purposes of this essay, Huang Ying was asked about the difference between his generation of theatre makers in China and those who preceded them, such as Tian Qinxin and Lin Zhaohua. The earlier generations, he suggests, were more "opposition"-conscious in their work, while he feels this generation is fortunate enough to be less bounded by such consciousness, because the notion of direct "opposition" in various forms is largely subdued nowadays. Huang's use of such a loaded term as "opposition" implies a binary mind-set in previous generations of theatre directors, perhaps due to prevailing social and historical factors. For example, Lin Zhaohua was reputed to be a kind of non-conformist, stressing the director's artistic independence and originality. This has often been understood (as in the anti-authoritarian elements of *Coriolanus*) to reflect a deliberate reaction against official art of the so-called "main melody."[51] Unlike Lin, Tian Qinxin is better known to be a "winner within the [official] theatre system" with "one foot standing within the [official] system, the other stepping outside."[52] However, her success in attaining this equilibrium is partially attributed to her ability to exploit such sentiments or ideas as a "Chinese Shakespeare" (in opposition to a Western/Anglo-Saxon Shakespeare) and through mobilising popular and youth culture references; that is to say a "pop Shakespeare" rather than a serious or highbrow version of the Bard.

Things have been different for Huang, Zhao and their peers born in the late 1970s or early 1980s. They have now reached their thirties and are mature enough to embark on independent careers. Over the past three swirling decades in modern China, many once distinct and ingrained binary relations have been dissolved or become blurred: high culture and popular culture, official and non-official, global and local, Western or Chinese. Thanks to this ongoing transformation, Huang Ying, Zhao Miao, and other young artists today are much more relaxed about defending or challenging certain "causes" or stances; they have become more accommodating, diverse, eclectic, and malleable, as have their theatre productions and, as a result, their "Shakespeares." Professor Zhang Xian from the Central Academy of Drama evaluates the significance of this young generation of directors in the following terms: "The creations of these directors have brought new blood with stimulants to the domestic theatre. Their creative vigour has not only become an important driving force for the development of drama, but made it possible for various dramatic concepts to be practised. The [old] pseudo-realist staging concept which used to be set as the orthodox will be smashed by these youths brimming with exuberance."[53]

Shakespeare's travels in the here and now

Alexa Huang has posed the question: "In an era when readers and texts travel far and wide and when theatre works are often sponsored by multinational organisations and toured to multiple countries, how are artists rethinking the meaning of the local?"[54] The 2014 NCPA series suggests that hybridity and pluralism are to the fore in this new era and that Chinese directors feel relatively free to experiment with Shakespearean plays and to claim them as their own and for the local context. How does that kind of new assertiveness sit alongside the announcement in 2014 by the UK's Royal Shakespeare Company (RSC) that with the help of a large government grant they would be "Taking Shakespeare to China" in 2016, the next anniversary year in the Shakespeare-soaked calendar? Greg Doran, artistic director of the RSC, wrote: "We're bringing Shakespeare's work to China, supported by the UK Government, as part of plans to boost business and cultural links between Britain and China." Once again in this context we seem to have returned full circle to a Shakespeare mandated by government commission and commercial goals. This project was supported by £1.5 million in UK government funding plus a further £300,000 towards the costs of performances. The intention is to translate all of Shakespeare's work into Mandarin Chinese, and in return to translate 14 seminal Chinese plays into English under the auspices and direction of the RSC, and for the company to tour its work throughout China in 2016 as part of the commemoration of the 400th anniversary of the death of both Shakespeare and Tang Xianzu, one of the greatest Chinese playwrights of the Ming Dynasty.[55] While the UK government rhetoric is one of mutual enrichment, the then Culture Minister Sajid Javid's announcement was linked to additional plans for exchanges with the British Museum, an emphasis that again locates Shakespeare as part of a heritage package rather than something associated with the "here and now" in China. Is that, in light of all we have said here about the shifting theatrical focus in China, the wise approach?

In a feisty article written in response to the 2012 World Shakespeare Festival in the UK which brought many global theatre companies and performers to London to perform Shakespeare, Emer O'Toole suggested: "We have reached the point that what's interesting about Shakespeare isn't Shakespeare at all – it's the themes and innovations that theatre artists bring to the texts."[56] Certainly Shakespeare on site in China seems to be exactly this space for experimentation and innovation, an understanding of and a response to which seems singularly lacking in the 2014 UK government initiative that appears instead to be premised on outdated models of an export culture and on an already tired notion of Shakespeare as heritage. Is the RSC in danger of promoting "retro" Shakespeare to a younger Chinese generation who are looking elsewhere for their cultural references and kicks? The future, in China at least, appears to be in the kind of hybridized, culturally resonant and relevant Shakespeare manifested in the work of Zhao Miao and Huang Ying, a Shakespeare resolutely already *in* China and one that does not need to be transported there. These homegrown domestic versions and interpretations of Shakespeare are in turn beginning their own global journeys, through international collaborations and performative circulations. This Shakespeare is resolutely walking out of China and not to it.

NOTES

1 Raymond Zhou, "All the World's a Stage," *China Daily*, April 18, 2014, 6–7, http://europe.chinadaily.com.cn/epaper/2014–05/02/content_17478974.htm.
2 See Susan Bennett and Christie Carson, eds. *Shakespeare Beyond English* (Cambridge: Cambridge University Press, 2013).

3 Cf. Sonia Massai, ed. *World-Wide Shakespeares: Local Appropriations in Film and Performance* (London: Routledge, 2005).
4 Both Huang Ying and Zhao Miao established their fame as talented young directors in the first Beijing Youth Drama Festival in 2008. Quite coincidentally, their respective productions, though a far cry from each other in terms of contents, happened to match each other by their names: *The Journey to the West* (Huang) and *The Journey to the East* (Zhao).
5 Mike Pearson, *Site-Specific Performance* (London: Palgrave, 2010), 3.
6 Cf. Craig Dionne and Parmita Kapadia, eds. *Native Shakespeares: Indigenous Appropriation on a Global Stage* (London: Ashgate, 2008).
7 Mimi Sheller and John Urry, "The New Mobilities Paradigm," *Environment and Planning D; Society and Space*, 38 (2006): 207–226, (214).
8 Li Ruru, *Shashibaya: Staging Shakespeare in China* (Hong Kong: Hong Kong University Press, 2003), 227.
9 For a superbly detailed account of the history of *Hamlet* in performance in China, see Li Ruru's "*Hamlet* in China: Translation, Interpretation and Performance," MIT Global Shakespeares http://globalshakespeares.mit.edu/blog/2010/04/05/hamlet-in-china-translation-interpretation-and-performance/. Intriguingly, Li notes that Ying Ruodeng, future Chinese Minister for Culture, was one of those who provided simultaneous interpretation through headphones for Chinese-speaking audience members at a Beijing performance.
10 Details derived from Li Jun, "Popular Shakespeare in China, 1993–2008," unpublished PhD thesis, Chinese University of Hong Kong, 2013, 17–19.
11 Li Jun, "Popular," 18.
12 Li Jun, "Popular," 16.
13 Murray J. Levith, *Shakespeare in China* (London and New York: Continuum, 2006), xv.
14 Li Jun, "Popular," 152. On Shakespeare as a global cultural brand, see also Kate McLuskie and Kate Rumbold, *Cultural Value in the Twenty-first Century: The Case of Shakespeare* (Manchester: Manchester University Press, 2014).
15 This festival was initiated in 2004. It is held every two years with different themes: Chekhov (2004), Ibsen (2006), Shakespeare (2008), "Asia" (2010), and "Europe" (2012) (this included a production of *Richard III* directed by Wang Xiaoying, which had been invited to the Globe to Globe festival in London in the same year), and the 2014 festival which had no particular theme but highlighted four Shakespearean productions: *Hamlet* by Lit Moon Theatre Company (USA); *A Midsummer Night's Dream* by Yohangza Theatre Company (South Korea, also part of the Globe to Globe programme); *Henry VI Part 3* by Bitola National Theatre (Macedonia); and *Taking Leave* (about the stage obsession of a veteran Shakespearean actor afflicted with Alzheimer's disease whose stock role is Lear) staged by the host theatre of NTC and directed by Wang Xiaoying.
16 The term *tian jia* appears in an article entitled "Xin (Tian Qinxin) and Yue (Dangnianmingyue) joined hands with contemporary artists in creating a *tianjia* stage" at http://yule.sohu.com/20080924/n259730639.shtml. The cost of sets and props were especially highlighted.
17 These remarks are selected from Tian's interview with He Dong from Phoenix TV [2008].
18 http://yule.sohu.com/20080916/n259587665.shtml.
19 See http://yule.baidu.com/show/2008–09–18/170308192820.html.
20 See, for example, Paul Edmondson, Paul Prescott, and Erin Sullivan, eds. *A Year of Shakespeare: Re-living the World Shakespeare Festival* (London: Arden/Bloomsbury,

2013); Paul Prescott and Erin Sullivan, eds. *Shakespeare on the Global Stage: Performance and Festivity in the Olympic Year* (London: Arden/Bloomsbury, 2015); and *Contemporary Theatre Review*, 23:4 Special edition on "The Cultural Politics of London 2012."

21 A fuller discussion of this particular production can be found in Julie Sanders and Li Jun, "Romeo and Juliet with Chinese Characteristics: Questions of Engagement in Twenty-first-century China," in *Shakespeare and Social Justice*, ed. David Ruiter (forthcoming).

22 http://www.mtviggy.com/articles/lin-zhaohuas-coriolanus-heavy-metal-shakespeare-in-china/.

23 See GaoYinan, "How Should Chinese Culture 'Go Out'?" at http://en.people.cn/90782/8163962.html.

24 Poonam Trivedi and Minami Ryuta, "Re-Playing Shakespeare in Asia; An Introduction," in *Re-Playing Shakespeare in Asia*, eds. Poonam Trivedi and Minami Ryuta (London: Routledge, 2010), 1–18 (2).

25 Trivedi and Minami, "Re-Playing Shakespeare in Asia," 4.

26 Li Jun, "Popular," 63. On "proximations," see the discussion of Gerard Genette's theories in Julie Sanders, *Adaptation and Appropriation* (London: Routledge, 2005), 20. Cf. Gerard Genette, *Palimpsests: Literature in the Second Degree*, trans. Channa Newman and Claude Dobinsky (Lincoln: University of Nebraska Press, 1997), 304.

27 Raymond Zhou, "Shakespeare on the Chinese Stage," *China Daily*, May 21, 2012, http://www.usa.chinadaily.com.cn. Zhou argued in the same article that Propeller's same-sex troupe would likely be well received due to kinships with the gender-restrictive tradition of Peking opera.

28 Jyotsna Singh, "Afterword" to Dionne and Kapadia, *Native Shakespeares*, 234.

29 The referendum and its "no" outcome was heavily reported and discussed both in Chinese mainstream media and on social media sites such as WeChat.

30 See, for example, http://baike.sogou.com/h624228.htm?sp=l61901995. On the Edinburgh award, see http://www.chinaculture.org/exchange/2014–08/07/content_555222.htm.

31 Interview with Zhao Miao, January 12, 2015 (for the purposes of this essay, the authors interviewed Zhao Miao by email and would like to thank the director for his generosity both with ideas and materials, including several of the supporting images for this article). There was also a 2011 version of the SanTuoQi *Romeo and Juliet* which was a more straightforward revival of the 2008 production. Li Lin, "The Physical Act," http://www.globaltimes.cn/content/854476.shtml.

32 Interview with Zhao Miao.

33 Ibid.

34 To take just those produced in recent years, for example, of special mention are: *Zhuluoji* ['Juliet & Romeo Season'] by Dream Workshop (2008), *Romeo and Juliet* co-produced by the Central Academy of Drama and School of Movie and TV of Jili College (2008), *Feng Kuang Shashibiya* [Crazy Shakespeare] by Shanghai Off-Broadway Theatrical Experimental Base (2011), a vampire version directed by famous avant-garde director Meng Jinghui (2011), and Tian Qinxin's above-mentioned touring production in 2014.

35 Interview with Zhao Miao.

36 For example, *Zhuluoji* (2008) highlighted its "crazy youth, fashion, humor, and other trendy elements" and its aim to "make classics crazy as well," http://epaper.jinghua.cn/html/2008–06/19/content_293926.htm and *Feng Kuang Shashibiya* (2011) trumpeted its "craziness": "[Our play] will let you feel exotic amour – crazy love, crazy jealousy, crazy hatred, crazy grudge," http://enjoy.eastday.com/e/20110808/u1a6041703.html.

37 Interview with Zhao Miao. This jibes with some of Tian Qinxin's statements about her 2014 production. See Sanders and Li, "Romeo and Juliet with Chinese Characteristics."
38 Interview with Zhao Miao.
39 http://www.stardaily.com.cn/3.1/1405/28/448777.html.
40 http://zhoukan.cc/2014/11/30/zhao-miao-running-away-is-to-see-ourselves/.
41 Interview with Zhao Miao.
42 Ibid.
43 For example, Huang was acclaimed as "the most pioneering youth playwright and director in Asia," who "not only owns a broad international vision, but also a solid foundation in Chinese traditional art," http://ent.ifeng.com/live/special/qingxijie/pinglun/detail_2011_09/01/8852621_0.shtml.
44 Many of these productions were directed when he was a postgraduate student studying directing at the Central Academy of Drama in the early 2000s.
45 This production, originating from a legendary novel of the Tang Dynasty, *A Story of a Dream*, debuted at Le Festival d'Avignon and ran for 24 performances, and was well received by audiences and deemed "the most Chinese play of the festival," http://ent.ifeng.com/live/special/qingxijie/pinglun/detail_2011_09/01/8852621_0.shtml.
46 Suzuki Tadashi has used medicalized *mise-en-scènes* in previous Shakespeare productions, most notably his seminal *King Lear* with a Russian cast from Moscow's Chekhov Art Theatre in 2004.
47 This in itself knowingly referenced both Suzuki's *King Lear* and Japanese popular culture traditions of "cosplay."
48 Julie Sanders, *Shakespeare and Music: Afterlives and Borrowings* (Cambridge: Polity Press, 2007), esp. Chapter 8 on "Contemporary and Hybrid Film Scores"; and Adam Hansen, *Shakespeare and Popular Music* (London: Continuum, 2010).
49 Taken from Li Jun's face-to-face interview with Huang Ying on November 2, 2014. The authors would like to thank Huang Ying for his cooperation and generosity during the research for this article.
50 Li Ruru, *Shashibaya*, 194.
51 The Chinese term for "main melody," *Zhu xuanlü* 主旋律, basically refers to artistic works which deal with uplifting topics so as to inspire and educate people to praise the Communist Party and socialism. With the evolution of this concept since its coinage after 1989, this term may now be loosely used for any artistic work which reflects *positively* the history, achievements, or culture of China and the brighter side of the society.
52 Zhang Zhuo, "*Yingjia* Tian Qinxin 赢家田沁鑫" [Tian Qinxin, the Winner], *China Weekly*, 10 February 2011, http://news.sina.com.cn/s/sd/2011–0210/114721932601.shtml; http://www.china.com.cn/culture/xiju/2010–05/10/content_20011257.htm.
53 Zhan Xian, "*Yi xijuyishu de mingyi: dui ruoganxijujie de gerenyinxiang* [In the name of dramatic art: personal impression of some drama festivals]," *China Drama*, Issue 12, 2009, 40–1.
54 Alexa Huang, "'No World without Verona's Walls?': Shakespeare in the Provincial Cultural Marketplace," in Trivedi and Minami, 251–68 (251).
55 Press Association, "RSC to Translate Shakespeare for Chinese Audiences," September 12, 2014, http://www.theguardian.com. The UK's Department of Culture, Media and Sport (DCMS) released this news alongside a package of commercial deals announced by the then Chancellor of the Exchequer George Osborne, emphasizing the business engagement angle of this creative endeavour.
56 Emer O'Toole, "Shakespeare, Universal? No, It's Cultural Imperialism," *The Guardian*, May 21, 2014, http://www.theguardian.com.

8 "What ceremony else?" Images of Ophelia in Brazil: the politics of subversion of the female artist

Cristiane Busato Smith

> Ophelia's importance as a cultural and critical body of texts lies not solely in her being a "symptom" or *effect* of the culture that represents her according to its own logic, ideology, and concerns, but also in how she is the *generator* or *site* of meaning or cultural shift, not merely a contingent reflection of an era's already existing preoccupations.
>
> (Peterson & Williams, 2012)

For at least two centuries, the fascination with Ophelia has taken her well beyond the realm of the text. Her image has not only seduced generations of visual artists but has captivated a number of prominent writers and film directors as well. The French symbolists, in particular, were fascinated by Ophelia, suggesting a lively interplay between poetic and visual depictions of the muse which can still be seen in contemporary art. Writers and artists alike have been intrigued, not only by the actual scenes of death and madness in Shakespeare's play, but also by the tantalizing cuts in its various editions[1] – cuts which seem to hold out the promise of more. In this sense, as Elaine Showalter argues,[2] the text itself has proved less interesting than a history of representations that far exceed its original boundaries. Today, Ophelia thrives in contemporary literature and art. Depictions of dead, drowning, mad, or repressed Ophelias, for example, proliferate across a wide range of twentieth- and twenty-first-century media: on the stage, in books and paintings, the screen arts as well as the internet in blogs, amateur videos, mash-ups on YouTube, games, and profile pictures.[3] Ophelia, "the young, the beautiful, the harmless, and the pious," retains a singular magnetism that continues to draw many into her tragic beauty.

While most scholarship devoted to the iconography of Ophelia traces her presence mostly in the Anglo-American world, her visual renditions have also found their way into different corners of the world and help chronicle how distinct cultures respond to the "myth of Ophelia" Showalter, 1991; Ziegler, 1997; Kiefer, 2001 in today's globalized world.[4] These representations establish a dialogue with the Victorian legacy but also move beyond: Ophelia is reimagined in Brazil as a dying/dead nymph, as a site of resistance to authority, and as a site of female trauma. These Brazilian Ophelias are no longer "a document in madness" (4.5. 178) but symbols of female agency and resistance. Some of the visual representations here analyzed take Millais's highly influential painting, *Ophelia* (1851–52),[5] as a point of departure while others invent alternative configurations for the heroine.

The aim of this essay is to investigate the very recent (2008–15) appearance of Ophelia in the Brazilian visual arts, which I shall investigate by analyzing images (mostly photographs) and performances (one installation and one solo performance) by three female artists. The idea is to evaluate the translatability of Ophelia in Brazilian art through the following questions: Is Ophelia capable of reflecting contemporary Brazilian feminist discourse? Could the emergence of images of Ophelia in Brazilian culture indicate a change in discourse about the "Brazilian woman"? How do these images rearticulate and/or reflect contemporary Anglo-American representations of Ophelia? In the absence of a history of Ophelia beyond the history of her representation, as per Showalter's (1985) memorable observation, what story can we tell about representations of Ophelia in Brazil?

Context: The Female Artist and Self-Representation

For many centuries, western art was overwhelmingly male, and the female body was represented from the perspective of the male gaze.[6] Even after 1850, when women were first admitted to art schools in Europe,[7] many artists still had a hard time finding a visual language that did not reproduce the stereotypes through which women had so long been represented. By the end of the nineteenth century, female artists were producing their first tentative self-images, challenging the established aesthetics of the representation of women.

One particularly significant example for the purposes of this research is the case of Elizabeth Siddal (1829–1862), an artist and model who posed as Ophelia for painter John Everett Millais (*Ophelia*, 1851-2). Married to Dante Gabriel Rossetti, a painter and poet, Siddal was one of the pre-Raphaelite painters' favorite muses. Her poses for her husband's painting and her own self-portrait well illustrate the different aesthetic inclinations of her day. In different paintings and drawings, Rossetti depicts his wife seated, cooking, and resting; passive, with her eyes half open, never looking directly at the observer. In *Beatrix Beata* (c. 1864–70), Rossetti paints a distant, melancholic, unattainable Siddal with her eyes shut. Dramatically different from the idealized style that her husband, Millais, and the other painters from the pre-Raphaelite school adopted to paint her, Siddal's[8] own self-portrait (1854) looks straight at the viewer and refutes the aestheticization of the female figure that was so in vogue in the Victorian era. Her much admired long, thick, auburn hair is held back by a darker-colored band. Her gaze is serious yet thoughtful. It is interesting that Siddal should choose to portray herself not as the famed beauty displayed in the famous pre-Raphaelite paintings, but in a more realistic way, looking more like the photographs of her taken in 1860.

The dichotomy inherent to the dual representations of Siddal in her positions as muse and artist – i.e. between the prevailing representation of the female vis-à-vis the way the female represents herself – has remained unresolved in the twentieth and twenty-first centuries, although one major difference is that female artists engaged in feminist issues have brought new topics into the mix, such as sexuality, suffering, disease, race, gender, and representation itself, taking an overtly political stance. This focus rejects the idea that artists – men or women – create from an abstract, universal vision that underpins their personal view, and evinces how creativity is directly affected by history, gender, sexuality, social class, race, and nationality. One of the most effective ways female artists have found to draw attention to their historical positions has been to use their own bodies in their art. A case in point is the series of self-portraits by Mexican artist Frida Kahlo (1907–1954) after the bus accident in which she broke her spine. In *The Broken Column* (1944), for instance, the artist depicts herself in a steel brace that holds in her broken spine at different places, with tears pouring from her eyes, and nails dug into her body, signs of her martyrdom. Another example[9] often associated with the iconography of Ophelia is the Silhouette (1973–1980) series by Cuban artist Ana Mendieta[10] (1948–1985), who brands her body on nature in different ways: on grassy ground, covered with grasses; on bare earth, surrounded by foliage or undergrowth; or even as a body floating in a murky stream.[11] Mendieta's "earth body art" aesthetic nonetheless prevents viewers from gleaning the same aesthetic pleasure they gain from looking at the Victorian paintings that represent fair Ophelia. The images of Mendieta's installations are too disturbing, and while they associate the female body and the earth, they also foretell of its transience, as all that remains is but a "silhouette."

In the late 1960s the advent of second-wave feminism heralded a new generation of female artists whose influence is still felt today. They manifested the popular slogan "the personal is political" in self-portraits like *Red Flag* (1971), a photo lithograph by American artist Judy Chicago (b. 1939) that portrays her from the waist down removing her tampon, or the photographic studies entitled *The Picture of Health?* by British artist Jo Spence (1934–1992), which document her breast cancer treatment. The core concern, as Borzello (1998) explains, is "to reclaim the female body from its imprisonment in art as a beautiful, voiceless object to be judged by male spectators" (167). Borzello stresses the importance of the strategy adopted by female artists of using their bodies in performances, photographs, and videos, because as authors, they now had the power to direct the viewer's response.

If the journey taken by European and North American female artists has involved repeatedly challenging the canon, what can we say of the women artists working in Brazil in the twentieth and twenty-first centuries? As Luana Tvardovskas explains, Brazil's historical and social process is very different than that of Europe or the United States, beginning with the military dictatorship, which marked a retrogression in the evolution of feminist discourse and all artistic expression.[12] Another obstacle was the lack of any systematic articulation of the feminists' claims, which meant that the movement was slow to get politically organized in Brazil. Despite all the hurdles, as of 1980, "feminist ideas were divulged in the country's social scene, the product not just of the action of their direct spokespersons, but also of a climate that was receptive to the demands of a society in a process of modernization" (Sarti, 42).[13] In the realm of the visual arts, this progress can be seen particularly since the 1990s with the emergence of Brazilian women artists tackling the statute of art and female subjectivity, like Márcia X (1959–2005), Anna Maria Maiolino (b. 1942), Rosana Paulino (b. 1967), Cristina Salgado (b. 1957), and Ana Miguel (b. 1956). Likewise, the fact that some exhibitions have been held of Brazilian female artists, even if not always with a specific feminist slant, is also indicative of this shift.[14] As for the academic world, the contributions to women's studies are substantial: mainly since the 1980s, universities, with the help of grants from foreign and government foundations, have been responsible for putting on courses, holding forums, conducting research, and creating periodicals in the area, contributing to the establishment and expansion of gender studies in the country. It is therefore no mere coincidence that the three artists analyzed in this study are scholars who do not just represent themselves as Ophelia but also reflect critically and theoretically on her in their publications.[15]

It is also no surprise that all three artists chose to represent themselves as Ophelia and to share with their Anglo-American peers not only the sense of women's socio-historical subordination, but also an awareness of how art practices have perpetuated this subordination.[16] Women artists' self-representation is particularly anchored in women's experiences and body politics. Besides using their bodies as political instruments for essential reinterpretations of the feminine, so clear in banal appropriations of Ophelia, the featured women artists have also made an effort to bring to light what the paintings of fair, dead Ophelia take every effort to keep hidden under a poetic veil.

THE EXORCISM OF PAIN: GABRIELA FREGONEIS'S OPHELIA

Gabriela Fregoneis is an actress and drama teacher. She has a master's degree in theater and is studying for a doctorate in performing arts at UNICAMP. She staged her *Metamorfoses de Ofélia* (Metamorphoses of Ophelia) in 2011 in a hybrid format that straddles both performance and art installation. Part of her master's project of the same name, it was organized, written, and performed by Fregoneis, who says she "does not regard it as a project on Ophelia *per se*, but rather, and mainly, a project about the metamorphoses of a Gabriela-Ophelia."[17] Intrigued by the ambiguities of Shakespeare's character and inspired by film and stage productions[18] of *Hamlet* that suggest that Ophelia had an incestuous relationship with Polonius and Laertes, Fregoneis focuses on the gaps in Ophelia's tragic story, which she sees as being essentially violent and traumatic in nature. In her postmodern interpretation of Ophelia, the violent actions/attitudes are inspired by Artaud's theater of cruelty and Heiner Mueller's *Hamletmaschine*, while Egon Schiele's animalesque representations[19] involving the female body are her main iconographic reference. From Brazil, Fregoneis draws on the dramatic language of Ophelia in *Ensaio.Hamlet* [Rehearsal.Hamlet] (2004) by the Cia dos Atores theater company, which seeks to instigate the audience's sensibilities through visual and auditory sensations.[20] As such, Shakespeare is a point of departure for the artist, who turns to other modern references to explore and discuss the relationship between the creative act and female sacrifice from a subversive viewpoint.

The installation was staged in a dark room and lasted around two to three hours. Punctuated by electronic music, over a thousand photographs were exhibited on three different walls exploring different aspects of Ophelia. Projected in slow and fast motion, the images narrated different stories set in an urban landscape. A post-modern Ophelia wearing black boots and a leather jacket over a mini-dress wanders along overpasses and railroads. In some of the photos, the model sits on the edge of an overpass with her legs hanging dangerously over the side, defying death. A more direct visual allusion to Ophelia's suicide are the photos of the railroad, where the artist lies on the rail tracks with her arms open, in a ritualistic offering that brings Millais's Ophelia to mind. In a given moment during the projection of the photos, a naked Gabriela-Ophelia enters the room and writes words on her body – *pain, trauma, cruelty*, and others – and interacts with the images. Handing the pen to audience members, she asks them to take part in the performance, writing words or sentences on her body that express the feelings the images produce. Her performances were designed to blur the boundaries between art and life, artist and viewer, and to catalyze an intense sensory experience.

Based on Freudian interpretations and film adaptations of *Hamlet*[21] that suggest Ophelia had an incestuous relationship with her father, Polonius, or her brother, Laertes, Fregoneis makes incest the subject of a sequence of photos. The recurring image of an Egyptian stool, associated in antiquity with the idea of sacrifice (Griffith, 1905, 290),[22] represents the place where the act took place. There are also images of the artist in different positions holding a bloody bull's heart (Figure 8.1), which also indicates incest. The more explicit examples show the artist holding the heart between her legs, with the blood staining Ophelia's characteristic white dress. She also used a bull's heart in the performance, handing it over to the audience, who reacted with revulsion. It is probably at this moment that Fregoneis draws a more direct association with *Ensaio.Hamlet*, namely Ophelia's death scene, where the character is literally reduced to a piece of meat to be ironed flat before being buried in a bucket. Both the bull's heart and the lump of meat are stage devices to subvert the strong tradition of aestheticizing the Shakespearean heroine's death. In Fregoneis's case, blood is also associated with rape: interspersed between the images, the words *father* and *brother* appear projected on the walls.

Incest is addressed not only visually but also metaphorically, if it is analyzed together with other groups of images. This act can therefore be interpreted as the symbolic "rape"[23] perpetrated by the patriarchal system that turns women into objects. This concept is supported visually by the constant blinking of the artist's unfocused gaze, which at the same time challenges, responds to, and confounds the male gaze, an ideology clearly adopted equally by romantic painters and by the pre-Raphaelites, who made Ophelia their principal muse. Fregoneis's visual interpretations are imbued with alternative ways of discussing and seeing Ophelia "through other eyes," and adopt the notion of "re-vision" that Adrienne Rich defended so vehemently in her essay "When We Dead Awaken."[24]

Rejecting the objectified representations of the female body and the male gaze, Fregoneis's Ophelias disturb us because they explore the antagonistic relationship between the female figure, loss, and pain. Adopting the strategy of exposing viewers to her pain, Fregoneis also confers on them the role of causer of pain. More than an aesthetic experience, the act is turned into a political strategy, since the Shakespearean heroine is appropriated and resignified in a political discourse whose strategies, rather than being enveloped in poetic imagery, are stark and defiant. Her artistic deed is therefore in harmony with theoretical feminist issues because it speaks out against the symbolical violence of oppression against the body, while investigating strategies for dismantling the legitimized truths about sexuality.

Figure 8.1   *Face do Amor* (2012)

A RE-VISION OF MILLAIS'S OPHELIA: PHOTOGRAPHS BY LUCIA CASTANHO

Lucia Castanho[25] is an artist and a professor of art at the University of Sorocaba (in São Paulo state). She has a master's degree in art and history and a doctorate in communication and semiotics. Her work consists primarily of photo essays, but also includes drawings and paintings[26] that portray the death of Ophelia.

Castanho's artistic work includes every stage of the creative process: from the design and making of her own costumes and accessories for Ophelia to the lighting and set design to communicate her subject matter. She started in 2009 with a painting of a floating Ophelia who seems to resist her own death in the water. The background is covered in roses that seem to emanate from Ophelia's luminous body. This painting inspired Castanho to pose and be photographed as Ophelia. For her, self-representation is not an expression of an artist's individual need, but "a representation of a character that incarnates the collective imaginary."[27]

For Castanho, as for most of the artists that have portrayed Ophelia, the story of this character is very much tied up with the story of her death – a death played out in three distinct sets of images: a) as a solitary figure standing beside a swimming pool or already in it, prefiguring her death; b) already dead, floating in the pool; and c) lying dead in a grave in the ground. Death, as in most of the visual representations of Ophelia, occupies a central position, even if for the artist Ophelia's suicide meant her liberation. Castanho's decision to represent her death in water reflects how haunted she was by Millais's Ophelia. Although many of her photos display a deliberate post-modern aesthetic that might challenge conventional visual perspectives on Ophelia, they also owe much to Millais, since they are mediated by the "citation" of the iconic painting, a central paradox in the iconographic history of Ophelia in the twentieth and twenty-first centuries. Like most of the visual reformulations of Ophelia in contemporary culture, Castanho's images run the risk of reactivating Edgar Allan Poe's aesthetic of the "beautiful dead woman"[28] that permeated Victorian English art.

In Castanho's representations of Ophelia's death, she appears in a modern swimming pool in a setting with the potential to desacralize and denaturalize the stream where Ophelia voluptuously succumbs to her death, celebrated in visual and textual representations of the drowning figure. In Figure 8.2, the body of a woman with the familiar white robe is floating in the water.

There are many parodies of Millais's Ophelia in the rich history of reproductions of this work. The modern interpretations include bathtubs and Jacuzzis operating as pop *mise-en-scènes* for Ophelia's watery grave. One lifeless Ophelia in a photograph, wearing a platinum-blond wig, floats face down in a Jacuzzi.[29] Breaking away from the mimetic tradition to which Millais belonged, the image is striking for the constructed nature of the photograph, in a self-reflective mode characteristic of post-modernism. This is manifested through the careful manipulation of light and color, which gives the final image an artificial effect. The seemingly doll-like model floats in the turquoise water of the Jacuzzi, creating a deliberately stylized expressive result. The photo also evokes the notorious bathtub episode, when Elizabeth Siddal almost literally incorporated Ophelia as she was modeling for Millais, lying in a bathtub of cold water. The allusion to Siddal is

Figure 8.2   *Ofélia Piscina 1* (2009)

important, as is the attempt to repress this reference, because unlike the tragic fate of Siddal (Smith, 2007), Castanho both narrates and stages Ophelia's death in her own way. By so doing she exerts her right and will to consolidate her identity as a woman artist, something Siddal was never able to do.

One image from the sequence of tomb photos portrays the body of a dead Ophelia wearing black. Recreating the "incomplete rites" of the heroine's funeral, the model's body is covered with dry leaves and twigs in a scene that brings to mind the earth body art of Cuban artist Ana Mendieta, mentioned earlier, which associates women with nature and suggests their symbolic fertility, making them assimilated by their natural element.

Interestingly, other incarnations of Ophelia by Castanho seem to take the character in slightly different directions. To a certain extent, there is a refinement of the swimming pool pictures, since these more mature Ophelias are more autobiographical in nature. The artist wanted to get away from the submerged Ophelias because they could undermine the impact of the moment of her death. As a result, the focus now shifts onto the artist's body, and especially her face, suspended above the water line and consequently far more perceptible. Equally striking is the white dress, which Castanho made meticulously from the cloth of her own wedding gown[30] (see Figure 8.3) in an attempt to release herself from the painful memories

Figure 8.3   *Ofélia Piscina 2* (2012)

of her aborted marriage.[31] Carefully arranged red, yellow, and white roses are scattered over the dead Ophelia's body, forming a bridal bouquet that creatively decorates her tulle dress. Her arms opened wide and her serene expression confirm that her death expresses an act of rendition and liberation, not a suicide. Yet is this elaborately staged bride a female figure of self-sacrifice that forges connections between the topics of love and marriage, sacrifice and death, perpetrating them? This post-modern image certainly brings Millais's painting to mind in its subject matter, form, and content, notwithstanding the absence of the romantic stream and landscape. In this updated scene, there is hardly any water in the swimming pool painted with stylized roses, some intentionally smeared, as if to draw attention to the photograph's artificiality. While Castanho seems to reject Millais's naturalistic stream, it is questionable whether this deliberately post-modern Ophelia effectively gets away from the death scene in the water as sacrifice and rendition.

A more recent series of photos and drawings seem to make a more robust, conscious effort to reject Millais in that they depict Ophelia in a swimming pool either partially submerged or with just her feet steeped in a red liquid that clearly alludes to blood. The artist has added a caption to the images: "Ophelia is not dead." In the artist's words:

> The desire to represent her dead cannot really be restricted by the limits of what had come before, namely the painting by Millais. . . . I also took pictures inside

the pool, with the water red like blood, and what I had in mind then was a video where I would wear the lining of my wedding gown, paint my legs with red watercolor flowers, and, upon coming into contact with the water, the paint would run and turn the water red.

(Castanho, 121)[32]

These new Ophelias by Castanho "are Opheliaized," to use Bachelard's term, in menstrual blood that runs down the artist's legs, one of the biological characteristics of the experience of being a woman that is now transformed into her lifeblood.[33] While this blood rejects the connotation of impurity inherited through the patriarchal system as a symbol of the female curse, it also stains the white fabric of Castanho's wedding gown, opening a biographical space that makes a bid to transcend the idea of patriarchal repression that marriage can represent for women.

Self-representation is actually an attempt by Castanho – and indeed all contemporary female artists – to attain transcendence and autonomy. Although her photographic work highlights the trope of the dead woman – the association between women and water/nature, and between the female and fluidity, concepts that Millais represents so well – this same practice can be interpreted as interventionist. Her images have the power to question the very nature of representation and, more importantly, the role of women artists in a structure of male domination. Ultimately, Castanho is artist, model, subject, object, observer, and observed.

LUCIA SANDER'S OPHELIA AND THE POLITICS OF INTERVENTION

The marriage of criticism and performance is what informs Lucia Sander's monologue, *Ofélia explica ou o renascimento segundo Ofélia & Cia.* [Ophelia explains or rebirth according to Ophelia & Co.] (2008). An actress and researcher with a doctorate in literature, Sander decided to put into practice the theories and ideas she had been teaching in her courses on adaptations of Shakespeare. She wrote, directed, and produced her solo performances, and staged them in different parts of Brazil and Argentina.

Irreverence and humor are the vehicles Sander uses to demystify and recontextualize the canonic texts, as well as the canonic interpretations of these same texts. As she explains, "Shakespeare's text does not just enable this modernization, it invites this approach" (Sander, 23). The fleeting nature of Ophelia is an incentive for alternative interpretations and performances. As such, Sander submits that Ophelia's madness is just as false as Hamlet's and that she could not have died in the way Gertrude describes. In her updated version, Ophelia is a survivor of the Danish massacre and is still haunted by the Danish court, who think she knows too much. This Ophelia swims out for her own safety and crosses oceans to reach Brazil four centuries later. She hides in the *favelas* of Rio de Janeiro, is involved in arms trafficking, and has become an actress and rapper.[34]

In the monologue, Sander interacts with Victorian paintings of Ophelia, which are projected onto the wall at the back of the stage. Wearing jeans and T-shirt, an Alice band of protuberant flowers in her hair and a gun at her waist, Sander intervenes and interferes dynamically with the nineteenth-century paintings. Some of her interventions take the form of ironic mimesis, where she imitates one of Ophelia's stylized gestures or poses in order to expose its artificiality. In another intervention, she brings to life the universe of a painting, namely *Ophelia* by Henrietta Rae.[35] This painting portrays the king and queen on the left-hand side and Ophelia on the right, but Rae had to alter the left-hand side many times before it was to the liking of her husband and other artists. Significantly, this is precisely the part of the painting that Sander leaves out in her performance. Instead, she focuses on the unaltered side, which shows the mad Ophelia offering some flowers (4.5). By eliminating the king and queen, the Brazilian artist not only symbolically censures the Danish court and the misogynistic ideology that prevented women from becoming artists but suggests that Ophelia's madness was the direct result of this same ideology.

In yet another visual interpolation, Sander evokes the complex status of Victorian actresses who played Ophelia on the stage (Figure 8.4). By placing herself (wearing dark glasses) between photos of actresses Helen Maud (1863–1937) and Nora de Silva (1868–1949),[36] who defied the heroine's traditional white raiment (sign of purity and innocence), swapping it for the black dress[37] that had been denied other actresses who came before, like the great Ellen Terry who enacted a bold Ophelia, Sander draws attention to her own role as Ophelia and her own art as an actor – and by extension, the very deed of acting.

Music is a different recourse Sander uses to intervene in the Ophelia story. She sings "How should I your true love know / From another one?" (4.5.23–40), one of the ballads Ophelia sings during her madness scene, explaining her unrequited love for Hamlet and the death of her father. This musical interlude goes beyond a mere strategy to help create a Renaissance atmosphere for the paintings; the ballad is replaced by an explosive, engaging rap song[38] that boldly contradicts the traditional love-struck ballad. The rap challenges Ophelia to take action and offers practical solutions for the character's conflicts. Through her song, Sander sends a message out to all contemporary "Ophelias" – young women who continue to be repressed or are the victims of abuse, self-mutilation, or other struggles such as those described in *Reviving Ophelia: Saving the Selves of Adolescent Girls* (1995).[39] It is through the same vicissitudes of life ("shoves of life") that Sander suggests Ophelia could survive and get stronger, "without hesitation, without inhibition, without

Figure 8.4   *Ofélia Explica*, 2008. Screen capture from *Ofélia Explica* (Sander 2009).

authorization." In other words, Sander conceives of a stronger, contemporary Ophelia who has little or nothing to do with the heroine Shakespeare created.

Indeed, Sander's iconoclastic performance stands up and challenges the prevailing representations of Shakespeare's heroine: they are all subject to the revisionist arbitration of the artist. Through her irreverent interventions in the Victorian paintings, Sander not only destabilizes the tradition that represents women as fragile *objets d'art* but also subverts it. With Sander, Ophelia has a chance to tell her own story, even if the voice she uses to do so comes in the form of an explosive rap from the *favelas* of Rio de Janeiro.

CONCLUSION

Since the eighteenth century, visual representations of Ophelia have proliferated. One intriguing feature of these different depictions is the irresistible attraction girls and young women have to her tragic story, a trend that began in the nineteenth century in the form of the popular *cartes-de-visite* and keepsake portraits (Smith, 2007). By engaging in dialogue with the visual arts, Victorian actresses also confirmed this trend. A case in point is Ellen Terry, one of the leading actresses of that century, who posed as Ophelia[40] for the first time when she was 16 years old, before she started working as an actress. Her three *cartes-de-visite* as the heroine were photographed after her compelling performance as Ophelia opposite Henry Irving in his 1878 production of *Hamlet*. It is clear that Terry wanted to be known and remembered as Ophelia. Stories reporting how actresses and models[41] identified with Ophelia are other indications of this trend. Although many may consider identification with a tragic figure who is inexorably linked to madness and suicide an odd phenomenon,[42] the fact is that the Ophelia archetype still has a strong hold on the popular imagination.

Representations of Ophelia were surprisingly slow to reach Brazil, yet when they arrived, they awakened sudden interest. Why? If the images of Ophelia "reflect the norms and stereotypes of the culture in which they are produced and received", if they mirror "where we are in history", they have the potential to signal a change in this culture.[43] Ophelia continues to both reflect and generate meaning about the feminine. Ultimately, the emergence of images of Ophelia in Brazil has coincided with a profound cultural and critical awareness of the politics of the female body, about how women are seen and how they see themselves.

In fact, the references that inform Gabriela Fregoneis's disturbing images and performance are multiple, as are the post-modern parodies of Millais's *Ophelia* by Lucia Castanho, and the irreverent interventions by Lucia Sander, revealing how influenced they are by European and Anglo-American culture. By aligning themselves with their Anglo-American peers in the cultural phenomenon of Ophelia representations, they speak out as Brazilian artists in the international scenario and the booming field of global Shakespeare. Meanwhile, these artists' work – forged culturally and historically – also articulates a special preoccupation with the female in Brazil that could not have been expressed so freely in the past. The recent emergence of these representations in Brazil indicates a socio-cultural environment that allows such concerns to be articulated.

The images produced by these Brazilian artists reaffirm the need to revisit Ophelia and bring forth a different historical interpretation on the display and representation of women's bodies in Brazil. Rewriting the story with their bodies is another way of rewriting the history of visual representations of Ophelia. It is also an attempt to exorcise the repression and violence against women that is still so deep-rooted in Brazilian culture. Self-representation becomes an effective strategy for breaking with this tradition, stopping women from being put in the role of objects and allowing them to become autonomous subjects.

Notes

1. See Cristiane Busato Smith, *Representations of Ophelia in Victorian England [Representações da Ofélia de Shakespeare na Inglaterra Vitoriana]* (CESh Centro de Estudos Shakespearianos. Belo Horizonte: Editora Tessitura, in press). Based on the author's doctoral thesis (2007), available at http://www.educadores.diaadia.pr.gov.br/arquivos/File/2010/artigos_teses/2010/Ingles/teses/busato.pdf.
2. Elaine Showalter, "Representing Ophelia: Women, Madness, and the Responsibilities of Feminist Criticism," in *Shakespeare and the Question of Theory*, eds. Geoffrey Hartman and Patricia Parker (New York: Methuen, 1985), 77–94.
3. As Iyengar and Desmet point out, the social media profile photos of girls depicting themselves as Ophelia encourage these girls to become cultural producers – either through identification with the Shakespearean heroine or through the very criticism these profile shots can make of the history of the representation of Ophelia. Sujata Iyengar and Christy Desmet, "Rebooting Ophelia," in *The Afterlife of Ophelia*, eds. Kaara Peterson and Deanne Williams (New York: Palgrave, 2012), 59–78.
4. On the iconography of Ophelia, see Showalter, "Representing Ophelia" and also Georgianna Ziegler, *Shakespeare's Unruly Women* (Washington: Folger Shakespeare Library, 1997) and Carol Salomon Kiefer, ed. *The Myth and Madness of Ophelia* (Amherst, MA: Mead Art Museum, Amherst College, 2001). On global appropriations, see, for instance, Alexa Huang, "The Paradox of Female Agency: Ophelia and East Asian Sensibilities," in *The Afterlife of Ophelia*, eds. Kaara Peterson and Deanne Williams (New York: Palgrave, 2012), 79–99; and Delphine Gervais De Lafond, "Ophelie in Nineteenth-Century French Painting," in *The Afterlife of Ophelia*, eds. Kaara Peterson and Deanne Williams (New York: Palgrave, 2012), 169–92.
5. No image of Ophelia's death has penetrated the popular imaginary as much as Millais's *Ophelia*. Anne Thompson and Neil Taylor, editors of the most recent reviewed edition of *Hamlet* (Arden, 2006), not only pay tribute to Millais by putting his depiction of the muse on the front cover but also – like many critics – classify the paintings of Ophelia as pre- or post-Millais. (Thompson & Taylor, 2006, 27–8). Exhibited for the first time in 1852 at the Royal Academy Exhibition, *Ophelia* is now part of the Tate Gallery collection in London. See http://www.tate.org.uk/art/artworks/millais-ophelia-n01506 (accessed April 2, 2015).
6. See John Berger, *Ways of Seeing* (London: Penguin Books, 1972); Griselda Pollock, Vision and Difference (London: Routledge, 2003); Frances Borzello, *Seeing Ourselves: Women's Self-Portraits* (London: Thames & Hudson Ltd, 1998); and Laura Mulvey, *Visual and Other Pleasures: Language, Discourse, Society* (London: Palgrave, 1975).
7. In Brazil, women were first granted admission to Academia Nacional de Belas Artes in 1892.
8. Historians of feminist art like Elisabeth Bronfen and Griselda Pollock have pieced together Siddal's story and claim an important place for her as a poet and painter in the history of art in the nineteenth century. See Elisabeth Bronfen, *Over her dead body: Death, femininity and the aesthetic* (Manchester University Press, 1992), and Pollock, Vision (2003).
9. See, for instance, Remedios Perni, "At the Margins: Ophelia in Modern and Contemporary Photography," in *The Afterlife of Ophelia*, eds. Kaara Peterson and Deanne Williams (New York: Palgrave, 2012), 193–212. See also Michael Duncan, "Tracing Mendieta," *Art in America* 87 (1999): 110–13; and Rose-Lee Goldberg, "Be My Mirror: Performance and the Moving Image," Saatchi Gallery, 2009.

10 Ana Mendieta heralds a genre known in the visual arts as "earth body art" or "land art."
11 These images of Mendieta's actually conjure up Gertrude's description of Ophelia's death, who "like a creature native and indued / Unto that element" was dragged to her "muddy death" (4.7).
12 See Luana Saturnino Tvardovskas, *Dramatização dos Corpos: Arte Contemporânea de Mulheres no Brasil e América Latina*. Ano de obtenção: 2013. Tese de doutorado. Unicamp, pp. 25–6.
13 Cynthia Andersen Sarti, "O Feminismo Brasileiro desde os Anos 1970: Revisitando uma Trajetória," *Revista Estudos Feministas*, 12, núm. 2 (2004): 35–50. Florianópolis: Universidade Federal de Santa Catarina.
14 See Tvardovskas, *Dramatização* (2013), 36.
15 See Lucia Castanho, "*Ofélia: Percurso Íntimo de uma Imagem Idealizada*," 175 f. Tese de Doutorado em Educação, Arte e História da Cultura. Universidade Presbiteriana Mackenzie, São Paulo, 2013; Gabriela Fregoneis, "Monólogos de Ofélia," in Congresso Internacional "Criadores Sobre Outras Obras – CSO'2010, 2010, Lisbon. Monólogos de Ofélia. Lisbon – Portugal: Universidade de Belas-Artes de Lisboa, 2010. v. 1. 125–9; Gabriela Fregoneis. "Faces de Ofélia," in Fazendo Gênero 9 - Diásporas, diversidades, deslocamentos, 2010, Florianópolis. Faces de Ofélia. Florianópolis: UFSC, 2010; Lucia Sander, *Ofélia explica ou o renascimento segundo Ofelia e cia* (Brasília: Minha Gráfica e Editora, 2009).
16 This perpetuation has come about through attitudes such as ignoring the work of women, objectifying women's bodies in paintings and films, romanticizing the sexual exploitation of women in narratives, employing criteria to exclude women's creativity, or even operating symbolic systems that consider the female as a dark rival for the male.
17 Gabriela Fregoneis, "Ofélia." Email to the author. November 17, 2011.
18 See, for instance, Tony Richardson's 1969 production of *Hamlet*, or the Korean adaptation of *Hamlet* titled *Ophelia: Sister, Come to My Bed* (1995, dir. Kim Kwang-bo).
19 Egon Schiele (1890–1918) was an Austrian painter linked to expressionism and known for his grotesque paintings of naked women and transfigured human beings. Schiele is believed to have had an incestuous relationship with his sister, Gertrude. He was arrested in 1912 for seducing a 13-year-old girl. During the trial the charges were dropped, although he was found guilty of immorality after "pornographic" drawings were found in his house. The biographical data on Egon Schiele are important for Gabriela Fregoneis, in that they sustain her interpretation of an incestuous relationship.
20 *Ensaio.Hamlet* is an important reference in Fregoneis's work on Ophelia, as seen in her reflections about the process of staging the play in her article, "Representação e Presentação no Teatro Stanislavskiano." (Gabriela Fregoneis, "Representação e Presentação no Teatro Stanislavskiano" *VI Jornada Latino-Americana de Estudos Teatrais*, Blumenau. VI (2013): 21–5).
21 One example is Tony Richardson's film version of *Hamlet* (1969), which suggests Ophelia had an incestuous relationship with Laertes. Another example is the Korean play by Jo Kwang-hwa titled *Ophelia: Sister, Come to My Bed* (2005), which also implies incest with Laertes.
22 See Brandford Griffith, "Native Stools on the Gold Coast." *Journal of the Royal African Society*, 4, n. 5 (1905): 290. The stool could also be an allusion to the ducking stools used to punish and/or torture transgressive women in Shakespeare's day. Offenders were chained to the stool, which was then dunked in water.
23 In *Against Our Will: Men, Women and Rape* (New York: Fawcett Books, 1975), Susan Brownmiller argues that rape is a crime that affects all women, since it is the unspoken

threat that represses all female activity. For Brownmiller, rape is therefore the core of patriarchal control.
24 See Adrienne Rich, "When We Dead Awaken: Writing as Re-Vision." *College English* 34:1 (1972): 18–32. The essay was written in 1971; it is reprinted in Adrienne Rich, *On Lies, Secrets, and Silence* (New York: Norton, 1979).
25 Lucia Castanho has a degree in art from Faculdade Santa Marcelina (1983), a degree in law from Faculdade de Direito de Sorocaba (1981), a master's degree in art education and the history of culture from Universidade Mackenzie (2005), and a doctorate from Universidade Presbiteriana Mackenzie (2013).
26 Lucia Castanho's work can be accessed on her blog: https://luciacastanho.wordpress.com.
27 Lucia Castanho, "Fotos," email to the author, November 21, 2011.
28 In "The Philosophy of Composition," published in 1846, Edgar Allan Poe states, "The Death Then of a Beautiful Woman Is Unquestionably the Most Poetical Topic in the World," in *Poemas e Ensaios*, ed. Edgar Allan Poe (São Paulo: Globo, 1999), 3. ed. revista.
29 Contemporary photographs of young Ophelias immersed in bathtubs and swimming pools are abundant on the internet. They are posted on blogs and Flickr groups like "Ophelia's pool," which also has a section of bathtub images. Also see the article "Ophelia in Bath Tubs and Swimming Pools" from the website Ophelia and Web 2.0 by Professor Alan R. Young, available at http://www.opheliapopularculture.com/home/ophelia-essay-title-page
30 Lucia Castanho, "Vestido," email to the author. December 15, 2014.
31 The use of autobiographical, domestic, and daily objects is a feature of the contemporary artist's work (Tvardovska, 75). According to Tvardovska, these elements "deconstruct the conservative nature of definitions like home, potentializing this space as a libertarian proposal" (78).
32 In: Lucia Castanho, *Ofélia:Percurso Íntimo de uma Imagem Idealizada*. 175 f. Tese de Doutorado em Educação, Arte e História da Cultura. Universidade Presbiteriana Mackenzie, São Paulo, 2013.
33 See Gaston Bachelard, *A água e os sonhos: ensaio sobre a imaginação a matéria*. Trad. Antonio de Pádua Danesi. São Paulo: Martins Fontes, 2002, 84.
34 This radical appropriation of Ophelia's story is nothing new. To cite one example, in Melissa Murray's play *Ophelia* (1979), Ophelia turns lesbian and runs off with a woman to join a guerrilla community.
35 Henrietta Rae (1859–1928) was a well-known Victorian painter who mainly portrayed literary themes. A feminist sympathizer, she kept her maiden name after marrying painter Ernest Normand. *Ophelia* (1890), like her other paintings, was submitted to the scrutiny of her husband and other male painters. Taking on board their suggestions, Rae made several alterations to the positions of the king's and queen's heads on the left-hand side of the painting. See Arthur Fish, *Henrietta Rae [Mrs. Ernest Normand]* (London, Cassell & Co., 1905), 57.
36 Photo on the right: Nora da Silva (*née* Angelita Helena Margarita de Silva Ferro) as Ophelia, photo by Hulton Archive/Getty Images, 1905; photo on the left: Mrs. Beerbohm Tree (*née* Helen Maud Holt) as Ophelia, photo-engraving, 1892. This scene would be more striking if Sander had projected photos of the actresses wearing black. In my research, I found photos of Nora da Silva as Ophelia, wearing black, http://intothebeautifulnew.tumblr.com/post/43860763072/ophelia-in-hamlet-1904-played-by-miss-n-de-silva (accessed September 15, 2015) but I found no images of Helen Maud wearing black.
37 Ellen Terry, *The Story of My Life* (London: Hutchinson and Co., 1908), 155–6.

38 Lyrics of Lucia Sander's rap: "You think the world's over / Well it's not / You're flat on the ground / You think you can't cope / But when life shoves you / You raise up your hand / And shove it back / Don't give up, don't give up / Without asking or warning your blood frees you / You join the gang / You let it all out / With no holds barred, no fear, no permission / Don't give up, don't give up / You think you're already dead / Look at me, look at me / What happened to you / But if the time's not right and / This moment's not yours / The sap don't dry up / No it don't / Ophelia, who'd have thought: singing rap in the *favela*! / Don't give up" (my translation).

39 In *Reviving Ophelia: Saving the Selves of Adolescent Girls*, Mary Pipher suggests that Ophelia dies because she can't grow up as an individual and so she loses her true "self," and is reduced to a mere object in the lives of others. See Mary Pipher, *Reviving Ophelia; Saving the Selves of Adolescent Girls* (New York: Ballantine Books, 1995).

40 The painting in question is *Ophelia*, c. 1864, by Ellen Terry's first husband, George Frederic Watts.

41 Some of the examples given by Showalter (1985) and Kiefer (2001) include the actresses Susan Mountfort and Henrieta Smithson (who also posed as Ophelia) and Lillian Gish, the model Elizabeth Siddal, and Russian painter Marie Bashkirtseff.

42 Coppélia Kahn argues that the contemporary representation of Ophelia on the internet is a complex problem for critics in that many versions (generally by adolescents) that bring to mind the pre-Raphaelite Ophelias offer no critical perspective (Kahn, 240). Kahn wonders what this continuing social fascination with the representation of Ophelia means, and recognizes the need for Ophelia to be represented in self-aware parodies so that "girls do not drown with her but rather, wonder why, in the playworld of *Hamlet*, her girlhood ends that way" (240). Coppélia Kahn, "Ophelia Then, Now, Hereafter," in *The Afterlife of Ophelia*, eds. Kaara Peterson and Deanne Williams (New York: Palgrave, 2012), 231–244.

43 See Kiefer, *Myth and Madness* (2001), 37–8 and H.R. Coursen, "Ophelia in Performance in the Twentieth Century" in Kiefer, 53–72 at p. 61.

9 Mapping Shakespeare in street art[1]

Mariacristina Cavecchi

Figure 9.1 The photograph of "Shakespeare toilet" (Matt from London) (Ian Press Photography) is published on the website The World's Best Photos of Shoreditch (www.flickr.com/photos/londonmatt/9580501367; last access 30 August 2016). CC creative commons.

On a wall in Shoreditch, an area of London that has become one of London's coolest urban areas and a hub of creativity, there is a graffito that has been photographed and published on the web, where it has been called (or tagged) "Shakespeare toilet" (Figure 9.1); next to the image of a fit-looking, well-muscled young man, sitting on a toilet in a thoughtful pose and busy with his smartphone, a notice written in black letters announces: "ON THIS SITE STOOD THE CURTAIN THEATRE (1577–1599) WILLIAM SHAKESPEARE FIRST PERFORMED "HENRY V" AND "ROMEO AND JULIET" AND ACTED ON STAGE HIMSELF".[2] The notice is inaccurate, since "The Curtain" vanished from historical records only in 1628 (and not in 1599), but, nonetheless, it briefly relates the fact that Shakespeare's company used this theatre for at least two years, from 1597 until "The Globe" on Bankside was ready, and that it was on its stage that *Henry V* and probably *Romeo and Juliet* were first performed. The writing on the wall probably appeared after the discovery, in June 2012, of the remains of "The Curtain" in Hewett Street, which caused great excitement, not just within the Shakespearean community.[3] As always with street art, it is difficult to ascertain precisely when and why this graffiti came into existence and therefore one can only make mere suppositions as to the occasion that gave life to it. However, despite its inaccuracy and the many unanswered questions it poses (first of all, whether the man on the toilet is actually meant to be Shakespeare), because of the references to the Curtain and to Shakespeare, Shakespearean scholars, who are perhaps too eager to find Shakespeare everywhere and who are, besides, not fully aware of the grammar and secrets of street art, might be tempted to interpret the whole wall as a desecrating, but at the same time a strikingly fresh, image of the Elizabethan playwright, conceived as a modern man dealing with a modern communication tool. Indeed, the whole wall seems to invite its viewers to embark on an exciting journey to track down the many new and different versions of Shakespeare's stories scattered in the walls not only of London but of the whole world.

Once that invitation has been accepted, one very soon realizes just how many traces of Shakespeare have been disseminated in the graffiti world; conversely, it becomes evident how the grammar of graffiti has often been used by theatre, cinema, advertising and visual art to bring Shakespeare and his work up to date for today's audiences. It is for this reason that I would like to propose a possible new methodology for approaching the study of Shakespeare through the analysis of verbal and visual quotations from his plays in graffiti and street art – two relatively new but important cultural phenomena.

Since its explosion in the mid- to late Sixties in Philadelphia and New York, graffiti writing has spread very quickly around the world, and within this medium the quotations of lines from Shakespeare have also very quickly proliferated and continue to do so, even though it is impossible to say when this Shakespeare-in-graffiti boom started. It is not likely that, at the beginning, the Elizabethan playwright was a source of inspiration for the first graffitists, who were mostly from the proletariat and part of gangs who generally intended to defend their territory or turf.[4]

Street art is nowadays the object of considerable academic interest, and quite a lot of quotations from Shakespeare can be spotted on the walls; but while the Tate Modern held an exhibition on street art in London in 2008, and *The Bridges of Graffiti* exhibition was part of the 2015 Venice Biennale, "Shakespeare and street art" is a field which has been largely neglected by Shakespeareans, even though it can, I believe, offer meaningful contributions to Shakespeare studies.[5] To my knowledge, there are no studies or databases devoted to this subject, which could indeed become another domain of intercultural Shakespeare reproduction well worth investigating; besides, it may contribute to fill in those "gaps" or "silences" in the study of Shakespeare's global reach highlighted by Alexa Huang.[6] It may also serve as the title for one chapter that remains missing in the two huge volumes of *Shakespeares after Shakespeare: An Encyclopedia of the Bard in Mass Media and Popular Culture*, Richard Burt's heroic attempt to archive the present cultural proliferation and fragmentation of Shakespeare in mass culture.[7] It is not my intention to write that chapter here, but merely to suggest how important it might be, and put forward some suggestions as to the reasons, the critical and theoretical tools and the methodology required for writing it.

First of all, the study of the relationship between Shakespeare and street art would allow us to tackle the work of the Elizabethan playwright from a very different vantage point, thus helping to gain a better understanding of the "process of negotiation, transposition, cooperation, revision, and contestation"[8] between Shakespeare and marginal subcultures. The practice of graffiti, which is the result of an unsanctioned, extemporary, individual and anonymous (generally, therefore, illegal) action, appropriates the most institutional of the authors and by this act of appropriation, frees his work from the stranglehold of institutions, both academic and theatrical. Undeniably, street art seems to have reinvented and reinvigorated the work of the Elizabethan playwright. On the one hand, it has offered and continues to offer a fuller and less predetermined Shakespearean experience, based on dismembered and/or disfigured Shakespeare lines and on unexpected images that are often difficult to interpret. On the other hand, it has restored his plays' subversive and destabilizing nature and their capacity to articulate a wide variety of complementary/conflicting meanings, some of which challenge the establishment.

Moreover, while it is site-specific and therefore underwrites local, traditional values, street art seems to respond as well to the need for a more transnational gaze, being the first truly global art movement; as street artist and gallery owner Charley Uzzell-Edwards (or "Pure Evil") explains, "It's fuelled by the internet. If someone is doing a piece in Panama, we'll know about it the next day."[9] It is precisely thanks to its global nature that this area of investigation may contribute to explore the way Shakespeare negotiates between global and local politics and aesthetics. Most artists are concerned with the physical, aesthetic and socio-political nature of their locations, and their aim is often "to play with the city by creating images that fit in the urban context and interact with the environment, to create a link between what they are painting and where they are painting it."[10] At the same time, however, the language they use is somehow quite accessible and universal. It is perhaps not accidental that the plays by Shakespeare most quoted from or referred to by graffiti writers are those that people know best, or that are most frequently staged: *Hamlet*, *Romeo and Juliet*, *Macbeth*. These are also the plays that fascinate these young artists because their main characters are generally the same age as them. Shakespeare's plays are torn to pieces and his lines and images, inevitably frozen by centuries of re-readings and by a myopic preoccupation with the canon, are re-appropriated on the walls in the form of fragments or tatters, either to express individual feelings or to tell stories of collective interest; thus, they come to share with street art the paradox of being at once criminalized yet acclaimed, accessible yet cryptic, anonymous yet identifiable, site-specific and at the same time global.

Finally, as street art is rooted in the creativity of youth culture, a reconnaissance, cataloguing and analysis of Shakespeare-related graffiti may also offer new incentives and motivation to students, who might gain a better understanding and appreciation of Shakespeare by perceiving him as alive and still meaningful.[11] It has been proved that, in the language classroom, the rebellious nature of graffiti "piques student interest and allows an introduction to learning to observe and analyse a culture."[12]

While I make a case for the relevance of the analysis of Shakespeare in street art, I am obviously aware of the methodological problems that researchers face when building a database of Shakespeare-related graffiti and developing a taxonomy of their locations, forms and intentions. I am moreover aware of the question of the legitimacy of this corpus. Just as Douglas Lanier has pointed out for film spin-offs and citations, "the line between legitimate and illegitimate offspring is never entirely clear."[13] It is not always easy to distinguish between the different uses of references to Shakespeare's works (whether these are unintentional or intentional, meaningful or superficial, explicit or hidden). An accurate study of Shakespeare-related graffiti should be grounded in a multidisciplinary analysis that requires not just the skills of Shakespeare scholars but also those of art historians and experts in urban studies or cultural studies, to name but a few. Furthermore, to understand the intentions that lie behind the references to Shakespeare's works, it is necessary not only to know the local cultures and the languages of the countries the graffiti belong to, but also to be aware of the different forms of graffiti and street art in terms of their structures, functions and aims. Therefore, just as for all other forms of Shakespearean quotations in the mass media, it would be crucial to assemble a multidisciplinary team of scholarly researchers.

A PROVISIONAL MAP

The first task is of course to carry out a reconnaissance and a mapping of all Shakespeare-related graffiti. This is obviously a very arduous task, since there is no systematic way of locating Shakespeare quotations in graffiti and street art, and, owing to their ephemeral nature, their whereabouts and duration are not easy to foresee. A first attempt to collect the Shakespeare-related graffiti occurrences is nonetheless possible thanks to the internet and its numerous search engines, so that, even though there is still no website specifically dedicated to the theme or an archive collecting Shakespeare-related graffiti, some of these works can be found while surfing the net.

After an initial collection and provisional filing of the material, it would be possible to distinguish between 1) a first corpus of the Shakespeare-related graffiti which is sprayed, scrawled, pasted or painted on to building walls, handrails, shop shutters or trains in capital cities, small villages or in the countryside; and 2) a second corpus of "fictional" Shakespeare-related graffiti, which proliferate in cinema, television, theatre and advertising.

Shakespeare in the streets

Following in the footsteps of Iain Sinclair's *Skating on Thin Eyes*, one might walk through the streets of London (and indeed of the whole world) armed with a camera and a notebook, "recording and retrieving the messages on walls, lampposts, doorjambs."[14] One might also surf the net in order to spot the many and various occurrences of Shakespeare in graffiti that are disseminated in its meanders, and might perhaps even venture to "tag" them, following the increasingly popular web practice for adding personal categorizations to artefacts of information. A first corpus of the Shakespeare-related graffiti may be made thanks to the numerous websites dedicated to graffiti art and photography. Just to name a few, Streetsy. com, Artcrimes and WoosterCollective.com collect thousands of pictures of street art from all over the world as well as artists' and fans' comments and ideas, while Flickr is a popular website where users can share and embed personal photographs.[15]

Thus, Shakespeare exists in the domains of both the street and the net, negotiating between the physicality and materiality of street art and the immateriality of its virtual replica, between the contingency of a precise location and the globality of the web dis-location, with implications that will be clearer soon. Compared to the often rewarding and totally unexpected experience of seeing graffiti in the street, the encounter with graffiti or street art via photographs posted online is obviously incomplete, and yet, it must be considered that, were it not for the numerous photographical publications and websites focused on graffiti, the movement would quite literally been lost. Besides, the internet is a powerful tool of dissemination, and therefore the primary vehicle for encountering the works. According to Zabou, a French artist living in London, "Instagram and Facebook gives [sic] you the potential to build a large audience very quickly. . . . People can be anywhere in the world and see what you're doing."[16]

After this preliminary reconnaissance, it might finally be possible to set up a first corpus of Shakespeare-related graffiti, "an unpredictable anthology" where the Elizabethan playwright would figure among the catalysts of what Sinclair calls the "spites and spasms"[17] of our contemporary life and one of the protagonists of what street artist Banksy, in his film *Exit through the Gift Shop* (2011), has defined as "the biggest counter-cultural movement since Pop."[18]

Unsanctioned Shakespearean lines or imagery spring up everywhere in unorthodox ways that question the traditional reception of the Elizabethan playwright and the process of negotiation between him and the city's subcultures. The very fact that in the streets these pieces appear suddenly and unexpectedly from nowhere and are often viewed quickly and distractedly while passing by implies a new and different way of encountering the Bard that goes against the common viewing experience we are used to when we see a play. It is also important that the Shakespeare who surfaces everywhere on the walls is a fragmented Shakespeare lurking in short but precise quotations from his plays, in desecrating and/or parodic echoes of his lines, or in lines which have been dismembered or slightly manipulated, so that the viewer is often compelled to make an effort to recognize their original source and interpret them. Moreover, uncontrolled as they are by any political or cultural institution, all these Shakespeare-related graffiti contribute to the unauthorized visual alteration of the city spaces and to graffiti writers' questioning of the boundaries between public and private uses of space; indeed, they, too, "infuse the public sphere with moments of fracture, spaces of disruption and subjective uses of territory."[19] Furthermore, Shakespeare-related graffiti, like most forms of street art, are relegated to and interact with those marginal spaces that are "unrestricted, unobstructed, exposed, empty, isolated, forgotten, unmanaged and bleak," "not necessarily liminal by way of geography, but rather by way of use."[20] Intriguingly, those interstitial spaces, or non-spaces, that "are part of the infrastructure that creates a city but does not define it (at least not from a consumption-driven capitalist standpoint)," might be considered as the modern equivalent of the "liberties" of Elizabethan London: those areas that were part of the city yet fell outside the jurisdiction of the Lord Mayor; places of anarchy that were similarly transformed into spaces of free expression and beauty by the creative outburst of theatre productions.

Another short documentary also worth remembering here is *Who Owns the Street* (2013),[21] by Australian graffiti artist Peter Drew, the author of a series of Shakespearean graffiti that will be discussed in the next paragraph. Drew explores the theme of the ownership of streets and public spaces and highlights the complex relationships between "graffiti writing" and "post-graffiti art." Notoriously, graffiti writing, or more colloquially "graff," is the movement "most closely associated with hip hop culture (though it pre-dates it),"[22] whose central concern is the "tag" or the signature of the author; what is generally known as "post-graffiti art" (or simply "street art") is characterized by "wide-ranging stylistic, technical and material innovations, which place less emphasis on lettering with markers and spray-paint and more weight on fashioning varied artistic interventions into the cultural landscape of a city."[23] Whereas graff is "functionally inaccessible to outsiders," who have no "direct path to entry into its meaning and purpose,"[24] and therefore is generally misunderstood and even despised by city councils and common people, post-graffiti art produces less visually cryptic art and considers the question of communication and community as a valuable one. Even though still illegal, the latter form of street art is often tolerated and sometimes is actually the result of commissioned public art projects.[25]

Street Shakespeare lives in a constant tension between the grammars of graffiti and post-graffiti: his works are appropriated by writers who spray-paint his verses or elaborate tags starting from the names of his characters, and by artists who explore more formal art techniques such as stencilling, printmaking and painting to create largely figurative works inspired by Shakespeare's plays.

After an initial collection and a provisional filing of the material, it will be possible to distinguish between two main groups of urban graffiti related to Shakespeare:

1A Shakespeare-related graffiti and/or post-graffiti that are the result of an extemporary, individual and anonymous action (generally illegal);
1B Shakespeare-related graffiti and/or post-graffiti that are part of precise artistic projects, such as Peter Drew's "Emoticon Hamlet" in Glasgow or Blub's "L'arte sa nuotare" ("Art knows how to swim") in Florence – which, incidentally, are also illegal.

SHAKESPEARE IN TATTERS EVERYWHERE

The first subgroup (1A) includes many very different kinds of works. First of all, we must consider that there are a large number of tags appropriating names of

Shakespearean characters as pseudonyms. Among these, the most frequently used are "Romeo" or "Juliet" and, since a tag name "can serve to convey an attitude or describe how writers want to represent themselves within the subculture,"[26] one might speculate on the reasons for such a choice. Does the writer want to stress any actual connection with the young characters in Shakespeare's play and their rebellion against the established order of the adult generation? One can never know for sure whether these tags evoking Shakespeare (even though perhaps they do so only to Shakespeareans) are marks of transgression and assertions of the graffiti writer's alter ego. According to Sinclair, one's tag is everything, "as jealously defended as the Coke or the Disney [logos]".[27] CAY161 once said: "The Name is the faith of graffiti."[28] It is a search for and affirmation of identity. Taggers understand their names as representations of the self, evolve their tags into individualized logos and, "like monks labouring on a Book of Hours,"[29] refine their art by infinite acts of repetition. Throwies,[30] essentially larger versions of tags consisting of outlined, traditionally "bubble" letters which are grouped together and sometimes filled in with a different colour,[31] represent another illegal manifestation of the writer's name that is executed at a frenetic pace as a way of publicizing and potentially making a name for oneself on the graffiti scene. They pop up from the walls, attacking the passers-by with their colourful energy and even perhaps forcing them to come to terms with their possible Shakespearean filiation. It is possible that these writers consider themselves as new Romeos and Juliets transgressing all laws and rules. It is also possible that they are playing ironically with a name that Shakespeare's Juliet unmasked as an arbitrary and meaningless convention: "What's in a name? that which we call a rose / By any other name would smell as sweet; / So Romeo would, were he not Romeo call'd, / Retain that dear perfection which he owes / Without that title" (*Romeo and Juliet*, 2.2.43–47).

Apart from the many tags and throwies inspired by Shakespearean names, the Shakespearean intertext on the walls is not easy to trace, even though it mostly consists of references to the better-known comedies and tragedies. Shakespeare's plays are most often quoted in support of individual and anonymous declarations of love. This is the case of Romeo's well-known "What light through yonder window breaks" (*Romeo and Juliet*, 2.2.2), written on the handrail of a staircase,[32] or of Helena's lines in *A Midsummer Night's Dream* (2.1), "I'll follow thee and make a heaven of hell. To die upon the hand I love so well," written with chalk on a wall in the countryside – a message, the latter, that was photographed and posted on Flickr with the comment: "I'm sure when Shakespeare was writing his sonnets, he thought 'hey, those couplets would look awfully good on a stone wall someday.' "[33] More philosophical considerations have been written on a wall in Leake Street in London, a road running under Waterloo Station also known as the

"Banksy Tunnel" or "Graffiti Tunnel." Hamlet's well-known lines to his friend Horatio, "There are more things in heaven and earth / Than are dreamt of in your philosophy" (1.5.167–8), are sprayed in red capital letters on a graffiti previously written by someone else.[34] Shakespearean verses can even be found on the walls in Italy, where political graffiti broke out in the years of the youth protest in the Sixties, even though the name of Shakespeare does not appear in the list of the people most quoted by graffiti artists made by the political police in Elio Petri's 1970 film *Indagine di un cittadino al di sopra di ogni sospetto* [*Investigation of a Citizen above Suspicion*]. Times have changed and today our walls tend instead to tell stories of economic difficulties and crisis, such as in Petruchio's lines in *The Taming of the Shrew*: "I come to wive it wealthily in Padua; If wealthily, then happily in Padua" (I.ii.75–76) . . . – a graffiti sprayed on a wall in Verona,[35] one of the richest cities in north-east Italy, which has nonetheless not been spared by the economic depression.

There are also many "post-graffiti" works. On a wall in Śródmieście, Danzica, Poland, a middle-aged couple are eloping with their orange cat in a car equipped with the meaningful numberplate "Romek & Julka,"[36] perhaps a presage of their star-crossed voyage. A wall photographed by Keith Palmer and posted on Flickr is also dedicated to the star-crossed lovers. The photo shows a colourful graffiti painted on a brick wall that comprises five different scenes illustrated in overlapping black frames: it is an abridged street version of *Romeo and Juliet*'s plot,[37] but we do not know how to explain it. We do not know who did it, or where or when, since the website does not give this kind of information. This is a recurrent problem. Again, we do not know the location of the graffiti written by a betrayed and injured lover who draws inspiration from Shakespeare's poetic vein, when he or she writes on a wall "Write that bitch a sonnet. Bitches love sonnets" next to the portrait of the playwright.[38] Neither have we known the location or the intentions behind Sonnet 116 written on a brick wall. The photo of this sonnet on the wall is posted on the BuzzFeed Community website, as one of "20 Awesome Examples of Literary Graffiti";[39] in the list there is also a blood-red stencil quotation from one of the witches in *Macbeth* written in capital letters saying: "SOMETHING WICKED THIS WAY COMES" (4.1.45). Street art being a form of art deeply rooted in the territory, the fact that we do not know where the graffiti are located makes the process of understanding the reasons behind them hard.

Thus, the same line can have a totally different meaning according to the urban context. Take the case of the above-mentioned quotation from *Romeo and Juliet* (2.2.2). The vaguely romantic aura associated with it seems to vanish or at least to create a striking contrast with its environment when the lines are written on the wall of what appear to be wartime ruins in the midst of which one can still see a heavy machine gun with the phrase "the war goes on" written on it.[40]

Even Hamlet's famous "to be or not to be" acquires new shades of meanings depending on its locations. On a white wall marked by a number ("-4") and a grey heart, a long quotation from the monologue ("To be, or not to be, that is the question. / Whether tis nobler in the mind to suffer / the slings and arrows of outrageous fortune / or to take arms against a sea of troubles / and by opposing end them"), written in black paint, can be considered as true to the original meaning as the expression of solitude and restlessness of a modern-day Danish prince,[41] who is perhaps counting the days that lead up to his suicide (-4), while other occurrences seem to give voice to feelings and messages that are very distant from those expressed in the original tragedy. A wall in Duszniki Zdrój, Poland, offers a comic adaptation of the same line by morphing it into a grammatically incorrect phrase: "two beer or not to beer," a dilemma that fits in the visual joke where two cartoon characters, one male and one female, drink two jugs of beer each while happily seated on a sort of red missile carrying the written "Shakebeer" and are perhaps ready to embark on an extraordinary journey into alcohol-fuelled unconsciousness.[42] More thoughtful distortions of the quote are to be found in a stencilled "T.B. or not T.B. / That is the question"[43] that evokes the spectre of tuberculosis, or in the stylized image of a man with an expression that may be repentance, regret or fear as he is apparently threatened by a large hand pointing at him. His arms, eyes and cheeks are red, and as he holds a skull in his hand, he asks himself, "To be or what?" as if afraid to give himself an answer.[44] A political use is made of these lines in one of the many graffiti that have flourished in the wake of the revolutionary wave of demonstrations, riots and civil wars of the so-called Arab Spring.[45] This[46] may be found on a wall in downtown Cairo, in Tahrir Square, which has been called "the epicenter of Egypt's revolution"[47] and which, like nearby Mohamed Mahmoud Street, has, since the 25th of January revolution, effectively become an open-air gallery showcasing street art on a wide range of political and social issues[48] (a phenomenon that is even more surprising if one considers that the Egyptian youth had never before written illegally on public surfaces).[49] This graffiti is quite different from the huge murals which may be seen on the walls of Cairo and is most probably not the work of a single artist but rather of various and extemporaneous participants. On this wall the most famous of all Shakespeare's lines, "to be or not to be," is quoted in connection with the demand for a political and social change ("together for a better Egypt") and is to be interpreted as a battle cry summoning the imminent 2011 Arab spring ("with our rivloution [sic] be or not to be"), as if to confirm both Shakespeare's vocation for playing a central role in the forging and articulation of many (not just the British) different national identities[50] and Margaret Litvin's argument according to which "to be or not to be" is the defining slogan of Arab politics; as she writes, Arab writers read this famous line "not as a meditation on the individual's place in the world but as an argument about collective political identity."[51]

A political intention may also have inspired the artist of the wall in Bree Street, Johannesburg. Here a portrait of Nelson Mandela stands between two quotations from *Macbeth*.[52] The lines on the left side of the portrait are those delivered by Macbeth when he is ready to kill Duncan and therefore calls upon the heavens to envelop the world in darkness: "Stars, hide your fires! / Let not light see my / black and deep desires" (*Macbeth*, 1.4.50–51); those on the right side – "And nothing is / but what is not" (1.3.142) – are uttered as an aside after the witches have told Macbeth the prophecy. Both are pithy passages expressing universal truths. The wall may have been painted after the revival of Msomi's critically acclaimed *uMabatha – The Zulu Macbeth* (1971) in post-apartheid Johannesburg in 1995 and may allude to Nelson Mandela's remark to Msomi about his epic rewriting of Shakespeare's Scottish thane as the warrior Shaka Zulu (1787–1828): "The similarities between Shakespeare's Macbeth and our own Shaka become a glaring reminder that the world is, philosophically, a very small place."[53] In 1995, following his release from prison and election as president of South Africa, Nelson Mandela encouraged Msomi to restage *uMabatha*, seeing it as "the perfect opportunity to highlight both the problems of, and vast opportunity for, change from so many years of apartheid in South Africa."[54] As is always the case, though, these are all speculations since one cannot know the precise intention behind the realization of this work, nor can one be sure that the pairing of Macbeth with Mandela is the coherent work of a single writer rather than the accidental result of different hands.

Understanding the reasons that motivate a piece of street art can be very hard. Sometimes graffiti quoting Shakespeare's verses are aware of their sources, while at others the verses are disembodied from the context of the quotation – they have become post-hermeneutic, they no longer have, that is, any meaningful relation to the Elizabethan playwright. Shakespearean scholars, however, may be tempted to interpret in Shakespearean terms any graffiti that vaguely echoes lines or images from his plays. What, for example, is one to make of the graffiti portraying a huge black cat spitting light blue flames paired with the word "MACBETH"?[55] Should one imagine that it has some kind of relationship with the Shakespearean tragedy, or not? It is a difficult question to answer, even though Shakespeareans will always be tempted to see Shakespeare lingering on. Maureen J. Haldeman's photograph of the wall where a second graffiti on the same subject was painted may offer some help (Ill. 9).[56] In this second case, next to the graffiti of the cat spitting Macbethian flames we find a comment sprayed in black paint that may indeed strengthen the connection between the graffiti and Shakespeare: "often enough luck will save a man if his courage hold". Though it sounds like a parody, the comment may somehow serve to relate the graffiti to the story of Macbeth, a brave soldier and an unlucky king, but even with this backing, we are still in the realm of suppositions and hypothesis.

Finally, this first sub-group of "Shakespeare in the street" includes a very important cluster of post-graffiti representing Shakespeare's face. The proliferation of images of Shakespeare's faces on our city walls, from New York[57] to Ekaterinburg (in Russia),[58] from Rio de Janeiro[59] to Hirai (in Japan),[60] seems to work similarly and affect the urban environment in the same way as tags do. In the above-mentioned film directed by street artist Banksy, *Exit through the Gift Shop*, another street artist, Shepard Fairey, who experimented with the power of repetition through his "Andre the Giant Has a Posse" (... OBEY ...) sticker campaign and his successful Barack Obama "Hope" poster designed for the 2008 presidential election, explains this strategy of overexposure: the more an image is "out there, the more important it seems, the more people want to know what it is. The more they ask each other."[61] Unsurprisingly, a poster of Shakespeare from the Droeshout portrait, wearing aviator sunglasses, appears in the film among other cultural icons of the past (Albert Einstein, Charlie Chaplin, Marilyn Monroe), appropriated and manipulated by French street artist Thierry Guetta (also knowns as Mr. Brainwash).

Confronted with the veritable dissemination of recognizable variations of the Droeshout portrait from the First Folio, in which Shakespeare's image is often "the subject of carnivalesque inversion,"[62] with a moustache, aviator glasses, a red tongue or grotesque pink gums with skull-like teeth, one may legitimately ask whether this manipulation may not itself be considered tagging, a mark of "tribal" and transgressive practice, such as Jean Baudrillard describes in his important essay on graffiti, *KOOL KILLER, or The Insurrection of Signs*: "a scream, an interjection, an anti-discourse, as the waste of all syntactic, poetic and political development, as the smallest radical element that cannot be caught by any organized discourse."[63] One might even eventually discover that Shakespeare's face, rather than being simply a commercially valuable marketing brand, might actually be something of far greater value: an image capable of investing streets, neighbourhoods and even nations with new life and meaning. This is what has been happening in countries such as Egypt and South Africa, and even in Afghanistan, where in 2005, after more than twenty years of war, Corinne Jaber staged a production of Shakespeare's *Love's Labour's Lost*.[64] This dissemination of spray-painted or stencilled images of Shakespeare faces, it should moreover be noted, shares the unique dynamic between authorship and anonymity which characterizes the practice of tagging; indeed, we may go as far as to say that the many anonymous graffiti versions of his faces and his plays prove Roland Barthes' assumption concerning the death of the author. On the one hand, a tag allows the writer to be recognized throughout a city while maintaining anonymity and at the same time gaining notoriety within the subculture. On the other hand, by their very nature, graffiti and street art seem to resist the idea of the individual author who, as Barthes argues, is responsible for "releasing a single theological meaning (the 'message' of the Author-God)" and is allied with other oppressive principles of authority in the dominant culture. Even though the walls of the world are scrawled with declarations of praise for or belief in Shakespeare ("in xeikspir we trust", "Shakespeare rules!"[65] or the more humorous "He was the top English writer or not"[66]), graffiti and street artists are rather more keen to consider as their interlocutor not Shakespeare/the Author, but the community of readers and viewers who engage with the full semantic potential of works that must considered as "multi-dimensional space[s]" where a variety of languages, "none of them original, blend and clash."[67] Thus, even if in an indirect and unintentional way, street Shakespeare ends up questioning the same idea of individual authorship on which most Shakespeare criticism is based and offering a uniquely modern vision both of the Elizabethan playwright's notorious "unconcern to preserve in stable forms the texts of most of his plays"[68] and of the Elizabethan collaborative enterprise of dramatic production in which Shakespeare was involved. In street art it often happens that various artists work together or even that, at different times, they add their logos or other images to an original work, sometimes actually changing its original meaning, as might well be the case with the above-described graffiti *Mandela and Macbeth* in Johannesburg.

STAGING SHAKESPEARE ON THE WALLS

The graffiti and post-graffiti in the second group (1B) are much easier to find and classify. As part of an artistic project, they are generally recorded and fully described on the net, even though the first spontaneous reaction on the street of the passersby is again one of surprise and puzzlement. This is the case of Australian artist Peter Drew's "Emoticon Hamlet," which was created in Glasgow, a city that has recently witnessed a boom in public art.[69] Between April and September 2013, Drew created a series of sixteen illegal wheatpaste figures accompanied by speech bubbles that depicted Hamlet's second-act soliloquy[70] and imagined the Danish prince as a modern character whose head had been replaced by a pixelated emoticon.[71] The emoticon faces spouting Shakespearean verses popped up across the streets of Glasgow, even though, not being part of a commissioned, legal project, some of them were quickly removed by the city council. According to Drew, the pieces were intended to surprise passersby who would encounter them by accident, and were "a way of questioning whether subtle and complex emotions, which once characterized great art, can have a place in the age of digital communication."[72] Although his message may not have been instantly interpreted by Glaswegian pedestrians, the artist hoped that the pictures would at least prompt questions: "I don't expect passersby to see the whole purpose of the project from one glance, but I hope they might enjoy the sight of it and feel curious to find out more."[73] By highlighting and examining the problem of the ordinary passerby's reception and responses to graffiti and to *Hamlet*, the "Emoticon Hamlet" project moreover questions the traditional reception of Shakespeare. After a first moment of surprise before this sudden and unexpected apparition, the viewer would recognize the unorthodox and disfigured representation of the Danish prince as familiar as and therefore much more sympathetic than the traditional representation of Shakespeare's character. Besides, because they were scattered throughout the city, the emoticon Hamlets dismantled the linear and logical sequence of the Shakespearean soliloquy in favour of a series of fragments; the possibility for the viewer to see all of them was left either to chance or to his or her own free will and initiative to go and seek out all the others. The accessible imagery of these pieces aimed at communicating with as many people as possible, though obviously at different levels, according to different cultural, political, social or ethnic backgrounds. Some viewers will have recognized the emoticon boy as the Prince of Denmark and his lines as part of his soliloquy in the second act of the tragedy; others won't. In any case, although some might see them without really looking at them, Drew's emoticon Hamlets, like most street art, function as reminders of free thought, free expression and individuality. By means of Shakespeare, the Australian artist aimed to reclaim public spaces for the community rather than leave them to the will of the council, and his "Emoticon Hamlet" project heated up debate about the legacy and legality of street art and its forms of negotiation with the urban space.[74] Indeed, Drew's art is an unsanctioned interventionist practice that rebels against established art forms and challenges Shakespeare's status both as a canon and as a potential global commodity.

Shakespeare also figures as one of the protagonists in "L'arte sa nuotare" ("Art knows how to swim"), a project by a Florentine street artist who, unlike Peter Drew, wishes to remain anonymous. The artist uses the pseudonym Blub, perhaps an onomatopoeic name suggesting the sound of the water bubbles he/she paints around the characters in his/her works.[75] Shakespeare is in fact one of the many Renaissance icons that have been intriguingly painted on the walls of Florence: among others are Dante, Lorenzo de Medici, Michelangelo's David, Botticelli's Venus, Pontormo's Musician Angel, Leonardo da Vinci's Mona Lisa and Lady with an Ermine.[76] Like these other figures, Shakespeare is also portrayed immersed in water and wearing a scuba mask; like them, he is part of the great visual saga cleverly staged on the walls of the city, despite his not being as obviously linked to Florence and its history as all the other characters.

According to Blub, "L'arte sa nuotare" is about the "two ways one can live life, like Eros and love or life and death. We can choose to be stuck with fear due to the crisis or we can choose to take it as an opportunity to overcome our limitations while being confident in the future and in our potential. So, even though it seems like we are all underwater it is time to learn how to swim!"[77] The Florentine street artist makes metaphorical play upon the present moment of economic and cultural crisis as a stimulus to do better and, accordingly, considers water as a symbol of the difficulties that art may encourage to overcome simply by putting on a mask and learning to swim. He/she paints his/her works directly on electricity and gas panels in the streets and alleys of the historic centre, paying great attention "not to upset the aesthetic equilibrium of the buildings on which the images are to be found," generally by contrasting blue paint with the Florentine yellow facades.[78] Each piece has a blue background, often with a gradient, and one or two figures painted in black ink. Shakespeare's portrait, however, like Dante's, is not monochromatic, and the inclusion of brown and orange for his Elizabethan clothes is more successful in capturing the attention of passersby. On the other hand, the familiarity of the icon makes him immediately recognisable when one unexpectedly bumps into him in via della Spada, a small street not far from Piazza Santa Maria Novella. One cannot but laugh at his new marine look. After some puzzlement, however, and upon closer inspection, one is challenged to question the significance of the work. Why is Shakespeare underwater? Why is Shakespeare included in a saga of Florentine characters? The first question is answered by Blub's explanation of the project, even though this explanation is only available on the web and therefore might be not immediately obvious to the passersby who may not grasp swimming as "a symbol that represents how we can use our resources."[79] Moreover, one could of course speculate on the image of a silent Shakespeare and draw the conclusion that by replacing his verses with bubbles coming out of his mouth, the artist may be suggesting that nowadays there are new and perhaps more visual ways to revive his poetry and meaning or, conversely, that his immortal verses are incomprehensible and yet still meaningful. The second question (Why Shakespeare in Florence?), however, can only be answered with mere conjectures. One may speculate that it is because some of his characters, such as Cassio in *Othello* or the Duke of Florence in *All's Well That Ends Well*, are Florentine, even though a more convincing speculation is that Shakespeare's indisputable iconicity is the reason for his presence on the walls of Florence. It is certainly no coincidence that one large "paste" of Blub's Shakespeare has been plastered into one of the outdoor niches of the walls of the church of San Filippo Neri, in Piazza San Firenze. Through this location, which makes Shakespeare appear as a saint, Blub may be mocking the "bardolatry" and the quasi-religious worship that surrounds the Elizabethan playwright. Finally, the street artist might have chosen

Shakespeare as one of the best examples of the longevity of art, despite the irony of presenting a series on the longevity of art through the medium of street art, which usually has a very short life.

Naturally, while Blub may intend his/her series ironically, he/she also seems particularly interested in exploring the relationship between past and present. As Blub explains, Renaissance art in Florence is "still strong and hides today's art that is alive and contemporary, so by using icons of the past with diving masks the theme presents a mix between the past and the contemporary world."[80] "L'arte sa nuotare" brings art out of the museums just like "Emoticon Hamlet" brings theatre out of the theatres and by this displacement allows the art of the past to live again in the city and be accessible to all in a direct and spontaneous manner.

Before closing this section on coherent artistic projects, it seems important to mention Marc Quinn's project *Love Paintings*, even though (or precisely because) it illustrates a very different case of the relationship between Shakespeare and graffiti. First of all, Quinn is not a street writer or a street artist at all, but an artist (actually, one of the most original exponents of Young British Art) who has understood the aesthetic (and economic) potentiality of street art and has therefore appropriated it just once for a precise project which involved the walls of Juliet's House in Verona in a side event of the 53rd International Art Exhibition–Venice Biennale (May–September 2009). Moreover, it seems important to bear in mind that, unlike Drew's and Blub's graffiti, forbidden and in fact sometimes removed from the walls, Quinn's graffiti move from the streets to the art galleries and museums and have therefore a very different aesthetic meaning and even value (having been turned into a commodity).

Notoriously, over the years, the walls of Juliet's famous house of Via Capello in Verona have been covered by multi-coloured graffiti, the messages left by thousands of couples pledging eternal love under the famous balcony from which William Shakespeare's Juliet is supposed to have talked to her Romeo – a place of phantasy and imagination, where the myth of Shakespeare's tragedy mingles with common people's dreams of love.[81] By the late 1990s, street art had become a mainstream phenomenon and big business,[82] and therefore, after having for long time been condemned and fought against by Verona's city council, the graffiti covering Juliet's walls were re-valued as popular art. In the wake of this new phase in the short history of street art when art dealers and gallery owners are capitalising on this new trend, the house of Via Capello has become a place where spontaneous and often uncontrolled graffiti art has met and intermingled with contemporary art, and with Marc Quinn's art in particular. By enabling the real and the unreal to coexist, the evocative spaces of Juliet's house and its graffiti were precisely what inspired Marc Quinn – who considers Juliet's house to be "a living functioning temple to the idea of love"[83] – and induced him to create his *Love Painting*.[84] These large-scale graffiti-saturated pictures were created out of those left by tourists who, while thinking they were leaving their mark on the courtyard wall, were actually writing on white canvases mounted in the entrance to the house. The scribbled declarations of love and post-its stuck to the walls with chewing gum, overlap and clash in spontaneous, graphic mosaics defined by Quinn as "ready-made paintings of pure emotion."[85] Whereas normally graffiti art is scatological and transgressive, these are "graffiti of dreams and aspiration"[86] which are reborn to the new destiny of being displayed worldwide in museums and in other public spaces, ranging from Juliet's house museum to the Aïshti Women's floor and People restaurant in downtown Beirut. It is a process which allows the pledges of the Veronese lovers to go global, and, at the same time, cleverly questions how legitimate it actually is to relocate within an art gallery a work of art created for a setting (the street) which is of critical importance to its value. Not only does Quinn's project highlight the evolution of street art from its subcultural and anti-establishment roots to commodity, but it daringly blurs the lines between street art and "real art."

Fictional graffiti

As far as "fictional graffiti" are concerned, though the survey of Shakespeare-related graffiti in cinema, theatre and advertising[87] might appear to be an easier task it does not, in fact, turn out to be so and is, once again, very often the accidental result of unrelated research.

Shakespearean theatre and cinema have often been seduced by the practice of graffiti, which have been used to update the Elizabethan playwright and sometimes to make him "cooler." An ongoing interchange and reciprocal contamination are detectable between Shakespeare-related street art and "fictional" graffiti which continue to produce original results, even though it must not be forgotten that the comings and goings between the spaces of the street and those of the theatre or the cinema inevitably pose some problems and even some questions, since they imply a continuous shifting from the uncodified and unsanctioned language of the streets to a language that has necessarily been "domesticated," losing its spontaneity, freedom, and illegality. Many writers consider graffiti as a rebellion against a system of consumption, and the illegal and free nature of their art is essential to their participation in subcultures. "No longer a transformation of the urban environment, nor a subversive addition to the cultural landscape of signage,"[88] they do not carry the same socio-cultural, personal or political weight, even though they are often used on stage as signs of transgression, subversion, or illegality, often evoking a marginal, bleak and unrestricted urban environment. As the celebrated godfather of the street stencil Blek le Rat says, graffiti in galleries, museums and – I would add – in theatres and cinemas are but "the shadow of the real thing."[89]

Obviously, the appeal to graffiti has been different according to the different directors, different periods and countries; plays and films may possibly be recorded and classified according to the functions graffiti play in them (political, ethnic, social or merely decorative) or to the identity of the artists who make them (whether they are, for example graffiti artists, students from art schools, actors improvising graffiti writing on stage, etc.).

IN THE THEATRE

Often theatre designers try their hand at painting graffiti, on other occasions they work together with graffiti artists or students from art schools to develop their sets. It is worth mentioning, for example, the graffiti-scrawled sets by Ralph Koltai, one of the greatest abstract theatre designers and an associate designer for the Royal Shakespeare Company, for Michael Bogdanov's modernized version of *Timon of Athens* at the Ruth Page Theatre of Chicago in 1997, or those by Czech designer Miloň Kališ for Lit Moon's internationally acclaimed production of *Hamlet* directed by John Blondell, Santa Barbara's adventurous director.[90] More recently, a genuine interest in the forms and grammar of street languages can be seen in David Leveaux's *Romeo and Juliet* at the New York Richard Rodgers Theatre (2013), where the set is dominated by a backdrop entirely overwritten with graffiti, designed by set designer Jesse Poleshuck, and, on the other side of the Atlantic, in Josie Rourke's *Coriolanus* at the Donmar Warehouse in London (2013), where set and costume designer Lucy Osborne makes the onstage use of graffiti-ing walls into a pivotal Brechtian gestus.[91]

Other times, there have been surprising co-ventures between playwrights and street artists and attempts have been made at "importing" onto the stage some of street art's freshness and spontaneity. One would argue that what makes the difference in the use of graffiti or post-graffiti work in a Shakespearean production is precisely the degree of engagement or the relationship they are able to create within the community of spectators and within the group of actors. One might, of course, remember the case of urban artist Will Powell's amazing graffiti for the set of the 2014 production of *The Bomb-itty of Errors*, a "rockin' hip-hoppin', high-energy, hilarious ad-rap-tation"[92] of *The Comedy of Errors*. This adaptation by Jordan Allen-Dutton, Jason Catalano, GQ and Erik Weiner, presented by Queensland Shakespeare Ensemble in association with the University of Queensland's O-Week, declares its close link to the world of graffiti from its title's reference to the practice of "bombing," which in graffitists' slang means to apply graffiti intensively to a location.[93] QSE, a community-based, nonprofit organisation in Brisbane (Queensland, Australia), whose aim is "to engage Southeast Queensland communities with Shakespeare in order to strengthen the connections and relationships between community members" and to create "evocative, engaging theatre that awakes the senses and impassions the lives of its audiences and artists,"[94] decided to enlist the help of Will Powell, who is, by the very nature of his profession, interested in contending and negotiating with the territory and its community.

Street artists' collaboration is often sought after by university productions, understandably so, since graffiti have entered world consciousness through the language of teenagers and youth culture. This was, for example, what took place with the gritty, hip-hop *Romeo and Juliet* at the Cornell University Schwartz Center for the Performing Arts in 2009, whose cast comprized Cornell students and professional actors. The set, designed by Kent Goetz, professor of theatre, film and dance and scenic designer, was a towering urban conglomeration complete with graffiti walls painted by the artists from the Ithaca High School led by local graffiti writer Jay Stooks of the Greater Ithaca Activities Center. Intriguingly, the graffiti were the result of both a participatory effort and spontaneous contributions and, according to Goetz, "by the time the set is fully decorated, so many hands, from so many different constituencies, will have played a part in realizing this design,"[95] offering a clear example of theatre's effort to import onto the stage some of the spontaneous and uncontrollable nature of street art, and also to advocate communal consciousness.

There are indeed many more examples of the use of graffiti writing in theatre, but here I would merely wish to suggest how important the study of the reciprocal influences between Shakespearean theatre and street art might be.

IN CINEMA

My final considerations will be focused on cinema and its fundamental role in fixing forever this ephemeral art generally doomed to being removed or modified either by the passing of time or by city councils' anti-graffiti campaigns. Functioning as a time machine, cinema proves an important source for understanding and documenting, not only the evolution of graffiti writing, but also the metamorphosis of the relationship between street art and the Elizabethan playwright.

Let us take just three films from different periods and countries as interesting examples of the way cinema records the graffiti practices that are tied to a particular historical and geographical context and appropriates them in relation to Shakespeare: Robert Wise and Jerome Robbins' *West Side Story* (1961), which mirrors the way New York's street gangs marked the boundaries of their neighbourhood through "tagging"; Derek Jarman's *The Tempest* (1979), which recalls the practice of writing on domestic walls that was very common both in Elizabethan times and in London in the Seventies; and James Gavin Bedford's *The Street King* (2002), set in a marginalized Hispanic community in Southern California, where the grammar of graffiti marks "a 'deterritorialisation' of Shakespeare as a fluid, transnational cultural origin from which myriad global identities can be oriented and accesses".[96]

West Side Story (1961) is both one of the earliest and most clearly illustrative example of the way Shakespeare was very quickly claimed by the emerging form of graffiti writing that grew up in Philadelphia and later in New York before 1965. Interestingly, the film, which is set in a gang-ridden West Side in New York City in the mid-1950s, translated social conflicts into ethnic struggle and depicted a racial confrontation and a fight between two youth gangs who expressed themselves by means of the newly born practice of "tagging." Invented in the 1960s as an attempt to claim public space by getting the writers' names out on the streets as a visual demonstration of their existence, tagging was largely associated with gangs whose members wrote on walls to mark out their territory. "Philadelphia gangs such as Dogtown and The Moon, as well as New York gangs such as the Black Spades and Tomahawks had a tradition of writing their gang name in their neighbourhoods so as to signal their presence on and control over a particular turf."[97] In the wake of such gang practices, the film visualises the crucial oppositions between the Jets, a heterogeneous group of young white European immigrants who call themselves "Americans" and are the self-appointed owners of the streets and the basketball court, and the newly arrived Puerto Rican Sharks, who want to settle in their territory, in the tags of the two gangs' names written on the walls and on the road surfaces to physically mark out the space they inhabit. Thus, in the scene where the Sharks are chasing after the Jets, the camera zooms in on a wall where a spray-painted shark with its mouth wide open and its sharp teeth is meant to show how dangerous all Puerto Ricans can be ("The Sharks bite hard"). Soon afterwards, the Puerto Ricans provoke the "Americans" and, in return, the Jets, who are unwilling to give up ("We fought hard for this turf and we ain't just going to give it up. . . . These PR's are different. They keep on coming like cockroaches"), declare their intention of expelling the Puerto Ricans from their territory by means of a graffiti stating, "Sharks stink".[98] Throughout the prologue the camera pans rapidly over the tags of the two gangs but so insistently that tagging emerges as something like the mark of a "pirate" – a word used by Lady Pink (Sandra Fabara), one of the leading participants in the rise of graffiti-based art, to define graffiti writers and herself: "Maybe we're a little bit more like pirates. . . . We defend our territory, whatever space we steal to paint on, we defend it fiercely."[99] Both the characters in the musical and the real-life graffiti writers are pirates, rule defiers for whom tagging provides a life-affirming element of risk; pirates who "will fight with knaves and for sure, if necessary, until death."[100] Such a risk is hinted at right from the start of the film, in a highly dynamic and kinetic sequence which foretells the tragic denouement of the story; however, as Baudrillard suggests, it is precisely through tagging that "a particular street, wall or district comes to life through them [tags], becoming a collective territory again."[101]

The grammar of graffiti writing was appropriated by Wise and Robbins to inject new life into *Romeo and Juliet* precisely because it was a practice initiated and kept alive primarily by the young and because it is one of the many expressions of youth's rage and rebellion against society. Instead, almost two decades later, in his 1979 adaptation of Shakespeare's *The Tempest*, Derek Jarman, British independent cinema *artiste maudit*, filmmaker, painter, stage designer, writer and gardener, would employ graffiti to link the magic of the Shakespearean romance with the punk culture of the seventies. His Prospero, interpreted by the poet Heathcote Williams and inspired by the Elizabethan mathematician and occultist John Dee, is primarily a learned white magician whose powers over the natural world derived from his knowledge of neoplatonic, hermetic and cabalistic philosophical traditions. Accordingly, Yolanda Sonnabend imagined and designed his "cell" in Stoneleigh Abbey as a repository of alchemical symbols derived from Dee, Bruno, Paracelsus, Fludd and Cornelius Agrippa – Agrippa's volume *Occult Philosophy* is open on his desk. Artist Simon Reade drew out magic circles on the floor that were "blueprints of the pinhole cameras he constructed in his studio,"[102] and the walls of Prospero's study are scrawled with magical signs that, according to the filmmaker, come "either from the *Occult Philosophy* of Cornelius Agrippa, or are the Egyptian hieroglyphs as they were used in the seventeenth century, as the writing of 'the Adepts.' "[103] One could of course speculate on the network of mysterious cabalistic signs chalked onto the walls by Prospero and suggest that these not only remind us of the fact that, as Juliet Fleming has revealed, drawing and writing on walls was widely practiced in the domestic interiors of Elizabethan England,[104] but also evoke London's political and counter-culture graffiti scene of the Seventies,[105] a scene first documented by Roger Perry's striking black-and-white catalogue of images, *The Writing on the Wall*.[106] As in the Elizabethan period imagined by Jarman, in late Seventies London, graffiti were "like a secret code," as Jon Savage puts it in his history of punk, *England's Dreaming* (1992): they were "the voice of the underdog. It was people telling you things you couldn't read in mainstream media and wouldn't necessarily think about. You'd get jokes, stoner and outcast humour, with serious points. It was another kind of language."[107] It is also worth mentioning that poet and dramatist Heathcote Williams' "agitational" graffiti were a feature on the walls of the then low-rent end of London's Notting Hill, a neighbourhood where graffiti was "the most enduring legacy of the 1968 student revolution,"[108] and that Williams was involved with the anarchist movement Albion Free State. In the Seventies squatters took over a corner of Notting Hill and declared it a utopian country, free from government control, a territory that, according to George Stewart-Lockhart, is perhaps "best described as 'the England of Peace and Love, which William Blake foresaw in his vision.'"[109] It would therefore be tempting to reconsider Jarman's island in his *Tempest* (which he described as "an island of the mind")[110] also in the light of the utopian Albion Free State and of its political manifesto, written on the city walls. Among the many quotes from this manifesto, the declaration "The only state is the state of your mind, the only government is your body," painted on the wall of the Meat Roxy,[111] foregrounded both the role of the individual within the political and social community and his/her ability to interpret the world. It is a claim in tune not only with Williams's own acknowledgement of the potential force of the practice of graffiti but also with his recognition in very poetical terms of the pivotal role of the viewer in the process of interpretation of a lark on the wall and, by extension, of the whole world: "A lark. The anonymity is appealing. It's not signature art. It's just a thought, which can either be the view of a lone crank or be the view of thousands. It's up to the reader to decide. They bubble up in an engagingly mysterious way. You think, 'What's that doing there? Who on earth wrote that?'"[112]

James Gavin Bedford's *The Street Kings* (2002) displays a completely different use of graffiti writing, which appears as the language through which the film re-appropriates and re-writes Shakespeare. Presented by a fleeting introductory credit establishing it as "based on" the tragedy of *Richard III*, which is in fact morphed to fit the style of Chicano gang subculture in Southern California, the film deals with the world of street art both in its plot and in its prologue. The protagonist, Rikki Ortega, who is modelled on Shakespeare's Richard III in his dual role of audience manipulator and playwright character, is shown as he moves towards becoming the "king" of the Ortega gang and of a drug cartel in Los Angeles, but also "the king of the streets" according to the meaning that was given by graffiti writers to the word "king" in the 1980s: "an accomplished and prolific writer" or "a master of style and technique."[113] As Mark Thornton Burnett suggests, it is significant that the film, which is a parodic reading of *Richard III*, "consistently favours narratives of 'writing' and/or 'lettering' that are culturally resonant."[114] On the one hand, Rikki is a street writer who at the beginning of the film spray-paints his signature onto a stone, suggesting perhaps that "the articulation of his identity is managed by acts of defiling and defamation: the protagonist marks himself by 'monsterizing' his environment in much the same way that he has been disfigured by the barrio experience";[115] on the other hand, both "writing" and "lettering" are metaphorically linked to the opening credits section of the film, which significantly shows a short sequence with a graffiti artist who begins to spray-paint on a barrio wall a Shakespeare head that bears a very close resemblance to the Droeshout portrait and then modifies it by adding a red bandana, a goatee, a gold crucifix earring and dark sunglasses. The graffiti is signed "LCN," the signature or tag of the brotherhood to which three members of the film's cast once belonged: Rikki, Alejandro and cop Juan Vallejo. The word *plata* (silver) is placed on the upper left of "the newly ethnicised Bard,"[116] while on the lower right we see the word *plomo* (lead); as Carolyn Jess-Cook observes, the "*plata o plomo*" phrase is a direct reference to Pablo Emilio Escobar Gaviria, the Colombian drug lord and leader of one of the most powerful criminal organizations, and to his strategy.[117] Intriguingly, this graffiti seems to both confirm street-writer Rikki's role as a playwright who is rewriting Shakespeare (as the narrator of the film he often, Richard-like, addresses the camera in order to establish a relationship with the off-screen audience) and also to reveal Shakespeare's dual role in the new millennium: that of "a cultural icon that unifies a linguistically, culturally and economically diverse global population" and "a locally specific symbol of the problems faced by marginalized Hispanic communities in Southern California."[118] Also interesting in this context is the fact that the opening sequence recalls the practice of promoting a film or a play through a piece of graffiti writing that is becoming progressively more common. One example of this might be the video showing the artistic process through which street artist Will Powell realized the graffiti that was used to promote the above-mentioned play *The Bomb-itty of Errors*, and which was posted on YouTube – once again a practice which created a dynamic interrelation between the streets, the stage, the screen and the internet community.[119]

Poetic, quotidian or coarse, subversive or commodified but always engaging, graffiti and post-graffiti art have set up a dialogue with Shakespeare in various ways to the point one may "fantasize" (just to quote Burt in his preface to *Shakespeares after Shakespeare*) about an archive that would include Shakespeare-related graffiti and post-graffiti and could contribute to the investigation of the Elizabethan playwright in a mediatized world.

Notes

1   All the illustrations referred to in this article are published on the website Tagging the Bard at https://sites.google.com/site/taggingthebard/home (accessed 1 April 2016).
2   The photograph of "Shakespeare toilet" (Matt From London) (Ian Press Photography) is published on the website "The World's Best Photos of Shoreditch," https://www.flickr.com/photos/londonmatt/9580501367 (accessed 1 April 2016).

3   Maev Kennedy, "Shakespeare's Curtain Theatre Unearthed in East London," *The Guardian*, 6 June 2012.
4   Andrea Nelli, *Graffiti a New York* (Milan: Wholetrain Press, 2012), 35–9.
5   Mariacristina Cavecchi, "Taggare il Bardo. Shakespeare e i graffiti," *Stratagemmi Στpaththmata. Prospettive teatrali. Shakespeare in the Maze of Contemporary Culture/ Shakespeare nei labirinti del contemporaneo*, special issue 24–25 (December 2012– March 2013), 227–53.
6   Alexa Huang, "Global Shakespeare as Methodology," *Shakespeare*, 9, no. 3 (2013): 272–90.
7   Richard Burt, ed. *Shakespeares after Shakespeare: An Encyclopedia of the Bard in Mass Media and Popular Culture* (Westport, CT, London: Greenwood Press, 2007).
8   Douglas Lanier, "Film Spin-offs and Citations," in *Shakespeares after Shakespeare*, vol. I, ed. Richard Burt (Westport, CT: Greenwood Press, 2007), 132.
9   "Street Art: Money on the Wall," *Courier*, September 3, 2014, http://courierpaper.com/2014/09/street-art-industry/ (accessed 13 December 2015).
10 Jana & JS in Frank Steam156 Malt, *Street Art London*, Årsta, Dokument Press & Frank Steam156 Malt, 2013, 69.
11 See M. Cavecchi, S. Soncini, eds. *Shakespeare Graffiti. Il cigno di Avon nella cultura di massa* (Milano: CUEM, 2002); R. Beach, D. Appleman, S. Hynds and J. Wilhelm, *Teaching Literature to Adolescents* (Aarhus, Denmark: Lawrence Erlbaum, 2006), 67.
12 Ann Williams-Gascon, *Teaching Culture with Graffiti*, http://www.frenchteachers.org/bulletin/articles/culture/cultureteachinggrafitti.pdf (accessed 13 December 2015).
13 Lanier, *Film Spin-offs*, 132.
14 'Skating on Thin Eyes' is Iain Sinclair's first walk in his *Lights Out for the Territory. 9 Excursions in the Secret History of London* (London: Granta Books, 1997), 1.
15 The problem with the image-hosting website Flickr, created by Ludicorp in 2004 and acquired by Yahoo in 2005, is that it never gives the name of the writer and sometimes it publishes photos without giving details such as the place where the photos were taken. Besides, it does not provide information about the graffiti or the graffiti writers who painted them, both of which would greatly contribute to a better interpretation.
16 http://courierpaper.com/2014/09/street-art-industry/ (accessed 13 December 2015).
17 Sinclair, *Skating*, 1.
18 Banksy's film *Exit through the Gift Shop* premiered at the 2010 Sundance Film Festival and was nominated for Best Documentary at the 2011 Academy Awards. Many reviewers questioned its legitimacy and wrote that it was Banksy's "prankumentary." The film contains exclusive interviews with and footage of Banksy, Shepard Fairey, Invader and many of the world's most infamous graffiti artists as they work on the city walls.
19 Wacławek, *Graffiti* (New York: Thames & Hudson, 2011), 73–4.
20 Wacławek, *Graffiti*, 114.
21 Drew's documentary is available at https://www.youtube.com/watch?v=SBDStTMiRhk (accessed 1 April 2016).
22 Cedar Lewisohn, "Street Art or Graffiti?," *Street Art: The Graffiti Revolution* (London: Tate Publishing, 2008), 15.
23 For a description of the differences and the relationships between graffiti and post-graffiti see Wacławek, *Graffiti*, 30.
24 Wacławek, *Graffiti*, 55.
25 As a matter of fact, Drew's docufilm underlines the contradictory position of city councils, such as that of Adelaide (and I would add of London as well) which on the one hand commission public artwork projects that have to be street-art-inspired, but on

the other prosecute street art and street artists, who go out at night to paint, because, ultimately, city councils can not control this creative output.
26 Wacławek, *Graffiti*, 15.
27 Sinclair, *Skating on Thin Eyes*, 1.
28 Nelli, *Graffiti*, 11.
29 Sinclair, *Skating on Thin Eyes*, 1–2.
30 Wacławek, *Graffiti*, 16–18.
31 See, for example: http://search.ldngraffiti.co.uk/image-detail.asp?imageID=7012 (accessed 1 April 2016) or http://artygraffarti.com/2015/02/25/vitamin-c-slack-pawk-romeo-brunswick/ (accessed 1 April 2016).
32 In Random Shakespeare Graffiti, http://stopitiloveit.com/random-shakespeare-graffiti/ (accessed 1 April 2016).
33 http://www.flickr.com/photos/cbeana/2794074852/ (accessed 1 April 2016).
34 The photograph is posted on Flickriver: http://www.flickriver.com/photos/duncan/6828316605/ (accessed 1 Arptil 2016).
35 The photograph is posted on https://christineestima.wordpress.com/2012/11/24/padua-part-2-street-art/ (accessed 1 April 2016).
36 The photograph of "Graffiti nach Shakespeare" is by Pitterkoeln (6 July 2009) and it is posted on the website Panoramio at http://www.panoramio.com/photo/24169049 (accessed 1 April 2016).
37 Keith Palmer's photo of the graffiti is posted on Flickr at https://www.flickr.com/photos/keifeh/7187732421/ (accessed 1 April 2016).
38 The photograph is posted on https://www.google.it/search?q=shakespeare+graffiti&newwindow=1&espv=2&biw=1621&bih=963&tbm=isch&tbo=u&source=univ&sa=X&ved=0ahUKEwigrtPfldbJAhVJShQKHSU-DpgQsAQIHg#imgrc=0GyJO2mX7rLfcM%3A (accessed 1 April 2016).
39 The graffiti is published on Flickr at https://www.flickr.com/photos/lausdeo/255463183/sizes/z/in/photostream/ (accessed 1 April 2016) and it is also included on the website BuzzFeed Community at http://www.buzzfeed.com/babymantis/20-awesome-examples-of-literary-graffiti-1opu (accessed 1 April 2016).O
40 The photograph of "the war goes on" by Kara O'Keefe is posted on Flickr at http://flickrhivemind.net/blackmagic.cgi?id=4317582866&url=http%3A%2F%2Fflickrhivemind.net%2FTags%2Fgraffiti%252Cshakespeare%2FInteresting%3Fsearch_type%3DTags%26textinput%3Dgraffiti%252Cshakespeare%26photo_type%3D250%26method%3DGET%26noform%3Dt%26sort%3DInterestingness%23pic4317582866&user=&flickrurl=http://www.flickr.com/photos/33689131@N04/4317582866 (accessed 1 April 2016).
41 The photo was taken on 21 March 2014 and is posted on Flickr: https://www.flickr.com/photos/mycophagia/14828682514 (accessed 1 April 2016).
42 "Two beer or not two beer" by Shakesbeer. On a wall in Duszniki Zdrój, Poland. Photograph by Edwinek, 31 August 2005, http://www.flickr.com/photos/44124436774@N01/52183532 (accessed 1 April 2016).
43 Graffiti stencil Shakespeare badger Hamlet tuberculosis. Photo by Matthew Gildley, London, 20 October 2006, posted on http://www.flickr.com/photos/29093703@N00/274686845 (accessed 1 April 2016).
44 http://www.flickr.com/photos/7680160@N04/4423320860 (accessed 1 April 2016) taken by DannyBoy on 6 March 2010.
45 In Tunisia, Egypt and Syria, in the months during and following the revolution, street art played a major role by reclaiming public spaces that used to be controlled by the

government and by letting artists and ordinary citizens express themselves freely for the first time in years. In all these countries street art has become a very important means of artistic and political expression and, even though I have not yet found many examples of graffiti and murals quoting Shakespeare, I am sure that a more thorough and systematic search might bring to light a wider group of Shakespeare-related material. As Graham Holderness wrote, quoting Nadia Al-Bahar, Shakespeare "was transplanted into Arab soil" and is quite frequently performed in modern Arab theatre (Graham Holderness, Arab Shakespeare, 25 July 2013, at http://globalshakespeares. mit.edu/blog/2013/07/25/arab-shakespeare/ (accessed 1 April 2016); Shakespeare may well also prove relevant to Arab street art.

46 The photo of the graffiti by Margarett Litvin was posted on the website Shakespeare in the Arab World on 9 September 2011, http://arabshakespeare.blogspot.it/2011/09/tahrir-graffiti.html (accessed 1 April 2016).

47 Ahmad Shokr, "The Eighteen Days of Tahrir," in *The Journey to Tahrir: Revolution, Protest, and Social Change in Egypt*, eds. Jeannie Sowers and Chris Toensing (London: Verso, 2012), 40.

48 Amenah AbouWard, "Tahrir Graffiti: History through Art," *The Independent*, 2 April 2012, http://academic.aucegypt.edu/independent/?p=3936 (accessed 1 April 2016).

49 Mia Gröndahl, *Revolution Graffiti: Street Art of the New Egypt* (Cairo, New York: The American University in Cairo Press, 2012), ix.

50 J.J. Joughin, *Shakespeare and National Culture* (Manchester: Manchester University Press, 1997).

51 M. Litvin, *Hamlet's Arab Journey: Shakespeare's Prince and Nasser's Ghost* (Princeton and Oxford: Princeton University Press, 2011), 9.

52 Mandela and Macbeth in Bree Street, Johannesburg, close to the Market Theatre. Artist unknown. Photo taken by Derek Smith (8 January 2014) and posted on https://www.flickr.com/photos/43066879@N06/11865872665/ (accessed 1 April 2016).

53 "'Umabatha – The 'Zulu Macbeth' Celebrates Origins of Zulu Nation With Drama, Music and Dance Oct. 2–5 at Wiltern." *UCLA Newsroom*. 19 August 1997, http://newsroom.ucla.edu/releases/UMABATHA-The-Zulu-Macbeth-1564, (accessed 1 April 2016).

54 Daniel Fischlin, Max Fortier, eds. *Adaptations of Shakespeare: An Anthology of Plays from the 17th Century to the Present* (New York: Routledge, 2000), 165.

55 The photograph is by ssamba and is posted on deviantART: http://ssamba.deviantart.com/art/macbeth-204307818 (accessed 1 April 2016).

56 The photograph is posted on fineartamerica: http://fineartamerica.com/featured/macbeth-maureen-j-haldeman.html (accessed 1 April 2016).

57 The poster of William Shakespeare with aviator sunglasses and with the unmistakable signature MWB, which is pasted up all over New York, is one of the works of Mr. Brain Wash, alias Thierry Guetta. The photograph, entitled "Shakespeare looking splendid," was taken by superk8nyc on 24 June 2007 in New York, and is posted on Flickr: https://www.flickr.com/photos/superk8/623118257 (accessed 1 April 2016). See also a clown-like skull of Shakespeare, painted on the shop-shutters in Wellington Court, New York. Photo by Luna Park (22 May 2010), posted on http://www.flickr.com/photos/54481803@N00/4631385928 (accessed 1 Apri l 2016). Another clown-like Shakespeare skull on a wall in Brooklyn, New York, holds a spray can. Photographed by Luna Park (23 January 2015) and posted on https://www.flickr.com/photos/lunapark/16366588806/ (accessed 1 April 2016).

58 The photo was posted in 2008 on https://www.flickr.com/photos/30741072@N00/2601054907/ (accessed 1 April 2016).
59 "In Xeikspir we trust." Photo taken by Cecília S. Unirio (24 September 2010, Rio de Janeiro) and posted on http://www.flickr.com/photos/15777455@N00/5354305544 (accessed 1 April 2016).
60 The photo is posted on http://reaperc.deviantart.com/art/Shakespeare-Graffiti-in-Japan-303699419 (accessed 1 April 2016). Two more Shakespeare faces are at https://coffeeandmissingstars.wordpress.com/2013/07/20/saturday-brings-you-shakespeare-graffiti/ (accessed 1 April 2016).
61 Shepard Fairey interviewed in *Exit through the Gift Shop*.
62 Douglas Lanier, *Shakespeare & Modern Popular Culture* (Oxford: Oxford University Press, 2002), 112.
63 Jean Baudrillard, "Kool Killer, or The Insurrection of Signs," *Symbolic Exchange and Death* (Paris: Gallimard, 1976; London: Sage, 1993), 79.
64 It was the first Shakespeare play performed in Afghanistan since the Soviet invasion in 1979 and the rise of the Taliban, and showed how Shakespeare had in fact written, without knowing it, an Afghan comedy (William C. Carroll, "*Loves' Labour's Lost* in Afghanistan," *Shakespeare Bulletin*, 28, no. 4 (Winter 2010): 443–58). This Shakespearean project is described by Qais Akbar Omar and Stephen Landrigan in their book *Shakespeare in Kabul*, London: Haus Publishing Limited, 2012.
65 "Shakespeare Rules!" photographed by Observe the Banana (7 July 2008) and posted on http://www.flickr.com/photos/55133504@N00/2677327706 (accessed 1 April 2016).
66 "He was the top English writer, or not," posted on https://coffeeandmissingstars.files.wordpress.com/2013/07/imag0322.jpg (accessed 1 April 2016).
67 Roland Barthes, "The Death of the Author," *Aspen* 5–6 (1967).
68 Terence Hawkes, *That Shakespearian Rag* (London: Methuen, 1986), 75–6.
69 Drew's project is discussed in M. Cavecchi, "Tagging the Bard: Shakespeare Graffiti On and Off Stage," forthcoming in *Shakespeare Survey*, 69 (November 2016).
70 ""I have of late, (but wherefore I know not) lost all my mirth; / and indeed, it goes so heavily with my disposition; / that this goodly frame the earth, seems to me a sterile promontory; / this most excellent canopy the air, look you, this brave o'erhanging firmament, / this Majestical roof, fretted with golden fire: / why, it appears no other thing to me, than a foul and pestilent congregation of vapours. / What a piece of work is man! / How noble in reason, / how infinite in faculty! / In form and moving how express and admirable! / In action how like an Angel! / In apprehension how like a god! / The beauty of the world! / The paragon of animals! / And yet to me, what is this quintessence of dust? / Man delights not me; no, nor Woman neither" (2.2.280–91).
71 See all sixteen of Peter Drew's graffiti at "Hamlet Emoticons" (1 October 2013), http://peterdrewarts.blogspot.it/2013/10/hamlet-emoticons.html (accessed 15 January 2016).
72 P. Drew interviewed by Rachael Fulton, "Much Ado about Graffiti As Street Artist Tackles Shakespeare Project," 19 May 2013, http://news.stv.tv/west-central/225789-shakespeares-hamlet-is-the-subject-of-peter-drews-glasgow-street-art/ (accessed 1 April 2016).
73 Drew in Fulton, *Much Ado*.
74 As a matter of fact, because his "Emoticon Hamlet" project was not part of Glasgow City Council's "Clean Glasgow Campaign" (the initiative which uses publicly funded street art to regenerate run-down areas), and therefore went against the council's

anti-graffiti policy, it was considered illegal and a potential cause for expulsion from the Glasgow School of Art, where he was completing his master's degree.
75 William Shakespeare by Blub ("L'arte sa nuotare"). Photograph by Luca Baratta, 2015.
76 One may also bump into Julius Cesar or the Pope in Rome; Amy Winehouse and Freddie Mercury in London; Pablo Picasso and Salvador Dalí in Spain. In Knokke-Heist, where Blub has recently taken part in the first important exhibition of "Italian Street Art" at the Cappelleschi Gallery, one may run into Belgian icons, such as Magritte, Jacques Brel and the young rapper Stromae (Paul Van Haver).
77 Tiana Kay, "Undercover Interview with Italian Artist Blub," Tiana's Travels, 9 December 2014, http://blog.tianakai.com/2014/12/street-art-florence-interview-with-blub/# (accessed 15 January 2015).
78 "Blub, Clet, Exit/Enter, UrbanSolid: The Top of Italian Street Art," http://www.cappelleschi.com/folder_web.pdf (accessed 1 April 2016).
79 Blub quoted by David Crowe, *L'arte sa nuotare [Art knows how to swim]* at http://www.cappelleschi.com/folder_web.pdf (accessed 1 April 2016).
80 Kay, "Undercover Interview with Italian Artist Blub."
81 The photo of the graffiti wall at Juliet's house in Verona was taken by Alice Equestri, September 2015.
82 Lewisohn, *Street Art*, 81.
83 D. Eccher, *Marc Quinn: Myth* (Milano: Charta, 2009), 70.
84 See Quinn's *Love Painting: Dan* (2009) at http://marcquinn.com/artworks/single/love-painting.-dan (accessed 1 April 2016).
85 Eccher, *Marc Quinn*, 70.
86 Ibid.
87 Even though I do not focus on advertising in this article, it is a fact that as soon as the marketing executives and advertising agencies against whom the street artists had been protesting perceived that street-art-style imagery had a hip-by-association rebelliousness attached to it, they started using the format to sell their products (Lewisohn, *Street Art*, 81). Thus, for example, Shakespeare and graffiti come together in the 2005 six-minute film for a jeans campaign from the fast-fashion clothing company H&M, where Romeo and Juliet's balcony scene is re-invented by the American director and photographer David LaChapelle so that it may be inscribed within the youth culture market. See La Chapelle's *Romeo and Juliet* at http://www.youtube.com/watch?v=ZKdWFC9T9ps (accessed 1 April 2016).
88 Wacławek, *Graffiti*, 60.
89 Lewisohn, *Street Art*, 70, 127.
90 Lit Moon's production of *Hamlet* began in Santa Barbara, California, in 2000 and was last seen there in March 2014. Images of the set are published at https://www.facebook.com/kalis.milon?fref=nf (accessed 1 April 2016).
91 For the analysis of graffiti writing in Leveaux's and Rourke's productions see Cavecchi, *Tagging the Bard*.
92 QSE's member Zac Kelty travelled to Dallas, Texas, in July 2012 to join the cast of Second Thought Theatre's production of *The Bomb-itty of Errors*. After a successful run in Dallas, he brought Heath Gage's banging new beats back to Brisbane and directed the QSE's workshop production of *The Bomb-itty* in September 2012. QSE produced it again in 2014, in association with University of Queenland's O-Week.
93 M. J. Whitford, *Getting Rid of Graffiti: A Practical Guide to Graffiti Removal* (London: Taylor & Francis, 1992), 1.

94 See the company's website at http://www.qldshakespeare.org/about_intro.html (accessed 1 April 2016).
95 Goetz interviewed by Susan S. Lang in "Real graffiti will splatter the set for upcoming 'Romeo and Juliet performances'", http://www.news.cornell.edu/stories/2009/11/high-school-students-contribute-graffiti-set-design (accessed 1 April 2016).
96 Carolyn Jess-Cooke, "Screening the McShakespeare in Post-Millenial Shakespeare Cinema," in *Screening Shakespeare in the Twenty-First Century*, eds. Mark Thornton Burnett and Ramona Wry (Edinburgh: Edinburgh University Press, 2006), 168.
97 Wacławek, *Graffiti*, 43.
98 The frames of the film are posted on https://www.google.it/search?tbm=isch&tbs= rimg%3ACTjxhQzgPfnNIjhcE1M3XGWDgNNHgfxz3WE6wmi6-bEttSHOcBYsx-VWbh0wB5AJrC4Cav_17dBrthBn0lwC5EjXfHSoSCVwTUzdcZYOAEbT76jNF1 tl1KhIJ00eB_1HPdYToR-x4csNGfaJ8qEgnCaLr5sS21IRGF_1ZFEi1vRzCoSCc5w FizH5VZuEUQlBHNAN9LOKhIJHTAHkAmsLgIR-x4csNGfaJ8qEglq_1_1t0Gu2E GREq9V8zldfIkyoSCfSXALkSNd8dEci5xjJEDnyA&q=west%20side%20story%20 tagging&ei=YTDbVKrQM4elyQTCsIHYAw&ved=0CAkQ9C8wA (accessed 1 April 2016).
99 Lady Pink quoted in J. Chang, *Can't Stop Won't Stop: A History of the Hip-Hop Generation* (New York: St. Martin's Press, 2005), 124.
100 G. Cesaretti quoted in Nelli, *Graffiti*, 43.
101 Baudrillard, *Kool Killer*, 81.
102 Derek Jarman, *Dancing Ledge*, ed. Shaun Allen (London: Quartet Books, 1984, 1991), 188.
103 Jarman, Ibid.
104 Juliet Fleming, "Wounded Walls: Graffiti, Grammatology, and the Age of Shakespeare," *Criticism*, Detroit, 39 (Winter 1997): 1; *Graffiti and the Writing Arts of Early Modern England* (London: Reektion Books, 2001), 38.
105 A recurrent feature of his cinema, the juxtaposition of the Renaissance with the late twentieth century may also be seen at work in *Jubilee* (1978), in which Queen Elizabeth I is accompanied by her court magician John Dee and Ariel through the world of the Seventies.
106 Roger Perry, *The Writing on the Wall* (London: Elm Tree Books, 1976).
107 Jon Savage, *England's Dreaming: The Sex Pistols and Punk Rock* (London: Faber and Faber, 2005).
108 Notting Hill History Timeline 11 Open The Squares 1968/69, http://www.vaguerants.org.uk/wp-content/pageflip/upload/TL/timelinechap11.pdf, (accessed 15 January 2016).
109 George Stewart-Lockhart, Foreword to Roger Perry, *The Writing on the Wall: Replica Reissue with Archive Shots and New Features* (London: Plain Crisp Books, 2015), 14.
110 Jarman, *Dancing Ledge*, 186.
111 Perry, *The Writing on the Wall*, 148.
112 Heathcote Williams quoted by Alexis Petridis, "Spraying the 70s: The Pioneers of British Graffiti," *The Guardian*, 3 February 2015, http://www.theguardian.com/artanddesign/2015/feb/03/the-writing-on-the-wall-1970s-pioneers-of-british-graffiti (accessed 13 December 2015).
113 Wacławek, *Graffiti*, 26.
114 Mark Thornton Burnett, *Filming Shakespeare in the Global Marketplace* (London: Palgrave Macmillan, 2007), 134.

115 Burnett, Ibid.
116 Jess-Cooke, "Screening the McShakespeare," 167.
117 "Plata o plomo," literally, silver or lead. Usually, if a politician, judge or a policeman got in his way, he would first attempt to bribe them, and if that didn't work, he would order them killed.
118 Jess-Cooke, "Screening the McShakespeare," 167.
119 https://www.youtube.com/watch?v=cNzTGx2A82g (accessed 13 December 2015).

10 Collaborations and conversations: the year in Shakespeare studies, 2012–2013

Elizabeth Pentland

If there was an overarching theme to Shakespearean scholarship in 2012 and 2013, it was collaboration. The essay that follows aims to address the events and conversations that drew our attention through the year – from the impact of Britain's World Shakespeare Festival, hosted in conjunction with the Summer Olympic Games, to the critical controversies over his lost play, *Cardenio*; from the contributions of stationers and booksellers to Shakespeare's reputation as a "literary dramatist" to the digital humanities initiatives that are reimagining the London of Shakespeare's day. Nearly all of the works surveyed below reflect in some way upon the collaborative relationships and communities that have shaped, or continue to shape, Shakespeare's work as we know it. Eighteen books and two digital projects are considered, but it seems most appropriate to begin, in this case, with a cultural event that drew international attention to the city where Shakespeare made his name more than four hundred years ago.

The year 2012 has been described as "unprecedented" for Shakespeare performance in the United Kingdom, thanks in large part to the Summer Olympic Games that during the spring and summer brought the world's attention to the stages of London and other cities. Two edited volumes, in particular, offer a wealth of information about these events and performances. The first, *A Year of Shakespeare: Re-living the World Shakespeare Festival* (Arden Shakespeare, 2013), edited by Paul Edmondson, Paul Prescott, and Erin Sullivan, gives an overview of the nearly "100 theatrical productions, television programmes, radio broadcasts, digital projects and museum exhibits exploring and showcasing the artistic output of the country's most famous literary son" (7). The World Shakespeare Festival took place within the larger context of Britain's Cultural Olympiad, which saw *The Tempest* repeatedly invoked by internationally recognized actors like Kenneth Branagh and Sir Ian McKellen during the opening and closing ceremonies of the Olympic and Paralympic Games. In the lead-up to the games, from April to June, London's Globe Theatre staged 37 of Shakespeare's plays and a reading of his narrative poem *Venus and Adonis* as part of its Globe to Globe Festival. Additionally, during the four weeks prior to the opening of the games, the BBC aired its four-part series *The Hollow Crown*, based on the second tetralogy of history plays (*Richard II*; *Henry IV, Part 1*; *Henry IV, Part 2*; and *Henry V*). The series showcased some of Britain's best acting talent under the direction of Rupert Goold, Richard Eyre, and Thea Sharrock. Through the summer, the British Museum held an exhibition called "Shakespeare: Staging the World," curated by Jonathan Bate and Dora Thornton, described by reviewer Kate Rumbold as "a marvellous evocation of a cultural moment that had Shakespeare in its midst, responding to events and shaping how others saw them" (256). Finally, "from March to November the Royal Shakespeare Company curated a festival of domestic and international Shakespeare collaborations with performances not only in Stratford-Upon-Avon and London but also in Brighton, Newcastle, South Wales, North Wales and Edinburgh" (7–8). The brief essays and reviews in *A Year of Shakespeare* describe and critically analyse all of the productions associated with the World Shakespeare Festival and set them against the wider backdrop of the 2012 Cultural Olympiad. While often the individual contributions, in a thousand words or less, can only gesture at the character of each event or performance, together they provide a fascinating account of the festival's range and cultural diversity as well as the questions or controversies, the range of responses, provoked by these productions.

Narrower in scope, *Shakespeare Beyond English: A Global Experiment* (Cambridge, 2013) edited by Susan Bennett and Christie Carson, is a collection of 40 essays offering a "complete critical record" of the Globe to Globe Festival, which saw "all of Shakespeare's plays" as well as *Venus and Adonis* performed in 38 different languages over a six-week period. The volume, described by Bennett as a "remarkable collaborative enterprise among an international group of scholars and theatre professionals" (2), explores the unique theatre-going conditions produced by the festival, which commissioned productions of Shakespeare's plays by international companies in languages other than English, and drew audiences from many of London's non-English-speaking communities (3). What does it mean, the writers and editors of this collection ask, to think about "Shakespeare 'beyond' his homeland and natural tongue" (2)? What were the challenges faced by these plays' performers and audiences? What did we learn about the expectations we bring to performances of Shakespeare and our assumptions about what and how his plays signify in today's world? While there is some unavoidable overlap between this volume and *A Year of Shakespeare*, the essays here are considerably longer and thus allow for more detailed consideration of each company's performance practices, and of the tensions between "global" and "local" signification that energized many of these productions.

Several other works take us beyond the borders of the United Kingdom to consider different facets of the burgeoning field of "Global Shakespeare" studies. Alexa Huang's German-language study, *Weltliteratur und Welttheater: Aesthetischer Humanismus in der kulturellen Globalisierung* (Transcript Verlag, 2012) sets Chinese Shakespeare performances within the context of world literature and world theatre. The book's aim is to examine the place and function of aesthetic humanism in globalized or transcultural literature and theatre. While the first part of the book draws connections between Western and Chinese humanisms through readings of modern and contemporary Chinese literature, the second explores ideas about transcultural theatre by showing how classical Chinese theatre is evolving in dialogue with Shakespeare's plays. Huang's study is concerned not just with the meanings attached to Shakespeare performances and the "idea of Shakespeare" at different times in China's history, but also with the ways that "Chinese Shakespeares" performed on European stages are reshaping the playwright's legacy there, too.

Ruth J. Owen's edited collection, *The* Hamlet *Zone: Reworking* Hamlet *for European Cultures* (Cambridge Scholars, 2012) brings together sixteen essays that consider the European legacies of Shakespeare's most influential tragedy. "No other translated play," Owen argues, "has had such a prominent role in the formation of national theatres and national identities in Europe, nor been used there so often to denounce political complacency and oppression" (1). Owen's collection is wide-ranging and truly international in its focus, with contributions by scholars working in Europe, the UK and the US. Perhaps because the project began with a conference on the reception of *Hamlet* in Europe, the essays focus not on Shakespeare's play *per se*, "but on its offspring: a cross-section from the rich tradition of drawing from *Hamlet* in European cultures to produce new, independent works, which include Hamlet theatre, Hamlet ballet, Hamlet poetry, Hamlet fiction, Hamlet essays, and Hamlet films" (1). Addressing topics that range from the re-workings of *Hamlet* by Spanish exiles in the 1940s to the "role of *Hamlet* behind Europe's Iron Curtain" to its use in early twenty-first-century Sweden to address issues relating to immigration and multiculturalism, and a German online project that takes up "contemporary concerns about surveillance," the essays work to show how, in effect, "*Hamlet* has become the common cultural currency of Europe" (5). An afterword by Ton Hoenselaars sets the collection's concerns against the long history of Europe's engagement with the play in order to suggest the myriad ways that "*Hamlet*'s ghost continues to haunt us" (201).

Aneta Mancewicz's *Intermedial Shakespeares on European Stages* (Palgrave Macmillan, 2014) also takes up the question of Europe's engagement with

Shakespeare, and especially *Hamlet*, but does so in order to theorize the interplay of onscreen and onstage action – or what Mancewicz calls "intermediality" – in contemporary productions that rely upon a mixture of live action, real-time recordings, and pre-recorded materials. Mancewicz argues that "digital intermediality transformed Shakespearean staging and European performance in the first decade of the twenty-first century" (5). Hers is the first study to take up this phenomenon, which sets continental European practices apart from the more text-based approaches typically seen in Britain and North America. The book draws examples from a decade of "British, Dutch, German, Italian, and Polish theatre in order to reflect a diversity of Shakespeare traditions across Europe" (14). Adaptations and re-workings of *Hamlet* figure prominently in four of the five chapters, alongside productions of *The Tempest* (*Der Sturm*, dir. Stefan Pucher, 2007), *The Merchant of Venice* (*Der Kaufmann von Venedig*, dir. Nora Somaini, 2007), *Troilus and Cressida* (dir. Ravenhill and LeCompte, 2012), *Macbeth* (Grzegorz Jarzyna, 2005), and the Roman tragedies (*Romeinse tragedies*, Ivo van Hove, 2007). The book's final chapter considers "non-digital intermedial effects" in productions of *Romeo e Giulietta* (dir. de Angelis and Lagani, 1999–2000) and *A Midsummer Night's Dream* (dir. Sean Holmes, 2010). For Anglophone readers, this study offers considerable insight into the work of companies and directors that aren't widely known outside Europe.

The Afterlife of Ophelia (Palgrave Macmillan, 2012), a collection of essays edited by Kaara Peterson and Deanne Williams, engages the critical legacy of Shakespeare's *Hamlet* more globally, exploring the "rich afterlife of one of Shakespeare's most recognizable figures." As Williams and Peterson argue, the enigmatic figure of Ophelia can be understood as "a screen on which a culture projects its preoccupations and reflects its values back onto itself" (2). The collection brings together essays that approach the topic of Ophelia's life both in and after *Hamlet* from the standpoint of print and performance history, literary appropriations and representations, cinematic adaptations, social media, nineteenth-century painting, and contemporary photography. As this list suggests, images of Ophelia surface across a wide range of media and cultural contexts from children's literature to French painting to East Asian literature, drama, and film. The essays in this collection reveal some of the fascinating ways Ophelia has been reinvented at different historical junctures, and how, in the process, she has served as a focal point for each era's or culture's constructions of femininity and madness.

If any single play stole the show in 2012 and 2013, it would have to be that famously "lost" collaboration of Shakespeare and his colleague John Fletcher: *Cardenio*. The release of no fewer than four monographs and essay collections on the topic coincided with the play's 400th anniversary. According to the records that survive, a play called "Cardenno" or "Cardenna" was performed at court in 1613, but the text, almost certainly based on an episode in Cervantes' *Don Quixote*, was not published in the seventeenth century (although there is an entry for it in the Stationers' Register for 1653) and the play, in the version performed during Shakespeare's lifetime, has not survived. In the eighteenth century, however, Lewis Theobald famously claimed to have rediscovered this lost work, and in 1727 he produced a stage version for the Theatre Royal, Drury Lane, called *Double Falsehood*. His play, according to the Royal Privilege, or licence, issued for its publication in December of that year, was adapted from a "Manuscript Copy of an Original Play of William Shakespeare." But the status of Theobald's play has been much debated. Indeed, even in Theobald's day, there were doubts about its authenticity. Was *Double Falsehood* an elaborate forgery? Or does it contain traces of the original seventeenth-century text by Shakespeare and Fletcher? What happened to the manuscript that Theobald claimed to have in his possession? And if *Double Falsehood* is the real deal, can we discern how much of the play, or what parts of it, were contributed by Shakespeare? Renewed interest in the play and its history in recent years has led some prominent scholars, including Gary Taylor and Stephen Greenblatt, to try and reconstruct the "lost" *Cardenio* from the text that has come down to us; the first academic symposium on the topic was convened in New Zealand in 2009. The monographs and essay collections released in 2012 and 2013 are a direct product of this renewed interest in the play and its fascinating textual and performance history.

The first of these to appear was Roger Chartier's monograph *Cardenio between Cervantes and Shakespeare: The Story of a Lost Play* (Polity, 2013). Originally published in a French edition by Gallimard in 2011, Chartier's study traces the evolution of the *Cardenio* story across three principal European contexts – English, French, and Spanish – from the first mention of the English play by Shakespeare and Fletcher in 1612 to the moment of its rediscovery by Theobald in the eighteenth century. Beginning with the context of Cervantes' reception in early seventeenth-century England – in Spanish-language editions, in Shelton's English translation, and in the aforementioned stage collaboration – Chartier shows us how the *Cardenio* story crossed borders and languages and literary genres, and was revived, adapted, and rewritten numerous times for changing audiences in Spain, in France, and in England, during a 100-year period when modern notions about authorship and ownership of texts were still taking shape. Moreover, Chartier's epilogue looks at the "*Cardenio* fever" that in recent years has "gripped" England and America, inspiring works of detective fiction and several stage productions that have sought, in various ways, to reconstruct the lost play. The result is a compelling work of cultural history: a nuanced and fascinating account of the paradoxical relationship between the "permanence of works" like *Don Quixote* and the "plurality of their texts" (185) – the various means, many of them ephemeral, by which the stories associated with "canonical" works circulate and continue to leave their imprint upon a culture.

If Chartier's book asks how we should "read a text that does not exist, or present a play the manuscript of which is lost and the identity of whose author cannot be established for certain," Gregory Doran, the acclaimed Royal Shakespeare Company (RSC) director, offers one possible answer. In *Shakespeare's Lost Play: In Search of* Cardenio (Nick Hern Books, 2012) Doran tells two interwined stories: that of his own quest to understand what happened to Shakespeare's "lost play," and the story behind his adaptation of the play for the RSC in 2011, a production that was the result of years of research and painstaking reconstruction. Doran writes engagingly, weaving journal entries and personal reflections into a narrative about the creative and scholarly processes that shaped his production. For those already familiar with the history of the lost play and its controversial rediscovery by Theobald in the eighteenth century, there is nothing really new about the facts Doran uncovers. The interest of this volume, however, lies in the way Doran puts the story together – the particular narrative at which he arrives – for it is this narrative that underpins his own adaptation of the play. The detailed account of Doran's artistic process is perhaps the most valuable contribution this volume makes to the ongoing discussion around *Cardenio*, not least for the way it illuminates the historical processes of adaptation and recreation that have shaped the story since the time of Cervantes, Shakespeare, and Fletcher.

Two volumes of scholarly essays also addressed the textual and performance histories of *Cardenio* in 2012 and 2013, both of them co-edited by Gary Taylor. *The Quest for* Cardenio*: Shakespeare, Fletcher, Cervantes, and the Lost Play*, edited by David Carnegie and Gary Taylor (Oxford, 2012), is a project that originated in a theatrical experiment and the scholarly conversation it generated. The production was Gary Taylor's *The History of Cardenio* (2009), a "creative reconstruction" of the lost play presented as an "unadaptation" of *Double Falsehood* (3); the colloquium that followed later that year was the first academic symposium dedicated to Shakespeare and Fletcher's lost play. Appropriately, then, this collection of twenty-six essays by an international cast of scholars and theatre practitioners takes up the controversy over Theobald's adaptation and its lost source from two angles: the theatrical and the editorial. Gary Taylor's contribution to the volume argues that it is possible to single out Theobald's "interventions" in *Double Falsehood*, and offers compelling evidence "that he did indeed possess a manuscript play by Fletcher and Shakespeare" (4). Other essays address the historical contexts, external and internal evidence for Fletcher's collaboration with Shakespeare (and the forms it might have taken), and the "intertexts and cross-currents" that shaped the early seventeenth-century play and its reception. Among the contributors to the volume is Brean Hammond, whose essay addresses the "furore" surrounding the publication of his Arden edition of *Double Falsehood* in 2010 (4). The twelve essays that make up the book's final section address various aspects of the play's performance history from its earliest command performances "up to the time of writing" (8).

A second volume of essays, *The Creation and Re-Creation of* Cardenio*: Performing Shakespeare, Transforming Cervantes*, edited by Terri Bourus and Gary Taylor, with a foreword by Roger Chartier (Palgrave Macmillan, 2013), explores further the collaborative nature of *Cardenio* and suggests that the original manuscript "was not 'lost' but was instead deliberately 'disappeared' because of its controversial treatment of race and sexuality." The fifteen essays that comprise the first part of the volume explore further the sources and contexts for Shakespeare and Fletcher's collaboration, including Fletcher's other borrowings from Cervantes, and revisit with a critical eye recent attempts to reconstruct the "lost" Shakespearean play – most notably Gregory Doran's production for the Royal Shakespeare Company and Taylor's own. The second part of this book reproduces the text of Taylor's collaborative "unadaptation" along with his preface to the work. Taylor calls his experimental playscript a "work in progress" that has been profoundly shaped by what he has "learned from theatrical collaboration" (239).

Theobald's *Double Falsehood* is among the plays included in *William Shakespeare and Others: Collaborative Plays* (Palgrave Macmillan, 2013), edited by Jonathan Bate and Eric Rasmussen for the RSC Shakespeare series. This anthology is designed as a companion to their edition of the *Complete Works*, and represents the first collected edition of the so-called Shakespeare Apocrypha in more than 100 years. Included are ten collaboratively authored works that have been, at one time or another, ascribed to Shakespeare and that appear to contain passages he wrote. As the editors remind us, "Theatre was, and remains, an essentially collaborative art form" (30). The collection raises important questions about dramatic authorship in Shakespeare's time, and discussion of the theatre's collaborative processes in this context is usefully framed by Jonathan Bate's "General Introduction" and an excellent essay by Will Sharpe providing "a comprehensive account of the Authorship and Attribution of each play" (5). Several of these plays – *Arden of Faversham*, *Edward III*, *Locrine*, *Sir Thomas More*, *A Yorkshire Tragedy*, and an adaptation of *Double Falsehood* (*Cardenio*) – have been staged in recent years by the RSC, and the volume contains a useful "From Script to Stage" section featuring interviews with actors and directors associated with these productions. Each individual play – edited from the first printed text (with the exceptions of *Sir Thomas More*, which is set from the revised manuscript, and *The Spanish Tragedy* and *Mucedorus*, for which the first printed editions with "additions" were used) – is given a brief introduction setting it within its generic and historical context, indicating its sources, and suggesting its significance for the

Elizabethan or Jacobean theatre. Each is accompanied, too, by a brief discussion of the uncertainties and most recent theories about its authorship. A "Key Facts" box provides readers with useful information about the play, including authorial attribution, linguistic medium (the proportion of verse and prose), dates of composition and performance, sources, textual status, and a list of major parts designed to show whether it was written as an ensemble piece or is dominated by a single character. Acknowledging the many uncertainties that remain about these play texts, the editors of this volume argue that "these works represent a fascinating part of the repertoire in which [Shakespeare] participated so centrally," and they "cannot fail to illuminate his theatrical world" (30).

Scholars also turned their attention to some other kinds of collaboration that took place within the walls of Shakespeare's theatres, with an innovative collection of essays that considers the practical question of how early modern plays were staged and how audiences would have experienced them. *Shakespeare's Theatres and the Effects of Performance* (Arden Shakespeare, 2013), co-edited by Farah Karim-Cooper and Tiffany Stern, explores in a series of fresh and engaging essays how stage effects were created in the Elizabethan and Jacobean theatres and the range of sensory experiences that would have been associated with play-going in the period. With contributions that explore topics from storm effects, stage blood, and costuming, to the scripts or parts that actors used, to the sounds, tastes, and smells that would have shaped the play-going experience, this groundbreaking collection works to recover the material and sensory world of the theatre in Shakespeare's time. The essays themselves are sharply focused and, at times, brilliantly evocative. With its focus on the material practices associated with the theatres – indoor and outdoor – and the technologies available to the playwrights and actors of the time, the volume greatly enriches our understanding of Shakespeare's plays and the conditions that shaped their earliest reception.

Playhouse manuscripts, which (quite literally) bear the marks of theatre's collaborative processes, also underpin an important new study on editorial practices in the field of early modern drama. Paul Werstine's *Early Modern Playhouse Manuscripts and the Editing of Shakespeare* (Cambridge, 2013) revisits the foundational work of W. W. Greg in order to demonstrate that the traditional thinking about Shakespeare's "foul papers" is fundamentally wrong. Working with nineteen playhouse manuscripts and three annotated quartos, Werstine analyses their material features – handwriting, inks, paper, annotations – for evidence of their provenance and their use in performance. The book's chapters, Werstine tells us, set "readings of the extensive work of W. W. Greg" alongside "detailed investigation of the MSS and printed texts that were repeatedly the objects of his study as he arrived at his conceptions of 'foul papers' and 'promptbooks'" (5). In attending to the contradictions in Greg's work, and in exploring what theatrical texts can tell us about early modern playhouse practices, Werstine calls for a new, "empirical" approach to the editing of Shakespeare's plays. There is considerable evidence, he suggests, that quarto editions of Shakespeare's works long thought to have been printed from the playwright's "foul papers" – for example, Q2 *Romeo and Juliet* and Q2 *Hamlet* – were instead based on playhouse manuscripts that had been used in performance.

Also concerned with the transition from stage to page, two books came out addressing another set of collaborations (and rivalries) that have shaped the way we read Shakespeare: those among the printers, publishers, and booksellers – the stationers – who first brought the playwright's works into print. *Shakespeare's Stationers: Studies in Cultural Bibliography*, edited by Marta Straznicky (University of Pennsylvania Press, 2013), brings together leading scholars in book history and the book trade to explore "the multiple and intersecting forms of agency exercised by Shakespeare's stationers in the design, production, marketing, and dissemination of his critical works." This collection begins from the premise that "the stationers who invested in Shakespeare's writings had motives that were not exclusively financial" and that the decision to publish any one of his works involved an act of "critical judgment that is discernible in the material text, not least in its very existence" (2). In this respect, the volume builds upon the work of Zachary Lesser (one of its contributors) in his *Renaissance Drama and the Politics of Print*, and on the histories of reading produced by such eminent scholars as Robert Darnton and Roger Chartier. The book's nine chapters each focus on the career of a different stationer whose work helped to turn Shakespeare into "the 'great Variety' of print commodities he would become in his first fifty years as a published author" (2). Their stories are fascinating and tell us much about the personalities, the politics, and the economics that shaped the book trade in early modern England.

Approaching the question of Shakespeare's career in print from a somewhat different angle, Lukas Erne's study *Shakespeare and the Book Trade* (Cambridge, 2013) presents the second part of a two-part argument about Shakespeare's attitude toward literary authorship that began with his groundbreaking 2003 study, *Shakespeare as Literary Dramatist*. In this new book, Erne is largely concerned with Shakespeare's presence and prominence in print during his own lifetime and in the years leading up to the publication of the First Folio (1623). Drawing on quantitative evidence for Shakespeare's success in print – how well his books sold in comparison to other dramatists', how many were reprinted and how often relative to his contemporaries) – Erne traces the emergence of "Shakespeare" as a marketable name in the developing book trade of late sixteenth- and early seventeenth-century London. Each chapter examines the phenomenon from a different perspective: what can larger patterns of authorial misattribution in the period tell us about Shakespeare's marketability? How did the bibliographic and paratextual makeup of Shakespeare's quartos shape the meaning of "Shakespeare" and his playbooks in early modern London? What do we know about Shakespeare's publishers and their role in shaping his literary reputation? And what can the earliest owners of Shakespeare's plays and poems tell us about the reception of his printed works? Shakespeare, Erne argues, was "far from indifferent to his popularity in print" and would have taken great interest in the processes by which his reputation as a literary author was made.

The English book trade also figures prominently in Michael Saenger's study *Shakespeare and the French Borders of English* (Palgrave Macmillan, 2013). Saenger's concern is with the trade in French language primers and, more broadly, the place (or status) of French in late sixteenth- and early seventeenth-century England. His book examines the "cognitive borders of the English nation, a set of borders that," he contends, "was as dependent upon languages and ideas as it was upon governments and shorelines" (5). Drawing on translation theory, economic criticism, and feminist and queer theory, Saenger sets early modern language primers in dialogue with Shakespeare's plays, not to study the playwright's representations of France *per se*, but instead to examine "how Shakespeare uses the idea of France to explore language and identity" (6). France, he argues, "is an intrinsic force in English identity" during this period (6). The book's first two chapters develop the methodological framework for Saenger's study; the remaining four "explore how the Anglo-French relationship shapes Shakespeare's models of history, comedy, and tragedy" through extended readings of *Richard II*, *Henry V*, *All's Well That Ends Well*, and other plays (10).

The study of foreign languages began for many students, of course, in the schoolrooms of early modern England. Lynne Enterline's masterful study *Shakespeare's Schoolroom: Rhetoric, Discipline, Emotion* (University of Pennsylvania Press, 2012) examines the material, discursive, and disciplinary practices that shaped the experience of early modern schooling, drawing upon the pedagogical materials of the time to illuminate the processes by which humanist educators sought to train up "proper English gentlemen" (1). But, as Enterline's study shows, there were often significant gaps between what educators claimed to be doing and what actually happened in the classroom – their teaching often had unintended consequences. Examining Shakespeare's plays and poems for the traces they bear of his own schooling, Enterline "brings evidence about the theatricality of everyday life in humanist grammar schools to bear on Shakespeare's representations of character and emotion – particularly expressions of 'love' and 'woe'" (1). The book's chapters each contribute to our understanding of the ways this education prepared Shakespeare (inadvertently, perhaps) for a career in the theatre, and enabled him "to invent characters and emotions so often taken to resemble modern ones" (1). But Enterline's study also cautions us to attend to the powerful contradictions that shaped the practices and processes of early modern schooling – many of which were quite "alien" to our own. "By contrast to the current tendency to accept humanist claims about their success in cultivating obedience and respect for authority and hierarchy," Enterline argues, Shakespeare's works suggest that we ought "to be cautious about taking schoolmasters entirely at their word" (8).

If Lynn Enterline asks us to reconsider Shakespeare's relationship to the classroom, David Goldstein's *Eating and Ethics in Shakespeare's England* (Cambridge, 2013) urges us to rethink our relationship – and Shakespeare's – to food. Goldstein's book argues that the sharing of food works to establish a community's boundaries and to both build and destroy relationships. The book's five chapters cover a range of early modern works and writers, beginning with Shakespeare before turning to other defining figures (Anne Askew, for example, and John Milton) and controversies of the period. Interestingly, Shakespeare's role in this book is to illustrate failures of commensality: Goldstein argues that "Shakespeare's plays demonstrate the vast gap between commensality and conviviality. If every act of inclusion means that someone else is excluded – left to starve, or to seek revenge – Shakespeare is more interested in those left out than in those invited to join the meal" (22). The book's opening chapters focus on two plays in particular, *Titus Andronicus*, "with its infamous cannibal banquet," and *The Merchant of Venice*, "which constantly mentions meals but never stages them" (22). The first play dramatizes the power of eating to "tear apart communities and physical bodies" (22); the second explores how meals and ideas about food sharing repeatedly fail in the play. Both plays ultimately ask us to consider how eating worked to divide as well as to unite communities in Shakespeare's time.

In the virtual realm, two collaborative digital projects explored the worlds of sixteenth- and seventeenth-century London. Pudding Lane's award-winning 3D representation of seventeenth-century London (before the Great Fire) made the rounds on social media in 2013 after it took first prize in Off the Map, a competition run by the British Library in association with two video game developers, GameCity and Crytek. This gorgeous three-minute video was produced by a group of six students at De Montfort University (www.openculture.com/2013/11/fly-through-17th-century-london.html). The students' blog offers considerable insight into their research for this project and their creative process: http://puddinglanedmuga.blogspot.co.uk/.

An ongoing project at the University of Victoria, The Map of Early Modern London (http://mapoflondon.uvic.ca/index.htm) continued its evolution as an interactive resource for researchers, teachers, and students of early modern culture. The project, begun in 1999, links "encyclopedia-style articles, scholarly work, student work, editions, and literary texts" to locations identified on a digitized version of the 1560s "Agas map" of London. Version five of the project was released in 2013, and in February 2014 the Pedagogical Partnership Project was launched with the aim of working with professors to develop teaching materials and collaborative modules that would allow students to research and develop new content for the site. This new initiative expands the educational scope of the project, so that in addition to learning about the landmarks, history, and culture of the city in which Shakespeare lived and worked, students can now connect the research they do in the classroom to a digital resource that will continue to enrich the study of Shakespeare's plays in years to come.

Along with these digital projects, the monographs and essay collections published this year contributed in some compelling ways to the ongoing project of reimagining Shakespeare's theatre, not least by underscoring the myriad collaborations and conversations that have shaped his plays and poems from their earliest, early modern iterations to the intermedial and intercultural productions we see on the world's stages today. We have, for some time, been moving away from the enduring myth of the playwright as "solitary genius," but perhaps what is most striking about this year's scholarship is the astonishing range of collaborations that have been described, theorized, debated, enacted, and enabled by international communities of researchers, teachers, editors, theatre practitioners, audiences, and of course students of Shakespeare.

WORKS REVIEWED

Bate, Jonathan, and Rasmussen, Eric, eds. *William Shakespeare and Others: Collaborative Plays*. Houndmills, Basingstoke and New York: Palgrave Macmillan, 2013.

Bennett, Susan, and Carson, Christie. *Shakespeare Beyond English: A Global Experiment*. Cambridge: Cambridge University Press, 2013.

Bourus, Terri, and Taylor, Gary. *The Creation and Re-Creation of* Cardenio. Houndmills, Basingstoke and New York: Palgrave Macmillan, 2013.

Carnegie, David, and Taylor, Gary. *The Quest for* Cardenio*: Shakespeare, Fletcher, Cervantes, and the Lost Play*. Oxford: Oxford University Press, 2012.

Chartier, Roger. Cardenio *between Cervantes and Shakespeare: The Story of a Lost Play*. Cambridge: Polity Press, 2013.

Doran, Gregory. *Shakespeare's Lost Play: In Search of* Cardenio. London: Nick Hern Books, 2012.

Edmondson, Paul, Prescott, Paul, and Sullivan, Erin (eds.). *A Year of Shakespeare: Re-living the World Shakespeare Festival*. London and New York: Bloomsbury Arden Shakespeare, 2013.

Enterline, Lynn. *Shakespeare's Schoolroom: Rhetoric, Discipline, Emotion.* Philadelphia: University of Pennsylvania Press, 2012.
Erne, Lukas. *Shakespeare and the Book Trade.* Cambridge: Cambridge University Press, 2013.
Goldstein, David. *Eating and Ethics in Shakespeare's England.* Cambridge: Cambridge University Press, 2013.
Huang, Alexa. *Weltliteratur und Welttheater: Ästhetischer Humanismus in der kulturellen Globalisierung.* Bielefeld: Transcript Verlag, 2012.
Jenstad, Janelle, director. "The Map of Early Modern London." http://mapoflondon.uvic.ca/index.htm.
Karim-Cooper, Farah, and Stern, Tiffany, eds. *Shakespeare's Theatres and the Effects of Performance.* London and New York: Bloomsbury Arden Shakespeare, 2013.
Mancewicz, Aneta. *Intermedial Shakespeares on European Stages.* Houndmills, Basingstoke and New York: Palgrave Macmillan, 2014.
Owen, Ruth J. (ed). *The* Hamlet *Zone: Reworking* Hamlet *for European Cultures.* Cambridge Scholars, 2012.
Peterson, Kaara, and Williams, Deanne. *The Afterlife of Ophelia.* Houndmills, Basingstoke and New York: Palgrave Macmillan, 2012.
Saenger, Michael. *Shakespeare and the French Borders of English.* Houndmills, Basingstoke and New York: Palgrave, 2013.
Straznicky, Marta, ed. *Shakespeare's Stationers: Studies in Cultural Bibliography.* Philadelphia: University of Pennsylvania Press, 2013.
Werstine, Paul. *Early Modern Playhouse Manuscripts and the Editing of Shakespeare.* Cambridge: Cambridge University Press, 2013.

Notes on contributors

Susan Bennett is University Professor in the Department of English at the University of Calgary, Canada. She is widely published in a variety of topics in theatre and performance studies, with particular interest in contemporary productions of Shakespeare's plays. Her recent books are *Performing Environments: Site-Specificity in Medieval & Early Modern Drama*, co-edited with Mary Polito and published by Palgrave in 2014, *Theatre & Museums* (Palgrave 2013), and *Shakespeare Beyond English*, co-edited with Christie Carson and published by Cambridge University Press (2013). In 2016, she is co-curating with Sonia Massai a digital archive of Shakespearean performances worldwide in the 400th anniversary year: performanceshakespeare2016.org. She is also general editor with Kim Solga of a new series for Bloomsbury Methuen called Theory for Theatre Studies, with its first titles appearing in 2017.

Tom Bishop is Professor and Head of English at the University of Auckland, New Zealand. He is the author of *Shakespeare and the Theatre of Wonder* (Cambridge, 1996), the translator of Ovid's *Amores* (Carcanet, 2003), and a general editor of *The Shakespearean International Yearbook*. He has published articles on Elizabethan music, Shakespeare, Jonson, Australian literature, and other topics, and is currently writing a book on Shakespeare's Theatre Games.

Clara Calvo is Professor of English Studies at the University of Murcia, where she teaches courses on Shakespeare, Jane Austen, and the Romantics. Her research interests include the afterlives of Shakespeare and Jane Austen, literary adaptation, and cultural memory. She is the author of *Power Relations and Fool-Master Discourse in Shakespeare* (1991) and has co-authored, with Jean-Jacques Weber, *The Literature Workbook* (1998). With Ton Hoenselaars, she has edited *European Shakespeares* (*The Shakespearean International Yearbook* 8, 2008) and a special issue of *Critical Survey* on *Shakespeare and the Cultures of Commemoration* (2011). With Jesús Tronch, she has edited *The Spanish Tragedy* for the Arden Early Modern Series (2013). She has recently edited, with Coppélia Kahn, *Celebrating Shakespeare: Commemoration and Cultural Memory* (Cambridge University Press, 2015). She is currently the President of the Spanish and Portuguese English Renaissance Studies Association.

Anna Stegh Camati earned a doctorate in English Language and Anglo-American Literature at the University of São Paulo. She is a full professor of Theatre and Drama Studies at the Master's Program in Literary Theory at UNIANDRADE University, Curitiba, PR, Brazil. She realized post-doctoral research in performance-oriented criticism of Shakespeare's dramaturgy at the Federal University of Santa Catarina. In 2011, with Tom Bishop, she coordinated a seminar entitled "Shakespearean Metamorphoses: Intermedial Transactions" at the 9th World Congress of Shakespeare, in Prague, Czech Republic. She has published articles about Shakespeare on the stage and screen in periodicals and books in Brazil and abroad, edited a collection of articles titled *Shakespeare sob múltiplos olhares* (2009 and 2016) and is co-editor of the periodical *Scripta Uniandrade* as well as regional editor for Brazil of the Massachusetts Institute of Technology's (MIT) Global Shakespeares digital archive.

Mariacristina Cavecchi is Senior Lecturer at Milan State University. Her main areas of interest include the twentieth- and twenty-first-century appropriations of Shakespeare's plays for theatre and cinema, prison Shakespeare, and Shakespeare in contemporary popular culture and modern British theatre. She is the author of *Cerchi e cicli. Sulle forme della memoria in* Ulisse (2012), and *Shakespeare mostro contemporaneo*. Macbeth *nelle riscritture di Marowitz, Stoppard e Brenton* (1998). She co-edited *Caryl Churchill* (2012); *Tra le lingue, tra i linguaggi. Cent'anni di Samuel Beckett* (2007); *Shakespeare & Scespir* (2005); *Shakespeare Graffiti* (2002); *EuroShakespeares. Exploring Cultural Practice in an International Context* (with Mariangela Tempera, 2002). She organized the international conference Shakespeare in the Maze of Contemporary Culture (Milan, 2012) and she is currently working on the appropriation of Shakespeare in graffiti art.

Jason Demeter is a post-doctoral fellow in the Literature and Languages Department at Marymount University specializing in Shakespeare and Renaissance literature. His broader interests are transatlantic and transhistorical, centering on the relationship between canonical Anglophone literature and American constructions of race and national identity. His current project considers manifestations of Shakespeare within the American Civil Rights and Black Power movements of the 1960s and '70s. He earned his PhD at George Washington University.

Alexa Huang (co-general editor of *The Shakespearean International Yearbook*) is Professor of English, Theatre and Dance, East Asian Languages and Literatures, and International Affairs at George Washington University in Washington, D.C., where she co-founded and co-directs the Digital Humanities Institute. Her latest book is *Shakespeare and the Ethics of Appropriation* (co-edited with Elizabeth Rivlin; Palgrave, 2014). She was the ACLS Frederick Burkhardt Residential Fellow at the Folger Library in 2015–2016.

NOTES ON CONTRIBUTORS

Margaret Jane Kidnie is Professor of English at Western University. She is author of *Shakespeare and the Problem of Adaptation*, and has published widely on Shakespearean performance, early modern manuscripts, and editorial practices; *Shakespeare and Textual Studies*, a volume of essays co-edited with Sonia Massai, was published in 2015. Kidnie's edition of Thomas Heywood's *A Woman Killed with Kindness* is currently in press and will appear in the Arden Early Modern Drama series.

Yu Jin Ko is Professor of English at Wellesley College. His publications have centered on Shakespeare, with an emphasis on Shakespeare in performance across the globe. He is the co-editor of *Shakespeare's Sense of Character: On the Page and from the Stage* and the author of *Mutability and Division on Shakespeare's Stage*. His other publications include reviews and articles ranging from essays on Asian adaptations of Shakespeare to the afterlives of Shakespeare's original conditions. He also teaches a MOOC (massive open online course) called "Shakespeare: On the Page and in Performance" through the online consortium edX.

Liana de Camargo Leão has an undergraduate degree from Universidade Federal do Rio de Janeiro and a PhD in English from Universidade de São Paulo. Since 2010 she has worked on digital projects as editor in the MIT Global Shakespeares archive and as coordinator of the Shakespeare website of the Federal University of Paraná, Brazil, which she founded and which in 2016 received recognition of cultural merit from the British Embassy in Brazil. Since 2014 she has been revising and preparing notes for the publication of *The Complete Dramatic Works of Shakespeare*, translated by Barbara Heliodora, to be published in 2017. She has contributed to several books on Shakespeare published in Brazil, the most recent being *A Brazilian Perspective: Shakespeare 400 Years: All the World Is a Stage* (Editora de Janeiro, 2016).

Li Jun is Lecturer (Senior Scale) at the University of International Business and Economics (UIBE), Beijing. He received his PhD in English Literary Studies from the Chinese University of Hong Kong in 2013. He is the author of *Popular Shakespeare in China: 1993–2008* (unpublished PhD thesis, 2013) and *An Attempt to Adapt Shakespeare in English by Using Chinese Xiqu Methods – on Julius Caesar Produced by UIBE* (UIBE UP, 2015). He is the director of ST@UIBE's *A Midsummer Night's Dreaming*, a back-to-back theatrical collaboration with Stage@leeds' *Dreaming under the Southern Bough*, performed in Leeds (July), Edinburgh (August), Shanghai and Beijing (September) in 2016.

Elizabeth Pentland is Associate Professor and Undergraduate Program Director in English at York University in Toronto, Canada, where she teaches courses on Shakespeare, adaptations of Shakespeare, early modern political theory, and the literature of travel. She is also Associate Performance Editor for the Internet Shakespeare Editions. Her research explores the forms and contexts of early modern transnationalism, with a particular focus on appropriations of French literature and political theory by early modern English writers. Her essays have appeared in several edited collections, including *Interlinguicity, Internationality, and Shakespeare* (McGill–Queen's, 2014), *Stages of Engagement: Drama in Post-Reformation England* (Duquesne, 2014), and, most recently, *Childhood, Education, and the Stage in Early Modern England* (Cambridge, 2017).

Julie Sanders is Professor of English Literature and Drama and Pro-Vice-Chancellor at Newcastle University, UK. She has published widely in early modern drama and literature and adaptation studies. Most recently she published the second edition of *Adaptation and Appropriation* (Routledge, 2015) and she is also the author of *The Cambridge Introduction to Early Modern Drama, 1576–1642* (Cambridge, 2014). Between 2013 and 2015 she lived and worked in Zhejiang as Vice-Provost of the University of Nottingham Ningbo China.

Cristiane Busato Smith is Editor for the MIT Global Shakespeares digital archive and an Arizona State University adjunct researcher. She has taught at both undergraduate and graduate levels in Brazil. She received her PhD from the Federal University of Paraná. She held a Visiting Fellowship at the Centre for Cultural Analysis, Theory and History (University of Leeds, UK). She has co-edited the journal *Scripta Alumni* and has been member of the editorial board of several journals. Over the past fifteen years, Dr. Smith has published chapters and articles on Shakespeare in South America, Europe, North America, and Asia. Her current research focuses on the field of global Shakespeares, especially on Brazilian adaptations of Shakespeare. She is the author of the book *Representations of Ophelia in Victorian England* (in press).

Ayanna Thompson is Professor of English at George Washington University, and she specializes in Renaissance drama and issues of race in/as performance. She is the author of *Teaching Shakespeare with Purpose: A Student-Centred Approach* (2016), *Passing Strange: Shakespeare, Race, and Contemporary America* (2011), and *Performing Race and Torture on the Early Modern Stage* (2008). She wrote the new introduction for the revised Arden3 *Othello*, and is the editor of *Weyward Macbeth: Intersections of Race and Performance* (2010) and *Colorblind Shakespeare: New Perspectives on Race and Performance* (2006). Professor Thompson has served as a Trustee of the Shakespeare Association of America and a member of the Board of Directors for the Association of Marshall Scholars.

Index

Note: Individual plays of Shakespeare are indexed under their titles.

Abe, Shinzo 116
Abraham, Chris 12–13
Academy of the People's Liberation
 Army 112
Adams Memorial Shakespeare Theatre 65
Adcock, Joel 55–6
Afful, Sarah 24–5; direction from Peter
 Sellars 17–18; modern identities
 and politics and 22–3
Afterlife of Ophelia, The 180
Ainé, Constant Conquelin 89
Alford, Joseph 118
Allen-Dutton, Jordan 164
All's Well That Ends Well 12, 161
A megera domada 93
American Library Association/Folger
 Shakespeare Library 8
Andrade, Oswald de 94
anti-Semitism *see Merchant of Venice, The*
 (Oregon Shakespeare Festival)
Antony and Cleopatra 90
Appel, Libby 49, 52, 54; modernized
 Merchant of Venice and 56–7, 59
Arab Spring 156–7
Arap, Fauzi 90
Artcrimes 151
artists *see* Ophelia
Ashland, Oregon *see* Oregon Shakespeare
 Festival
Asian Shakespeare Internet Archive 31,
 38, 41
Assis, Machado de 89
As You Like It 90
Auden, W. H. 58
Auerbach, Erna 79
authenticity, perception of 31, 35–6
Autran, Paulo 90
Azevedo, Álvares de 89

Babbage, Edward 79
Bachelard, Gaston 139
Bandeira, Manuel 93
Banksy 152, 155, 158
Barber, C. L. 58
Barrault, Jean-Louis 89
Barthes, Roland 90–1, 158
Bate, Jonathan 82, 183
Baudrillard, Jean 158, 167
Beatrix Beata 131
Beaumont Theater 12
Bedford, James Gavin 166, 168
Beijing Youth Drama Festival 110
Ben-Ami, Jacob 89
Bennett, Susan 178
Bernhardt, Sarah 89
Bessell, Jacqueline 6
Billington, Michael 93
Blanes Museum Gardens 94
Blek le Rat 164
Blondell, John 164
Bloom, Harold 58
Blub 153, 160–2
Boal, Augusto 90
Bogdanov, Michael 164
Bomb-itty of Errors, The 164, 169
Borzello, Frances 132
Bowmer, Angus L. 50
Boyle, Danny 83
Branagh, Kenneth 83
Brazil 6–7, 65; *Sua Incelença, Ricardo
 III [His Excellency, Richard III]*;
 feminist discourse in 130; history
 of Shakespearean productions
 in 87–94; political upheaval in
 89–90; post-dictatorship period
 91–2; regional theaters in 92,
 93–4; street theater in 92–3,

195

104–5; television in 91; *see also* Ophelia
Brecht, Bertolt 22, 90
Bridges of Graffiti, The 149
British Council 1–2, 7, 8–9
British Museum 2, 5, 6, 81; "Shakespeare: Staging the World" 5, 81–4
Broken Column, The 131
Brown, Frank Chouteau 69, *71*
Brunel, Isambard Kingdom 83
Buckle, Richard 75–81
Buliung, Evan 12–13
Burt, Richard 149
Butterfly Lovers, The 117
BuzzFeed 155

Cabral de Melo Neto, João 102
Caetano, João 88, 89
Caixa-Preta [Black-Box] 92
California Pacific International Exposition 65, 75
Calvo, Clara 5, 6
Camargo Leão, Liana de 6
Camati, Anna Stegh 6
Canadian Broadcasting Corporation (CBC) 17
"Cannibalist Manifesto" 7, 94
Cardenio 177, 180–4
Cardenio between Cervantes and Shakespeare: The Story of a Lost Play 181–2
Carlson, Ben 12
Carneiro de Mendonça, Anna Amélia 94
Carson, Christie 2, 178
Castanho, Lucia 135–9
Catalano, Jason 164
Caymmi, Dorival 102
Cena Contemporânea in Brasília 94
Central Academy of Drama (Beijing) 111, 124
Cervantes, Miguel de 181
Chamber Play, A: actors 17–18, 17–20; Canadian Broadcasting Corporation coverage of 17; directed by Peter Sellars 13–24; as immersive experience 24; Masonic Concert Hall setting 13–16; modern identities and politics in 22–3; raw emotion displayed in 20, 23–5; removal of Shakespeare's plot points from 18–20; stage design 13–16; transition into "new dawn" 25–6

Chaplin, Charlie 158
Chartier, Roger 181–2, 185
Chicago, Judy 132
Chicago World's Fair 6, 65, 75
Chile 94
China: assumptions about Western identity of Shakespeare and 113–14; Beijing Olympics 113; collaborations with Japan 115–16; *Coriolanus* production in 109, 114–15; Huang Ying and 7, 110, 116, 120–4; Lin Zhaohua and 109, 114–15, 123–4; *Macbeth* in 109, 110, 115, 121–3; *Midsummer Night's Dream* in 109–10, 115–16; *Ming* production in 112–13; National Centre for the Performing Arts 109–11, 112; *Romeo and Juliet* in 7, 109, 110, 114, 116–20; Royal Shakespeare Company travel through 109, 115, 124–5; Shakespeare Society of China 111; Tian Qinxin and 112–14, 123–4; *Weltliteratur und Welttheater: Aesthetischer Humanismus in der kulturellen Globalisierung* and 179; Zhao Miao and 7, 110, 116–20
China Daily 109
Cia dos Atores theater 133
Cimolino, Antonio 3, 13, 14, 24
cinema and graffiti 165–9
Clowns de Shakespeare 7, 87, 93, 94, 95; *see also Sua Incelença, Ricardo III [His Excellency, Richard III]*
Collor de Mello, Fernando 91
Comedy of Errors, The 164
Complete Works of Shakespeare 111
Confucianism 33, 34
Connerton, Paul 66, 83
Coriolano 90
Coriolanus 109, 114–15, 164
Cornell University 165
Craveiro, J. C. 88

creative cannibalism 94
Creutzenberg, Jan 36
Crucible Theatre 12
Cruz, Ulysses 91
Crytek 187

Daily Tidings, The 54
Darnton, Robert 185
Davidson, Martin 1, 2, 9
Dee, John 167
Demeter, Jason 4, 8
Deng Xiaoping 110, 112
DeVille, Abigail 13, 14–15
Diaghilev, Sergei 79
Dias, Gonçalves 89
Diaz, Enrique 91
DiCaprio, Leonardo 117
Dom Casmurro 89
Donmar Warehouse 164
Don Quixote 181
Doran, Greg 124–5, 182
Double Falsehood 181, 183–4
Drew, Peter 153, 159–60
Dromgoole, Dominic 110
Ducis, Jean-François 88
Dunsinane 109
Durst, Walter George 91

Earl's Court exhibition 6, 69–75, 77, 79, 80
Early Modern Playhouse Manuscripts and the Editing of Shakespeare 184–5
Eating and Ethics in Shakespeare's England 187
Edinburgh Fringe Festival 116, 118, 120
Edmondson, Paul 177
Edwards, Michael Donald 55–9
Einstein, Albert 158
El Cid 121
Eliot, T. S. 37
Elizabeth I, Queen 81
Elmore, Richard 49
"Emoticon Hamlet" 159–60, 162
England's Dreaming 167
Ensaio.Hamlet [Rehearsal.Hamlet] 91, 133, 134
Enterline, Lynne 186–7
Erne, Lukas 185–6
Evans, Tony 76, 77

Exit through the Gift Shop 152, 158
Eyre, Richard 178

Facebook 152
Fagundes, Patricia 91
Fairey, Shepard 158
Fausta, Itália 89
Feiler, Yael 60–1
feminism: art and second-wave 131–3; discourse in Brazil 130, 142; Fregoneis' Ophelia and 133–4; Lucia Castanho and 135–9; Lucia Sanders and 139–43
Festival Internacional de Expressão Ibãrica (FITEI) 94
Festival Internacional de Santiago a Mil 94
fictional graffiti 163–4
Filho, Antunes 90–1
Fleming, Juliet 167
Fletcher, John 180–1
"400 Dreams – Shakespeare in Space" 8
400th anniversary of Shakespeare's death 1–3, 8
Fraga, Guti 92
Frateschi, Celso 91
Fregoneis, Gabriela 133–4, 142
Freudian interpretations 134
Fudan University 111

GameCity 187
Gasparani, Gustavo 92
Georgiadis, Nicholas 79
Gielgud, John 76, 77
Globe and Mail, The 19
Globe Theatre 1, 5, 6, 178; Earl's Court exhibition 6, 69–75, 77, 79, 80; "Shakespeare: Staging the World" exhibition 5, 81–4; Shakespeare Exhibition, Stratford-upon-Avon, 1964 reconstruction 75–81; Shakespeare Village in Boston and 67–9; worldwide replicas of 65–7
Globe to Globe Festival 2, 5, 7, 8, 110, 178
Goad, Jonathan 12–13
Go-Between, The 68
Goetz, Kent 165
Goldstein, David 187
Gomes, Celuta Moreira 88

Gonzaga, Luiz 97
Good Person of Setzuan, The 121
Goold, Rupert 178
Gossett, Suzanne 5
GQ 164
graffiti *see* street art
Greenblatt, Stephen 181
Greg, W. W. 184–5
Grieg, David 109
Grisolli, Paulo Afonso 91
Grupo Galpão 6, 92–3, 104
Gualtieri, Giacinta Pezzana 89
Guetta, Thierry 158
Guinness, Alec 12, 14
Guthrie, Tyrone 11–12, 14
Guthrie Theater 12

Habima National Theatre 5
Haldeman, Maureen J. 157
Hamlet 133, 150; in Brazil 88, 89, 90, 91, 92; in China 111; discussed in *Intermedial Shakespeares on European Stages* 180; *Hamlet Zone: Reworking Hamlet for European Culture, The* 179; Ophelia and 133, 134, 142; street art featuring 156, 159–60, 164
Ham-let 91
Hamlet, Korean performances of 1, 3–4; appeal of 29–30, 32; communal folk activities in 34–5; cutting and compression in 42–3; as folk drama 39; ghost and possession of spirit featured in 36–8, 40, 43–4; gravediggers in 41–2; *gut* in 35, 37, 42, 43–4; history of 29; Horatio in 39–41; Jung-ung Yang's production 30, 32, 34, 42–5; Korean aesthetics in 30, 37; Korean funeral practices and 35–6; Korean sentiment of *han* and 32–3, 34, 35, 45; opposition between local and universal in 31; perception of authenticity in 31, 35–6; shamanism in 33–5, 43, 44–5; stage settings 35–6, 44–5; Youn-taek Lee's production 29–42
"*Hamlet* across Space and Time" 111

Hamlet sincrético [Syncretic Hamlet] 92
Hamlet Zone: Reworking Hamlet for European Culture, The 179
Harlem Duet 24
Hartley, L. P. 68
Hathaway, Anne 81
Hawkes, Terence 80
Hazlitt, William 58
Heliodora, Barbara 88, 92
Henry IV 178
Henry V 97, 115, 148, 178
Herz, Daniel 92
Hilliard, Nicholas 81
Hirst, Michael 83
Hobsbawm, Eric 96
Hollar, Wenceslaus 69, 81
Hollow Crown, The 178
Huang, Alexa 3, 7–8, 149, 179
Huang, Alexander 124
Huangliangyimeng [Cooking a Dream] 121
Huang Ying 7, 110, 116, 120–4, 125

Im, Yeeyon 29
In Focus 57, 58
Ingalls, James F. 13
Instagram 152
Intermedial Shakespeares on European Stages 179–80
International Festival in Londrina (FILO) 94
International Festival in São Josã do Rio Preto (FIT) 94
International Festival of University Theatre in Blumenau (FITUB) 94
International Space Station 8
intervention, politics of 139–43
Irving, Henry 142
Isozaki, Arata 65

Jacobi, Derek 111
Japan 65
Jarman, Derek 166, 167, 168
Jefford, Barbara 90
jeop-shin 38
Jewish Journal, The 53
Jewish Transcript 54
jinogigut 35, 37, 42, 43–4

João VI, Dom 88
Johnstone, Dion 24–5; direction from Peter Sellars 17–18, 19–20; modern identities and politics and 23–4; raw emotion displayed by 20, 23–5
Julius Caesar 89, 90
Jun, Li 7

Kahlo, Frida 131
Kalis, Milon 164
Karim-Cooper, Farah 184
Kennedy, Dennis 31
Kidnie, Margaret Jane 3
King Lear 89, 113
Kirwan, Patrick 69
Ko, Yu Jin 3–4, 8
Koltai, Ralph 164
Korean performances *see Hamlet*, Korean performances of
Kwon, Miwon 9

Laboucane, Josue 12
Lage, Roberto 91
Lanier, Douglas 75, 150
"L'arte sa nuotare" 160–2
Latin America 6
Latour, Bruno 80
Lecoq, Jacques 118
Lee, Hyonu 32, 41, 42
Lee, Youn-taek 29–42, 45; Horatio character and 39–41; *jeop-shin* employed by 37–8
Lesser, Zachary 185
Let Us Make Friends with Shakespeare 111
Leveaux, David 164
Levenson, Jill L. 16
Levith, Murray 112
Li Jun 112
Lincoln Center 12
Lindström, Trish 17, 23–6; direction from Peter Sellars 17–18; raw emotion displayed by 20, 22
Lin Zhaohua 109, 114–15, 123–4
Li Ruru 111, 112
Lit Moon 164
Litvin, Margaret 156–7
Loncraine, Richard 97

Love Paintings 162–3
Love's Labour's Lost 158
Lowenthal, David 65–6, 72, 75
Lu Gusin 111
Lula da Silva, Luiz Inácio 91
Lurhmann, Baz 117
Lutyens, Edwin Landseer 69, 72, 74
Luzhu [Pot-stewed] 121

Macbeth 7, 150; in Brazil 88, 90, 91; in China 109, 110, 115, 121–3; discussed in *Intermedial Shakespeares on European Stages* 180; *Dunsimane* sequel to 109; street art featuring 155, 157–8
MacGregor, Neil 5, 82
Magalhães, Gonçalves de 88
Magno, Paschoal Carlos 89
Maiolino, Anna Maria 132
Mancewicz, Aneta 179–80
Mandela, Nelson 157
Mandela and Macbeth 159
Mantel, Hilary 83
Map of Early Modern London, The 187–8
Marchioro, Marcelo 91
Márcia X 132
Mars, Bruno 13
Martinez Correa, José Celso 91
Masonic Concert Hall, Oregon: sound in 16–17; stage design 13–16
Massai, Sonia 4, 30
Maud, Helen 140
McKellen, Ian 178
Measure for Measure 89
Mendieta, Ana 131, 137
Merchant of Venice, The: in Brazil 88, 90; discussed in *Eating and Ethics in Shakespeare's England* 187; discussed in *Intermedial Shakespeares on European Stages* 180
Merchant of Venice, The (Oregon Shakespeare Festival) 4–5; David Zaslow and 52–4, 56, 60; Jerry Turner and 51–2, 54, 55; modernized by the Oregon Shakespeare Festival 49–51, 55–9; protests and complaints about

49–55; public outreach by OSF on 56–9; study of history 59–62; young audiences 53–4
Metamorfoses de Ofélia 133
Midsummer Night's Dream, A: in Brazil 89, 90, 91–2; in China 109, 110, 115–16; discussed in *Intermedial Shakespeares on European Stages* 180; in Los Angeles 109; Stratford Festival of Canada 3, 11–13 (*see also Chamber Play, A*); street art featuring 154
Miguel, Ana 132
Millais, John Everett 130–1, 133, 136, 138
Ming 112–13
Misanthrope, The 121
Moffat, William 54
Moiseiwitsch, Tanya 12, 14
Monroe, Marilyn 158
Morte e vida severina 102–4
Much Ado about Nothing 93; in China 111
Muito barulho por quase nada [Much Ado about Nothing] 93

Nabuco, Joaquim 89
Nadajewski, Mike 24, 25; direction from Peter Sellars 17–18, 19; raw emotion displayed by 20, 22
NASA 8
National Centre for the Performing Arts, China (NCPA) 109–10; *Ming* 112–13; "Salute to Shakespeare" 110–11, 112; 2014 series 115–24
National Geographic 81
National Theatre of China 7, 112
National Theatre of Scotland 109
NCPA *see* National Centre for the Performing Arts, China (NCPA)
Nestruck, J. Kelly 14, 23
New York Times 67, 68, 77
Ng, Eleine 31
Noite de Reis [Twelfth Night] 93
Nora, Pierre 66
Nós do Morro [We from the Hillside] 92
Nunbit Theatre 35
Nunes, Celso 90

Obama, Barack 158
Occult Philosophy 167
O'Connor, Marion 69, 70, 71, 74
O'Doherty, Brian 77
Olajide, Thomas 12
Oliveira, Jessé 92
Oliveira e Silva, J.A. de 88
Olympic Games, London 2, 8, 81, 83, 177–8
Ophelia: fascination with 129–32, 141–2; female artists representing themselves as 132–3; Gabriela Fregoneis' 133–4, 142; Lucia Sander's 139–43; "myth of" 130; re-visioned in photographs by Lucia Castanho 135–9
Ophelia (painting) 130
Oregon Shakespeare Festival (OSF) 4–5, 8; history of 50–61, 62–3n1; modernized *Merchant of Venice* production 49–50, 55–9; public outreach by 56–9; study of *Merchant of Venice* and 59–62; young people and 54–5; *see also Merchant of Venice, The* (Oregon Shakespeare Festival)
Ortiz, Tareke 13
OSF *see* Oregon Shakespeare Festival (OSF)
Otello 116
Otelo da Mangueira 92
Otelo de Oliveira 91
Othello 24, 161; in Brazil 88, 89, 92; in China 116
O'Toole, Emer 125
Ouzounian, Richard 16–17
Owen, Ruth J. 179

Papp, Joseph 92
Patterson, Tom 11
Patton, William 55
Paulino, Rosana 132
Pearson, Mike 1–2, 110
Pena, Martins 89
People's Art Theatre 113
Pericás, Luiz Bernardo 96
Perry, Roger 167
Peter Grimes 77

Peterson, Kaara 129, 180
Petri, Elio 155
Piccolo Teatro de Milano 89
Picture of Health, The 132
Pilbrow, Richard 80
place: experiences and meanings of 2; street art as specific to 149–50
Poe, Edgar Allan 136
Poel, William 69, 74–5
Poleshuck, Jesse 164
politics of intervention 139–43
Porto Alegre em Cena 94
Powell, Will 164, 169
Prescott, Paul 177
"Proximal Dreams: Peter Sellars at the Stratford Festival of Canada" 3
Pudding Lane 187

Queensland Shakespeare Ensemble 164–5
Quinn, Marc 162–3

Raleigh, Walter 58
Rasmussen, Eric 183
Rauch, Bill 59
Red Flag 131–2
Redgrave, Vanessa 90
Renaissance Drama and the Politics of Print 185
Renaud, Madeleine 89
Reviving Ophelia: Saving the Selves of Adolescent Girls 140
Rich, Adrienne 134
Richard II 178
Richard III: in Brazil (*see Sua Incelença, Ricardo III [His Excellency, Richard III]*); in China 7; film, 1995 97; *The Street Kings* and 166, 168–9
Richard Rodgers Theatre 164
Richardson, Ralph 76, 77, 90
Robbins, Jerome 166
Robbins, Tim 109
Robertson, Toby 111
Rocha, Roberto 90
Rogue Valley Jewish Community 51
Romeo and Juliet 148, 150; in Brazil 6, 88, 89, 90, 91, 92; in China 7, 109, 110, 114, 116–20; discussed in *Intermedial Shakespeares on European Stages* 180; street art featuring 154, 155, 162–3, 164, 165; *West Side Story* and 166–7
Romeu y Julieta 6, 89, 90, 91, 92
Rosling, Tara 12
Rossetti, Dante Gabriel 130
Rossi, Ernesto 88
Rourke, Josie 164
Rowse, A. L. 80
Royal Dramatic Theatre 60
Royal Shakespeare Company 2, 7, 75–6, 90, 178, 182; travel in China 109, 115, 124–5
Ruth Page Theatre 164
Rylance, Mark 93

Saenger, Michael 186
Salgado, Cristina 132
Salvini, Tommaso 88–9
Sander, Lucia 139–43
Sanders, Julie 7
Santiago, Silviano 94
SanTuoQi 109, 116, 118, 120
Sauter, Willmar 60–1
Savage, Jon 167
Schiele, Egon 133
scholarship, Shakespearean (2012–2013) 177–88; *Afterlife of Ophelia, The* 180; on *Cardenio* 180–3; digital projects 187–8; *Early Modern Playhouse Manuscripts and the Editing of Shakespeare* 184–5; *Hamlet Zone: Reworking Hamlet for European Culture, The* 179; *Intermedial Shakespeares on European Stages* 179–80; *Map of Early Modern London, The* 187–8; Olympic Games and 177–8; *Shakespeare and the Book Trade* 185–6; *Shakespeare and the French Borders of English* 186; *Shakespeare as Literary Dramatist* 185–6; *Shakespeare beyond English* 178–9; *Shakespeare's Schoolroom: Rhetoric, Discipline, Emotion* 186–7; *Shakespeare's Stationers: Studies in Cultural Bibliography*

185; *Shakespeare's Theatres and the Effects of Performance* 184; *Weltliteratur und Welttheater: Aesthetischer Humanismus in der kulturellen Globalisierung* 179; *William Shakespeare and Others: Collaborative Plays* 183–4
School for Scandal, The 121
Sears, Djanet 24
Seattle Post-Intelligencer 55
Segurado, Livia 94
self-representation *see* Ophelia
Sellars, Peter 3; on *Chamber* as a "new dawn" 25–6; direction of *Chamber Play* 13–26; Masonic Concert Hall as setting for production and 13–16; openness to modern identities and politics in Shakespeare performances 22–3; work with actors 18–19
Sewol ferry disaster 33
Shakespeare: Staging the World 82
"Shakespeare: Staging the World" 5, 81–4
Shakespeare, William: birthplace 72–4; 400th anniversary of death of 1; scholarship in 2012–2013 177–88
"Shakespeare and His First Folio" 8
Shakespeare and the Book Trade 185–6
Shakespeare and the French Borders of English 186
Shakespeare and the Jews 58
Shakespeare as Literary Dramatist 185–6
Shakespeare Beyond English 2, 178–9
Shakespeare in the Present 80
Shakespeare National Theatre Memorial Fund 74
Shakespeare Passport app 8
Shakespeares after Shakespeare: An Encyclopedia of the Bard in Mass Media and Popular Culture 149
"Shakespeare's England" exhibition 6
"Shakespeare's Legacy 400" 8
Shakespeare's Lost Play: In Search of Cardenio 182
Shakespeare Society of China 111
Shakespeare's Restless World 82

Shakespeare's Schoolroom: Rhetoric, Discipline, Emotion 186–7
Shakespeare's Stationers: Studies in Cultural Bibliography 185
Shakespeare's Theatres and the Effects of Performance 184
Shakespeare street art *see* street art, Shakespeare
Shakespeare Theatre Association 8
"Shakespeare toilet" 147–8
Shakespeare Village, Boston 67–9
shamanism, Korean 33–5, 43, 44–5
Shanghai Dramatic Arts Centre 7
Shanghai Youth Theatre 111
Shapiro, James 58
Sharrock, Thea 178
Shaw, Deborah 2
Sheller, Mimi 111
Shi Ge [Hymne à la disparition] 116
Showalter, Elaine 129, 130
Siddal, Elizabeth 130–1, 136–7
Silva, Aguinaldo 91
Silva, Nora de 140
Sinclair, Iain 151, 152, 154
Sirinsky, Marc 56
site-specificity and spatial organization in *Sua Incelença* 95–104
Skating on Thin Eyes 151
Skirball Center for the Performing Arts 7
Soares, Jô 91
Sonho de uma noite de verdão [A Midsummer Night's Dream] 91–2, 93
Sonnabend, Yolanda 167
Soushenji [Tales of Gods] 121
spectatorial positionality 31
Spence, Jo 132
Stern, Tiffany 184
Stewart-Lockhart, George 168
Stooks, Jay 165
Stratford Festival of Canada 3, 26; *Chamber Play* directed by Peter Sellars at 13–26; *Midsummer Night's Dream* performed by 11–13; Antonio Cimolino and 3, 13, 14, 26; Chris Abraham and 12–13; origins of

11–12; two productions of *Dream* presented by 13–14
Straznicky, Marta 185
street art, Shakespeare 147–51; academic interest in 149; analysis of Shakespeare in 150–1; in cinema 165–9; emergence of 148–9; "Emoticon Hamlet" 159–60, 162; fictional graffiti 163–4; intertext and meanings 154–7; "L'arte sa nuotare" 160–2; *Love Paintings* 162–3; as part of artistic projects 159–3; provisional map of 151–3; as site-specific 149–50; tags in 153–4, 158–9; in the theatre 164–5; youth culture and 150
Street Kings, The 166, 168–9
Streetsy.com 151
Street Theatre Troupe 29, 35, 42; *see also Hamlet*, Korean performances of
Strindberg, August 19
Sua Incelença, Ricardo III [His Excellency, Richard III] 6, 7, 87, 93; alternating scenes using circus ring 98–9; closure of 102–4; dialogue 100–1; music 97–8, 101–2; operatic approach 99–102; site-specificity and spatial organization in 95–104; *see also* Brazil
Sullivan, Erin 177
Sunday Times, The 74, 75, 77

Tadashi, Suzuki 116
Tagg, Alan 76–7, 80
tags, graffiti 153–4
Taming of the Shrew, The 12, 89, 93; in China 109–10, 121; street art featuring 155
Tang Xianzu 125
Tartuffe 120–1
Taylor, Gary 181
Teatro de Estudante do Brasil 89
Teatro Municipal 90
Teatro Stabile di Genoa 89
Tempest, The 83, 90, 166, 167, 168, 177–8; discussed in *Intermedial*

Shakespeares on European Stages 180
Tempo Festival in Rio de Janeiro 94
Terry, Ellen 140, 142
Theatre O 118
Theatro Lyrico Fluminense 88
Theobald, Lewis 181
Theseus, Duke 65
Third International Drama Season 112
Thompson, Ayanna 4, 8
Thornton, Dora 82
Three Dark Tales 118
Tian Qinxin 112–14, 123–4
Timon of Athens 115, 164
Titus Andronicus 187
Trabulsi, Gabriel 89
Troilus and Cressida 180
Trono de sangue 91
Tudors, The 83
Turner, Jerry 51–2, 54, 55
Tvardovskas, Luana Saturnino 132
Twelfth Night 50, 90; in Brazil 93

Ueba Troupe 93
uMabatha-The Zulu Macbeth 157
Ur-Hamlet 90
Urry, John 111
Uruguay 94
Uzzell-Edwards, Charley 149–50

Victoria and Albert Museum 6
Vigny, Alfred de 88
Villela, Gabriel 92, 93, 96
Visit, The 121
Visscher, Claes Janszoon 69

Weiner, Erik 164
Weltliteratur und Welttheater: Aesthetischer Humanismus in der kulturellen Globalisierung 179
Werstine, Paul 184–5
West Side Story 166–7
"When We Dead Awaken" 134
Whitechapel Art Gallery 74–5
Who Owns the Street 153
Williams, Deanne 129, 180

Williams, Heathcote 167–8
William Shakespeare and Others: Collaborative Plays 183–4
Winter's Tale, The 115
Wise, Robert 166
women artists *see* Ophelia
WoosterCollective.com 151
World Shakespeare Festival (WSF) 2, 8, 177
Worth, Irene 12
Worthen, W. B. 20
Writing on the Wall, The 167

Xi you ji [The Journey to the West] 121

Yamamoto, Fernando 94
Yang, Jung-ung 30, 32, 34, 42–5
Year of Shakespeare: Re-living the World Shakespeare Festival, A 177
Yi Liming 109
Yohangza theater 3, 32, 34, 42; *see also Hamlet*, Korean performances of
Yong, Li Lan 31, 32
Yonhuidan Gureepe 3, 29, 30; *see also Hamlet*, Korean performances of
YouTube 129, 169

Zabou 152
Zacconi, Ermete 89
Zaslow, David 52–4, 56, 60
Zaushu [Jujube Tree] 121
Zhang Xian 124
Zhao Miao 7, 110, 116–20, 125
Zhou, Raymond 115
Zydower, Astrid 80